JOAN CRAWFORD, CIRCA 1933

BETTE DAVIS IN *EX-LADY*, 1933

FOREWORD BY ROBERT OSBORNE

INTRODUCTION BY MOLLY HASKELL

TEXT BY ANDREA SARVADY

EDITED BY FRANK MILLER

Leading
LADIES

THE 50 MOST UNFORGETTABLE ACTRESSES OF THE STUDIO ERA

CHRONICLE BOOKS
SAN FRANCISCO

All of the films in this book, along with countless other classics,
can be seen every day, completely commercial-free, on
Turner Classic Movies.

A concerted effort has been made to trace
the ownership of all material included in this book.
Any errors that may have occurred are inadvertent
and will be corrected in subsequent editions,
provided sufficient notification is sent to the
publisher in a timely manner.

Library of Congress Cataloging-in-Publication Data available.
ISBN 0-8118-5248-2

Manufactured in China.

Designed by Affiche Design

Distributed in Canada by Raincoast Books
9050 Shaughnessy Street
Vancouver, British Columbia V6P 6E5

10 9 8 7 6 5 4 3 2

Chronicle Books LLC
85 Second Street
San Francisco, California 94105
www.chroniclebooks.com

Cover photographs, L-R (top): Grace Kelly, *High Society*; Katharine
Hepburn, *Sylvia Scarlett*; Jean Harlow, *Bombshell*; Joan Crawford,
Chained; (bottom) Bette Davis, *Jezebel*; Ava Gardner, *Mogambo*;
Ginger Rogers, *Top Hat*; Marion Davies, *Cain and Mabel*.

ACKNOWLEDGMENTS

As with all great film productions, this book reflects the collaborative efforts of many: from the Academy of Motion Picture Arts and Sciences & Margaret Herrick Library, Sue Guldin and Faye Thompson; from The Everett Collection, Glenn Bradie and Ron Harvey; from The Kobal Collection, Jamie Vuignier and Ayzha Wolf; Photofest, Howard Mandelbaum; from the Warner Bros. Corporate Image Archive, Cynthia Graham and Jeff Stevens; from Turner Image Management, David Diodate, Brandy Ivins, Christopher Grakal, Melissa Jacobson, Cynthia Martinez, Sam Morris and Kim Vardeman

TCM contributors to project development and management and to editorial and research include, Carrie Beers, Kristin Ramsey Clyde, Tanya Coventry, Katherine Evans, Alexa Foreman, Talia Gerecitano, Hadley Gwin, Darcy Hettrich, Tom Karsch, Scott McGee, Chris Merrifield, Dennis Millay, R. Anna Millman, Robert Osborne, John Renaud, Charles Tabesh, Lee Tsiantis, and Eric Weber.

Thanks to our friends and colleagues for their relentless enthusiasm and commitment to TCM: Anne Borchardt, Brooks Branch, Creative Branding Group; Aubry Anne D'Arminio; Britt Else, Signal, Inc.; Dianna Edwards; Roger Fristoe; Molly Haskell; Frank Miller; Andrea Sarvady; Michon Wise.

FOREWORD
ROBERT**OSBORNE**

Yes, yes, we all agree that when it comes to movies, one couldn't find a better way to spend time than sitting in a darkened theater watching the unscrambling of the mystery of Rosebud, or seeing that baby carriage bobble down the Odessa steps, or watching H.A.L. 9000 create mischief in *2001: A Space Odyssey*. Those moments, and a few others, deliver the kind of visual magic that have made the world of cinema so revered, so celebrated, so fascinating to all of us.

But, hey, simply gazing at Audrey Hepburn, Gene Tierney, or Sophia Loren has its compensations, too. There's something to be said for the pure, unadulterated pleasure of watching the countless screen heroines whose main virtue is the fact they are beautiful, or fascinatingly complex, or heart-stoppingly talented—sometimes, in a few rare instances, all three of the above. That's what this book is all about.

We chose fifty of the great leading ladies to spotlight in this book, all of them from the so-called studio era, because it's when glamour reigned supreme, when the first genuine movie queen bees were born and developed and, most importantly, prized by both Hollywood and the insatiable moviegoing public. It was the time critics now refer to as the golden era of motion pictures—when each studio had an identity and style of its own, not only with the films it made, but with the stars it created.

MGM, for instance, was all about glamour and class; for years, never did a speck of dust ever appear in an MGM movie, nor was a hair out of place on the head of an MGM leading lady. Warner Bros., meanwhile, specialized in urban action, gangsters and gutters; their ladies were usually tough babes, sassy and always busy filling ashtrays. The look of Fox product and their female stars was equally distinctive. And so it went. What each movie studio had in common was a stable of stars and a penchant for beautiful women— the more oomph the ladies had, the better.

In this book, you'll find a wealth of examples, along with the reasons these particular ladies stand out from the pack. You'll notice they all have several things in common, such as a strong, identifiable persona and a sense of style that set standards other women in society gravitated toward. Each is also absolutely distinctive. No one ever mistook Sophia Loren for Ingrid Bergman, or Barbara Stanwyck for Katharine Hepburn. Each also epitomizes a different style of leading lady—from the fragile grace of a Lillian Gish to a boisterous Debbie Reynolds, from a sunny Doris Day to a cool Grace Kelly to that prime candidate for Valium, Bette Davis.

A few of them were well defined as actresses with a capital A, but you'll also find some who, on first glance, might be dismissed as sex symbols—until you look more closely at their work. Was anyone funnier than Mae West in her prime? Or Marilyn Monroe in *How to Marry a Millionaire?* Jean Harlow in *Dinner at Eight?* Singing stars such as Judy Garland and Doris Day also gave triumphant performances worthy of awards and praise in, respectively, *I Could Go on Singing* and *Love Me or Leave Me.* Esther Williams was no Anna Magnani, but her athletic prowess and natural charm not only enchanted moviegoers for two decades, but also the great playwright Eugene O'Neill, who once told Lillian Gish that Esther was his favorite of all movie actresses— the best reason he knew, above all others, for going to the movies.

The most difficult part of coming up with this roster of fifty exceptional women was to keep the list down to a manageable number. We realize that many of your favorites from Hollywood's golden age—Lucille Ball, Joan Fontaine, Judy Holliday, Jennifer Jones, Patricia Neal, Jane Powell, Jean Simmons, and Shirley Temple, to name a few—are not represented here. The final list was the subject of passionate debate for the TCM staff working on this project. We wish there was room to include them all. But we hope, in the final analysis, you'll agree with us when we borrow a phrase uttered by Spencer Tracy, in *Pat and Mike*, when he said, ". . . but what there is, is *cherce*."

INTRODUCTION
MOLLY**HASKELL**

"We had faces then!" These words, hurled with high diva disdain by Gloria Swanson in the famous mad scene in *Sunset Boulevard*, referred to the stars of silent film, her own glorious era, who had to withstand and embrace the most intense close-ups, without the disguises and softening effects an increasingly sophisticated technology would bring. They were simply more naked under the camera's ruthless gaze. Moreover, in the absence of sound, their faces had to convey information that would later be rendered in speech. But the stars who had voices, too, weren't exactly deficient when it came to close-ups. What's remarkable about both groups, as exemplified by the fifty represented in this book—women so magnetic we still regard them with awe, their wattage miraculously undimmed by time—is how much more they were (and had) than pretty faces.

Beyond beauty (itself less important than being photogenic) was luck, talent, personality, "It," and, when they'd made it to even the lower echelons of stardom, a whole apparatus of studio personnel dedicated to displaying them, literally and figuratively, in their best and most dazzling light: Lighting cameramen who knew their angles, costume designers whose wardrobes illuminated their strengths and concealed their weaknesses, makeup artists with an equivalent dexterity regarding facial features, writers who could create stories and dialogue tailored to each star's idiosyncratic personality, and, finally, directors for whom they were often muses as well as stars, and for whom all the other assets were arrows in a quiver whose ultimate purpose was not just a movie but also a great and seamless poem of love, an irresistible erotic artifact.

What made all this possible was, of course, the studio system, blamed often as a factory that crassly exploited its stars as properties but without which they would never have realized the spellbinding potential that makes their very existence, the charms of their movies, seem even more wondrous today than it did at the time. Yes, it was a capitalistic and paternalistic system in which moguls ruled over fiefdoms such as MGM, Warner Bros., Paramount, and Universal, and treated their stars like indentured servants in a gilded cage. They rose at an unholy hour, went to the studio, made one film after another, and had their private lives supervised and spun by a host of studio publicists.

But for their trouble, they not only had faces—they had careers! Just compare the erratic professional lives of actresses today: These women are not protected by a contract, they're subject to the whims of producers geared to teenage audiences, they star in a movie every two or three years (if they're lucky, and always excepting the prolific Nicole Kidman), and, for their part, they're determined to have "normal" lives as wives and mothers. If the stars of the studio era had refused to travel to some distant location unless accompanied by nanny and children, the studio heads (their bosses) would have laughed in their faces.

The discovery process, no less haphazard then than it is today, might begin with someone being spotted in a beauty contest or a Broadway play, as a cover girl or a model, or sitting, as legend has it, at the counter in Schwab's drugstore—or in "foreign" films, which included British ones. The burning of Atlanta was already being filmed for *Gone with the Wind* when agent Myron Selznick brought Englishwoman Vivien Leigh to producer and nephew David and said, "Here's your Scarlett O'Hara"—a part every actress in Hollywood had schemed, tested, and fought for.

Generally, the path to stardom was less quicksilver and more of a trial-and-error process, as the newcomer was subjected to a battery of screen tests in which potential was gauged and questions posed: How could this woman fit in with the kinds of films the studio made? What type did she represent: Working-class dame, or refined lady? Aristocrat, or siren? Nice girl, or seductress? Good girl, or bad girl? She might start out in one category and wind up in another. Jean Harlow, miscast early on as a society lady, migrated to the opposite end of the spectrum, becoming the quintessential pre-Code sexy broad, an enchantingly forthright good-time girl who would do or say almost anything.

Type, elaborated and enriched by each individual's special qualities, evolved into a persona, a signature so distinct that you knew what you'd get when you went to a Bette Davis film (melodramatic intensity and willfulness) or a Norma Shearer film (refinement, with a little modern toying with adultery). Types were plentiful; stars were relatively few. There were a lot of wisecracking blonds, but Jean Arthur had a special quality, a vulnerability transmitted by the catch in her voice; Claudette Colbert and Irene Dunne were impeccably ladylike, but a special snap and savvy went into their covert sex appeal.

Indeed, one of the qualities that characterizes these stars in their full blossoming is an uncanny mix of simplicity and complexity, an ability to retain their type but go beyond it, sometimes in contradictory ways: there are hints of abandon, of fires banked, lurking in most proper damsels (think Grace Kelly or Deborah Kerr), as there are aspirations and yearnings in the more earthbound and less ethereal, like Shirley MacLaine and Kim Novak. For all their femininity, there was in most of the greats a touch of masculinity: consider the androgyny in Garbo's sleek, boyish beauty or in husky-voiced Barbara Stanwyck's no-nonsense style.

Add to the mix a huge amount of luck. Legion are the stories of almost stars and might-have-beens: if slender, dark, and lovely Jean Simmons had not been prevented by producer Howard Hughes (who owned her contract) from starring in *Roman Holiday*, we might talk today of a Jean Simmons type rather than an Audrey Hepburn type. Instead, an unknown Dutch-British girl, also slender, dark, and lovely, emerged to steal our hearts.

There was something else we know nothing of today: reticence—both on and off the screen. From time immemorial, the studios controlled the stars' images and protected these gods and goddesses from the press. There was no TV—and, consequently, no celebrity interviews, no talk shows that would expose their "humanity," their scandals, their boringness. There were fan magazines, whose job it was to worship the beloved, and according to which Joan Crawford, say, was a wonderful housewife and mother—a far cry from the monster with coat hangers of her adopted daughter's revisionist book *Mommie Dearest* and its film adaptation. As ridiculous and contrived as these fan-magazine stories were, their idols were kept idealized, magical. And when the stars appeared in public, they were like visiting royalty; today's intimate, one-on-one junket interviews were unknown.

And, perhaps most important, this distance, this reserve, was deeply characteristic of the films themselves. Sex never entered the picture except as subtext, as eyes locked in an amorous gaze, a single passionate kiss as consummation. There was no grappling, no nudity, no body doubles. There was the matter of, for example, Greer Garson's artificially fatted calves for her showgirl scenes in *Random Harvest*, but, essentially, the stars were unknowable in the carnal sense, nice girls were virgins, and saying no was a huge and essential ingredient of women's power. Foreplay was 90 minutes of sparkling conversation, or smoldering looks, or comic obstacles, all designed to forestall and stand in for the actual commingling. This very lack of fulfillment created a continuous sense of yearning on the part of viewers, whose identification with the stars was a far more intense communion than our more fickle, celebrity-gossip fixation on the stars today. In the space where "nothing" happened, everything happened.

The downside was that the stars felt constricted by their rigid placement in the studio grid, by their lack of freedom, and by the narrowness and mediocrity of the roles they were sometimes obliged to play. Bette Davis and Olivia de Havilland famously fought back, simply walking out on Warner Bros., forcing the studio to renegotiate their contracts. They had clout back then, as well as faces! Those were the days when women were essential to the filmmaking process, commanded salaries equal to their male counterparts, and appeared in equal numbers on annual lists of box office favorites, very different from the current lopsided situation in which for every lone "bankable" woman like Julia Roberts, twenty male stars constitute a significant box office draw and can sell a picture.

Still, a shortcoming of a "system" of filmmaking, almost by definition, was its exclusion of actresses who didn't fit into the preset molds, those women who were just a little too exotic, too sophisticated, too worldly, or too unrepentantly pleasure seeking for the morals and taboos of Hollywood. Louise Brooks, playing amoral vamps with good humor, was tantalizing under German director G.W. Pabst, but she lost half her brazen and ambiguous allure in American movies, and even European stars like Marlene Dietrich and Greta Garbo, who had found their niche in the heady precensorship days, suddenly found themselves out of fashion in the more standardized and sanitized movie world of the mid- to late thirties. The puritanical bias that kept sex out of movies (especially from 1933 on, under the reign of the Production Code) also barred sexy women who might contaminate innocent Americans. Off screen, prudery was on the ascendancy, as an outraged public crucified Ingrid Bergman for having an adulterous affair and a child (with Roberto Rossellini) and virtually drove her from the country.

Probably the fallout would have been milder had the same actress not become an icon of saintliness as the nun in *The Bells of Saint Mary's*. But this film, along with such classics as *Notorious* and *Gaslight*, showed what Hollywood could do right! Look at Bergman in a pre-Hollywood Swedish film such as *Intermezzo*—she's just out of drama school, overly made up, gesturing and acting for all she's worth. Once under the tutelage of Selznick and the other behind-the-camera geniuses, however, she learns to be "natural." Off comes the makeup (redundant, in her case), and the gesticulations disappear. In the beauty of her stillness, she absorbs the camera's gaze and learns the language of the close-up, where the merest traces, flickers of expression, convey an agony of longing.

Movies are a medium of surfaces, but those surfaces must convey depths, and the eyes are, of course, the windows of the soul. With Vivien Leigh, a similar transformation takes place. A pretty but undistinguished English actress with a few black-and-white melodramas under her belt suddenly appears on wide screen and in color, and the arguments over who should have played Scarlett are instantly moot. Here was everything one could demand of Margaret Mitchell's memorable heroine: the delicious Southern accent, the tiny waist, the mixture of Irish tough and Southern belle, of charm, competence, and conniving, all somehow fused into one entrancing vixen, but first and last were those green cat's eyes, Leigh's most dazzling feature, and one to which only the comparatively new Technicolor process could do justice.

Thanks to the glories of television and the new video technologies, we can revisit the cinematic past as if it were yesterday, form new crushes and affinities, discover the delights of Jean Arthur or Rosalind Russell as freshly minted leading ladies. Still, it is not just technology that renders these women so vibrantly contemporaneous and important. What makes them more than just a curiosity to the young, and, for older viewers, more than just a walk down Memory Lane, is that they also illuminate our lives, provide a missing part of the puzzle of women's "liberation."

At a time when very few women worked at all, and it was taken for granted that they were subordinate to men in marriage, here were women who radiated power on screen, and as actresses and star "commodities" were making salaries equal to men. Even when stories dictated that, under the rules of romantic contrivance, they capitulate in the end, we were left with a quite different sense of them as heroic free spirits, contravening any and every implication of submission. And in these stories, they struggled with many of the same anxieties that beset us today, juggling friendship and ambition and the need for love, making choices both wise and foolish, carving out individual paths.

Today's young women, benefiting from wider professional opportunities and greater sexual freedom, and operating under the assumption that we've "come a long way, baby" from the benighted eras of our mothers and grandmothers, are often staggered by the incredible presence of these earlier stars—their strength of mind, their confidence, their brio and female swagger. These icons of a bygone era seem, in many ways, more authoritative, more at ease in their skin, than stars today. We may find ourselves returning to them for inspiration and as an antidote to our present-day anxieties, forming as they do an ongoing historical basis for a belief in women's potential.

I'm fully convinced that we've absorbed them into our collective bloodstream, that these exceptional women are part of the atmosphere breathed by even those who never saw them firsthand, and a lot of what we are and enjoy today we owe to the images they so radiantly provided. Cloaked in seductive femininity, the leading ladies of the studio system projected an aura of power and independence that was itself a flag of protest planted in the soil of inequality.

Frank Capra called her his favorite actress for the depth and humanity she brought to her comedic roles, but it was her husky, tremulous voice that spun her gentle kookiness into gold.

JEAN
ARTHUR

Some stars find their niche almost as soon as they arrive in Hollywood. Others, like Jean Arthur, require years of false starts to establish what they do best. Though a late bloomer, when Jean arrived she was one of the best of the best. After leaving high school to become a model, Jean soon found herself in Hollywood, playing earnest cowgirls and saucy flappers in silent films. The talkies should have brought her into full blossom, showcasing her tremulous, husky voice. But Paramount, her studio during these early years, didn't know what to do with her. When they let her go, Jean headed to Broadway, where she got her first decent reviews and honed her comedic skills. Theatrical success brought Columbia calling, and studio head Harry Cohn promised her bigger and better roles. After she appeared in a few tiresome weepers, director John Ford cast her in *The Whole Town's Talking* (1935), a comedy that showcased her particular charms. Yet it was work with director Frank Capra that many feel brought out her best in films like *Mr. Deeds Goes to Town* (1936) and *You Can't Take It with You* (1938). Jean's voice and soulful eyes added depth to her comic roles, suggesting a pained spirit behind the laughter. Her natural poise, combined with her capacity for deep feeling, made her an everywoman for the masses, whether playing Calamity Jane in Cecil B. DeMille's *The Plainsman* (1936) or a struggling salesgirl in *Easy Living* (1937). But success didn't really satisfy Jean. Painfully shy, she balked at the demands of stardom. After making two comedies with director George Stevens, *The Talk of the Town* (1942) and *The More the Merrier* (1943), a salary dispute with Cohn sent her back to Broadway. She quit the stage production of *Born Yesterday* during previews, reinforcing a growing reputation for difficult behavior, and then toured with Boris Karloff in *Peter Pan*. She only returned to Hollywood twice, for director Billy Wilder's spoof of post-war Germany, *A Foreign Affair* (1948), and Stevens's new take on the Western, *Shane* (1953). Sporadic stage and television work, along with teaching, occupied her for many years. She resisted efforts to open up her life to public prying, so reclusive in her final years she was called "America's Garbo." Even after her death, she remains one of Hollywood's greatest enigmas, an icon who never shared herself with audiences except through her roles.

Born
Gladys Georgianna Greene
October 17, 1900
Plattsburgh, New York

Died
June 19, 1991
Carmel, California,
of heart failure

Star Sign
Libra

Height
5'3"

Husbands
Photographer Julian Anker
(1928, annulled after one day)

Producer Frank Ross Jr.
(1932–49, divorced)

Essential
JEANARTHURFilms

MR. DEEDS GOES TO TOWN
(1936) Columbia
The first of Arthur's three films for director Frank Capra, a heart-warming account of an unassuming Vermont man (Gary Cooper) who inherits a fortune and creates a controversy by passing it on to the needy. Arthur is the hard-boiled reporter who goes soft after falling for the guy.

YOU CAN'T TAKE IT WITH YOU (1938) Columbia
The whimsical Moss Hart–George S. Kaufman play about a family of crackpots, turned into an Oscar-winning film by director Frank Capra. As the "normal" daughter, Arthur falls in love with James Stewart and learns not to be embarrassed by her crazy but lovable family.

MR. SMITH GOES TO WASHINGTON (1939) Columbia
The final entry in Arthur's Capra trilogy, a tale of a neophyte senator (James Stewart) who fervently fights corruption in the government. Arthur again plays the cynical one, a secretary this time, who is transformed by her man's idealism.

THE TALK OF THE TOWN
(1942) Columbia
A literate comedy about a law professor (Ronald Colman) and a falsely accused fugitive (Cary Grant) who compete for the hand of a pretty schoolteacher (Arthur). Arthur shows off her unique comedy style under the direction of George Stevens, later to direct her in a dramatic role in *Shane* (1953).

THE MORE THE MERRIER
(1943) Columbia
A witty account of a wartime housing shortage in Washington, D.C., that forces Arthur to share an apartment with a handsome guy (Joel McCrea) and an old codger determined to play Cupid (Oscar winner Charles Coburn). Arthur received her only Oscar nomination for this performance, once again directed by Stevens.

MR. SMITH GOES TO WASHINGTON, 1939

STYLENOTES

Although she seems a strange choice for the role, Jean was one of the four actresses to appear in the final round of screen tests for the role of Scarlett O'Hara in *Gone with the Wind* (1939). While the other three actresses dressed in studio costumes, Jean insisted on wearing a "scarlett" dress she had personally commissioned from costume designer Irene.

When Jean was displeased with a look created for her, she didn't mince words. On one set she actually tore up a wig and dress that didn't suit her.

Jean used many tricks to stay youthful. Even her closest friends were fuzzy on the details of where and when she was born, and she often wore a veil in public.

Jean claimed to be fairly disinterested in clothes until meeting up with designer Nolan Miller. Miller created elegant hats and satin coats for *The Jean Arthur Show* before going on to make costumes for both *Dynasty* and *Charlie's Angels*.

behindthescenes

THE FAMOUSLY PRIVATE JEAN COULDN'T IMAGINE WHY ANYONE WOULD WANT TO INTERVIEW HER. SOMETIMES SHE WENT AS FAR AS AGREEING TO MEET WITH A JOURNALIST BUT WOULD THEN CHANGE HER MIND, EVEN AFTER THE REPORTER HAD TRAVELED FAR FOR THE INTERVIEW. SHE WOULD THEN OFFER TO PAY WHAT THE WRITER WOULD HAVE RECEIVED FOR THE ARTICLE.

BORN YESTERDAY WAS NOT THE ONLY BROADWAY PRODUCTION THAT JEAN WALKED OUT ON. SHE ALSO QUIT DURING REHEARSALS OF *THE FIRST MONDAY IN OCTOBER,* A COMEDY ABOUT THE SUPREME COURT THAT HAD BEEN WRITTEN FOR HER, AND *THE FREAKING OUT OF STEPHANIE BLAKE,* WHICH NEVER EVEN MADE IT TO OPENING NIGHT.

FOR SEVERAL MONTHS IN 1966, JEAN STARRED IN THE *JEAN ARTHUR SHOW,* PLAYING A FEMALE LAWYER WHOSE SON WAS ALSO IN THE PROFESSION.

An overnight sensation in her first film, *To Have and Have Not*, publicists dubbed her "the Look" but it was really the whole package—the sultry glance, the husky voice, and the brash attitude.

LAUREN
BACALL

One of the screen's most independent women, Lauren Bacall grew up in a middle-class family in the Bronx. Her childhood interest in dance gave way to a passion for acting early on, and she studied at the American Academy of Dramatic Arts, where the young Kirk Douglas became a lifelong friend. Her first stage shows didn't do well, so to make ends meet she turned to modeling. A *Harper's Bazaar* cover caught the eye of producer-director Howard Hawks's wife, Slim, leading to a screen test for Bacall and the chance to make her screen debut as the star of *To Have and Have Not* (1944). An attack of the jitters forced her to hold her head down to keep it from shaking. But somehow all that came together to turn her into one of the sassiest, sexiest creatures ever to stalk the screen. Lauren won a horde of fans, not the least of them her leading man, Humphrey Bogart. Bogie and Baby, as they called each other, married a year later, while working on their second film with Hawks, *The Big Sleep* (1946). They would team up twice more before Bogart fell victim to cancer in 1957. On her own, Bacall moved to New York and reestablished herself as a stage star, first in the comedy *Cactus Flower* (1965), and later as the Tony award–winning star of the musicals *Applause* (1970), based on the classic film *All About Eve,* and *Woman of the Year* (1981). She also penned a best-selling 1979 autobiography, *By Myself,* which won a National Book Award. With her star persona intact, Lauren managed to make her screen appearances notable events. She joined an all-star cast for the Agatha Christie thriller *Murder on the Orient Express* (1974), comforted a dying John Wayne in *The Shootist* (1976) and capitalized on her Broadway fame as a musical star stalked by *The Fan* (1981). More recently she won an Oscar nomination (after over fifty years in films) for her role as Barbra Streisand's glamorous mother in *The Mirror Has Two Faces* (1996) and has joined rising star Nicole Kidman in a pair of dramas, *Dogville* (2003) and *Birth* (2004). Even in her eighties, Lauren continues to possess one of the sexiest voices in the business, putting her in demand for commercial voice-overs for everything from cat food to luxury cruises.

Born
Betty Joan Perske
September 16, 1924
Bronx, New York

Star Sign
Virgo

Height
5'8½"

Husbands and Children
Humphrey Bogart
(1945–57, his death)
two children,
Stephen and Leslie
Jason Robards Jr.

Essential
LAURENBACALLFilms

TO HAVE AND HAVE NOT

(1944) Warner Bros.
Bacall's sizzling on-screen introduction to future husband Humphrey Bogart, in the film version of the Hemingway story about a skipper-for-hire caught up in the French resistance. Bacall, as a sexy pickpocket dubbed "Slim," created a sensation by being even tougher than her smitten costar.

THE BIG SLEEP

(1946) Warner Bros.
A reteaming of Bogart and Bacall in a private-eye yarn so convoluted that even original author Raymond Chandler couldn't explain the plot. Once again, what counts is the potent sexual chemistry, as Bacall's wealthy divorcée trades lusty gazes and double entendres with Bogart's Philip Marlowe.

DARK PASSAGE

(1947) Warner Bros.
A new, gentler angle on the Bogie-Bacall on-screen relationship, with Bogart as an escaped convict unjustly accused of his wife's murder and Bacall as a lonely heiress who helps him hide.

KEY LARGO

(1948) Warner Bros.
The fourth and final entry in the Bogart-Bacall series, a film treatment by writer-director John Huston of the Maxwell Anderson play about a gangster (Edward G. Robinson) who commandeers a crumbling Florida hotel. Bacall plays a war widow drawn to Bogart's world-weary yet idealistic veteran.

HOW TO MARRY A MILLIONAIRE

(1953) 20th Century-Fox
The first CinemaScope comedy, with Bacall joining Marilyn Monroe and Betty Grable as a trio of Manhattan gold diggers. Bacall is the smart, cynical one—who nonetheless follows her heart and gives up rich William Powell in favor of the attractive but supposedly poor Cameron Mitchell.

CIRCA 1944

STYLENOTES

Lauren Bacall's trademark look was a winning combination of natural beauty and sophistication. Her brows remained unplucked, her teeth unstraightened. Yet she dressed perfectly for her body type—tall, thin, flat chested—in slightly mannish suits, belted and snug, that showed off her nice waist and legs.

When Lauren became pregnant in the late 1940s, she designed a maternity wardrobe that was decades ahead of its time: suits and skirts that capitalized on her changing figure rather than concealing it.

Whether worn dressed up or down, Lauren's jewelry collection is simple and elegant. When she and Humphrey Bogart were courting, he gave her a gold bracelet with a whistle, in honor of her famous line in *To Have and Have Not*.

Down-to-earth Lauren has this view of aging: "I think your whole life shows in your face and you should be proud of that."

behindthescenes

LAUREN BACALL IS THE COUSIN OF FORMER ISRAELI FOREIGN MINISTER SHIMON PERES. THEY EVEN SHARE THE SAME SURNAME, PERSKE.

PRODUCER-DIRECTOR HOWARD HAWKS MODELED LAUREN'S SCREEN PERSONA ON HIS WIFE, SLIM. MUCH OF BACALL'S DIALOGUE, MANNER OF DRESS, AND SPEAKING (THAT FAMOUS DEEP VOICE) WERE PATTERNED AFTER SLIM. THEN, TO HAWKS'S ANNOYANCE, BACALL FELL FOR A BALDING BOGART INSTEAD OF HIM.

LAUREN GOT HER STAGE NAME BY ADDING AN *L* TO HER MOTHER'S MAIDEN NAME, BACAL.

Forever remembered as *Casablanca*'s luminous Ilsa Lund, she radiated a truth and goodness that she found hard to escape even in her most controversial roles.

INGRID
BERGMAN

As a shy, young orphan in Sweden, Ingrid Bergman dreamed of becoming an actress. She started appearing in films while still a teenager, eventually rising to stardom. Her film *Intermezzo* (1936), in which she played a classical pianist in love with a married violinist, brought her to the attention of independent producer David O. Selznick. Many foreign stars were happy to come to America and be remade by Hollywood, but Ingrid would have none of it. When Selznick brought her to the States to star in an American version of *Intermezzo* (1939), she insisted on maintaining her natural hair color, eyebrows, and makeup. Selznick saw the publicity value in her position and sold her as a natural, fresh-faced heroine. *Intermezzo* was a hit, but Ingrid soon chafed at being typecast as a good girl. When Selznick loaned her to MGM to costar with Spencer Tracy and Lana Turner in *Dr. Jekyll and Mr. Hyde* (1941) she fought to switch from the leading lady role to the sluttish barmaid originally earmarked for Turner. The switch was made and she walked off with the film. But, despite her attempts to vary her roles, her typecasting as "St. Ingrid" continued, thanks largely to her performances as a World War II resistance fighter in *Casablanca* (1942) and as a nun in *The Bells of St. Mary's* (1945). However, her reputation was changed forever when she and Italian director Roberto Rossellini, both married to other people, fell in love while filming *Stromboli* (1949) in Europe. The affair triggered an international scandal, particularly when they had a child out of wedlock. Suddenly St. Ingrid was vilified on the floor of Congress and exiled from Hollywood. It wasn't until the marriage was on its last legs that 20th Century-Fox asked her to star in *Anastasia* (1956). The same audiences who had rejected Bergman now welcomed her back. She moved gracefully into mature roles, still radiating that essential goodness and emotional truth that had made her a star. She also returned to the stage in classics by Eugene O'Neill and George Bernard Shaw. Ingrid scored a particular triumph when she finally joined forces with Swedish director Ingmar Bergman for *Autumn Sonata* (1978). Even as her health was declining, she courageously took on the role of Golda Meir in the television miniseries *A Woman Called Golda* (1982), winning an Emmy for what would be her final performance.

Born
August 29, 1915
Stockholm, Sweden

Died
August 29, 1982
London, England,
of lymphoma complications
following a
breast cancer operation

Star Sign
Virgo

Height
5'9½"

Husbands and Children
Dr. Aron Petter Lindstrom
(1937–50, divorced)
daughter, Pia

Roberto Rossellini
(1950–57, divorced)
three children, Roberto Ingmar,
Isabella, and Isotta

Swedish stage
producer Lars Schmidt
(1958–76, divorced)

Essential
INGRID**BERGMAN**Films

INTERMEZZO

(1939) Swedish Film Production/ Scandinavian Talking Pictures Bergman's U.S. film debut, a remake of her 1937 Swedish film of the same title about a beautiful young pianist who falls for a famous married violinist (Leslie Howard).

CASABLANCA

(1942) Warner Bros.
The quintessential World War II romantic melodrama, with Bergman and Humphrey Bogart creating screen magic as star-crossed lovers reunited in the international hot spot after her marriage to resistance leader Paul Henreid.

GASLIGHT

(1944) MGM
Director George Cukor's film version of Patrick Hamilton's stage thriller about a Victorian bride whose ruthless husband (Charles Boyer) tries to convince her she's losing her mind. Bergman won the first of her three Oscars for her harrowing portrait of a woman on the brink of madness.

NOTORIOUS

(1946) RKO
Bergman's second teaming with director Alfred Hitchcock, and her first with Cary Grant, in a sexy espionage thriller about a "bad girl" who marries a neo-Nazi (Claude Rains) so she can spy on him. Grant is the American secret agent who engages Bergman in a memorable love-hate relationship.

ANASTASIA

(1956) 20th Century-Fox
Bergman's triumphant Hollywood comeback after a European exile occasioned by her affair with Italian director Roberto Rossellini. She won her second Oscar for a radiant performance as the woman who may or may not be the daughter of Czar Nicholas of Russia.

CASABLANCA, 1942

STYLENOTES

Costume designer Edith Head accessorized some stars to the nines, but she felt Ingrid Bergman looked best in simple lines: the less ornamentation, the better.

Ingrid refused to cap her teeth or pluck her eyebrows but happily chopped off her hair to portray Maria in *For Whom the Bell Tolls.*

Producer David O. Selznick wisely dealt with Ingrid's insistence on a natural appearance by publicizing her as the only natural girl in Hollywood.

At 5'9½", Ingrid Bergman towered over other actresses—and some male stars, too. When one producer, sizing her up, asked her to take off her heels, she had to explain, "I'm wearing flats." Shorter leading men like Humphrey Bogart had to wear lifts to work opposite her.

behindthescenes

INGRID GOT HER BIG HOLLYWOOD BREAK BY ACCIDENT. A SWEDISH COUPLE PRAISED THE FILM *INTERMEZZO* TO THEIR SON, A NEW YORK ELEVATOR OPERATOR. HE MENTIONED THE FILM TO ONE OF THE RESIDENTS OF THE BUILDING WHERE HE WORKED—WHO JUST HAPPENED TO BE A TALENT SCOUT FOR INDEPENDENT PRODUCER DAVID O. SELZNICK.

WHEN INGRID MET WRITER ERNEST HEMINGWAY TO DISCUSS HER ROLE IN *FOR WHOM THE BELL TOLLS,* HE WARNED HER THAT SHE WOULD HAVE TO CUT HER HAIR OFF. "TO GET THAT PART," SHE SAID, "I'D CUT MY HEAD OFF!" HER HAIRCUT PLAYED A SIGNIFICANT ROLE IN FILM HISTORY. WARNER BROS. COMPOSER MAX STEINER HAD CONVINCED THE STUDIO TO LET HIM WRITE A NEW SONG FOR *CASABLANCA,* BUT THAT WOULD HAVE REQUIRED BRINGING INGRID BACK TO RESHOOT SCENES IN RICK'S CAFÉ AMERICAIN, AND THE STUDIO HAIRDRESSERS COULDN'T MATCH HER ORIGINAL HAIRSTYLE. THE RETAKES WERE CANCELED, AND THE SONG "AS TIME GOES BY" STAYED IN THE FILM.

ROBERTO ROSSELLINI AND INGRID BERGMAN, CIRCA 1950

Hollywood's first "It" girl, she was a come-hither goddess with enough energy and charm to light every soundstage in Hollywood.

CLARA
BOW

A tragic heroine long before she ever made a movie, Clara Bow was born dirt poor in one of New York's most notorious slums to an insane mother and an abusive, alcoholic father. Too raggedly dressed to be accepted by the other girls in the neighborhood, she became a tomboy, which may have signaled the birth of her trademark high spirits. Clara escaped poverty by going to the picture shows, but when she won a part in a silent movie, her mother tried to save her girl from the depravity of Hollywood by attempting to slit her daughter's throat as she slept. After a string of supporting roles, Clara played her first flapper in 1925's *The Plastic Age* and made the role her own. With bobbed hair that refused to behave, darkly shadowed eyes, heart-shaped lips, and a fizzy flirty attitude, she was the embodiment of the Jazz Age, the girl who threw her corset and conventional morality out the window. With *It* (1927), the country fell in love—and lust—with the naughty girl next door. But though the public loved her on screen as the independent, hard-living and -loving party girl, off screen Clara's image was tarnished by her constant string of boyfriends and affairs. She further alienated Hollywood insiders by telling the press every sordid detail of her childhood at a time when movie stars never admitted to having such problems. Yet she had her fans; many colleagues have hailed her as the best actress ever to work in silent films, impressed by her ability to enliven cardboard plots with her high-energy improvisation. Trouble arrived with the talkies; according to legend, her raucous delivery blew out the mikes with her first line. Moreover, she refused to change her Brooklyn accent and drove soundmen wild trying to keep up with her improvisatory acting. Then, just as she adjusted to the new medium, another scandal hit. Clara caught her secretary embezzling from her and turned her in, but during the trial the former friend told all (and invented a bit more) about her many affairs. With the Great Depression calling into question Jazz Age excesses, Clara's career was over. After making fifty-eight films in just over a decade, she was a has-been at the age of twenty-six. Problems with weight and mental illness made any hope of a comeback impossible. Clara died alone at the age of sixty.

Born
Clara Gordon Bow
July 29, 1905
Brooklyn, New York

Died
September 26, 1965
Los Angeles, California,
of a heart attack

Star Sign
Leo

Height
5'3"

Husband and Children
Cowboy star Rex Bell
(1931–62, his death)
two sons, Rex Anthony and
George Robert

Essential
CLARABOWFilms

MANTRAP
(1926) Paramount
As the flirtatious bride of a much older backwoodsman in the Canadian town of Mantrap, Bow can't help flirting with a famous lawyer who shows up on vacation.

IT
(1927) Paramount
The film that sparked Bow's nickname, "the 'It' Girl." Bow plays a shopgirl who employs her bountiful charms in landing the handsome owner (Antonio Moreno) of the store where she works.

WINGS
(1927) Paramount
The first Best Picture Oscar winner, director William Wellman's silent epic about two World War I aviators (Buddy Rogers and Richard Arlen) in love with the same Red Cross nurse (Bow). To get Bow out of her uniform and into something sexy, the writers devised a sequence in which she poses as a Parisian tart to rescue Rogers from a drunken revel.

DANGEROUS CURVES
(1929) Paramount
A circus story, with Bow as a young bareback rider who loves a high-wire artist (Richard Arlen) and consoles him after his partner (Kay Francis) spurns him and he turns to alcohol. Brooklyn accent intact, Bow shares a comedy act with Arlen as part of his rehabilitation.

THE SATURDAY NIGHT KID
(1929) Paramount
A tale of two sisters, Bow and Jean Arthur, who work at a department store while keeping their eyes open for marriageable men. When both girls fall for wealthy Bill (James Hall), bad sister Arthur overplays her hand and the uncharacteristically restrained Bow claims him in the end.

WINGS, 1927

STYLENOTES

Best known as a perfect example of the playfully sexy Roaring Twenties flapper, Clara favored a short bob under cloche hats, low-cut dresses designed for boyish figures, and skirts designed to flash some leg while doing the Charleston.

Hollywood designer Travis Banton was the man behind some of Clara's most sophisticated movie gowns, but the actress drove Banton crazy by cutting up his designs. "She slit his necklines and cut off his sleeves," recalled fellow flapper icon Louise Brooks. "Clara was quite beyond Banton, and quite right."

Clara's mass of tangled, slept-on red hair was her most famous attribute and her most artificial. When fans of the new star found out she put henna in her hair, sales of the dye tripled.

Clara applied her red lipstick in the shape of a heart. Women who imitated this shape were said to be putting a "Clara Bow" on their mouths.

behindthescenes

ROMANCE NOVELIST ELINOR GLYN DUBBED CLARA BOW "THE 'IT' GIRL" AFTER THE FILM VERSION OF HER NOVEL *IT* BECAME A ROUSING SUCCESS. SHE GAVE INTERVIEWS EXPLAINING THAT "IT" WAS "THAT STRANGE MAGNETISM THAT ATTRACTS BOTH SEXES." WHEN ASKED TO NAME THOSE WHO HAD "IT," GLYN POINTED TO ONLY THREE INDIVIDUALS IN HOLLYWOOD: REX THE WONDER HORSE, THE DOORMAN AT THE AMBASSADOR HOTEL, AND CLARA BOW. ACTUALLY, PARAMOUNT HAD PAID HER TO HELP BOOST CLARA'S CAREER.

DIRECTORS LOVED WORKING WITH CLARA ONCE THEY GOT USED TO HER FREE-SPIRITED METHODS. SHE RARELY FOLLOWED DIRECTION, BUT SHE COULD BE COUNTED ON TO INVENT JUST THE RIGHT BUSINESS AND MOVEMENTS ON THE SET. HER IMPROVISATIONS WERE SO FREE THAT THE CAMERAMEN OFTEN HAD TROUBLE KEEPING HER IN FRAME.

CLARA PREFERRED PLAYING POKER WITH HER COOK, MAID, AND CHAUFFEUR OVER ATTENDING HER MOVIE PREMIERES.

CLARA BECAME A LIFELONG INSOMNIAC AFTER HER MOTHER TRIED TO KILL HER IN HER SLEEP.

NOT ONLY DID CLARA KISS AND TELL; SHE DID SO IN LANGUAGE THAT WOULD MAKE A SAILOR BLUSH.

A VISIBLY NERVOUS CLARA HAD TO DO A NUMBER OF RETAKES IN THE WILD PARTY (1929), HER FIRST TALKIE, BECAUSE HER EYES KEPT WANDERING UP TO THE MICROPHONE OVERHEAD.

IT, 1927

Beautiful, headstrong, and erotically charged, she and her sleek, bobbed hairstyle defined the 1920s flapper just as her meteoric rise and fall mirrored the fortunes of the Lost Generation.

LOUISE
BROOKS

Louise Brooks was raised to read and think and dance, and to turn those skills into a life of culture and fame. At sixteen, she left home for New York City to take the world of modern dance by storm. Yet rebellious Louise could only be herself, and as a result she was eventually kicked out of Ruth Saint Denis's dance company for her impertinent attitude. Louise, ever resilient, soon found work all over as the toast of London's Piccadilly Circus, as a Ziegfeld girl, and, eventually, as an aspiring film star. Signing with Paramount, Louise made six pictures in 1926. Her offscreen carousing led colleagues to dismiss her as a tawdry vamp, but her look and boundless enthusiasm made her a Jazz Age icon. With her keen intelligence and intuitive acting, the charismatic, critical actress found little to admire in Hollywood. Embittered over studio politics and itching for a new adventure, Louise shocked the industry by abandoning Paramount to work with director G. W. Pabst in Berlin. In typical fashion, Louise had no idea of the coup she had scored: Pabst's search for an actress to play the sexually ravenous Lulu in *Pandora's Box* (1928) rivaled Hollywood's later search for Scarlett O'Hara. The story of a sexually free spirit who innocently destroys everyone who falls within her orbit made Louise an international sensation. She shared her character's innocence, thinking that Hollywood would tolerate her continued defiance. Yet a final run-in with Paramount proved to be too much, and Louise's film acting career ended in 1938. She returned to Kansas and tried teaching dance, but her tempestuous manner was ill suited to encouraging young performers. Back in New York, she lived in obscurity and destitution until former lover Bill Paley, the founder of CBS, set up a monthly stipend that supported her for the rest of her life. More than two decades passed, with Louise's spectacular career a fading memory, until the persistence of her admirers and a noteworthy article in The *New Yorker* brought her back into the public eye. During the last twenty years of her life, Louise lived in Rochester, New York, and became a sought-after film historian and accomplished writer.

Born
Mary Louise Brooks
November 14, 1906
Cherryvale, Kansas

Died
August 8, 1985
Rochester, New York,
of a heart attack

Star Sign
Scorpio

Height
5'2"

Husbands
Director A. Edward Sutherland
(1926–28, divorced)

Playboy Dearing Davis
(1933–38, divorced)

Essential
LOUISEBROOKSFilms

A SOCIAL CELEBRITY

(1926) Paramount
Silent comedy-drama with Brooks
as a small-town manicurist who
goes to New York with her boyfriend
(Adolphe Menjou), a barber who
poses as a French count.

LOVE 'EM AND LEAVE 'EM

(1926) Paramount
Silent film version of a stage
comedy cowritten by George
Abbott about two competitive
sisters (Brooks and Evelyn Brent).
Brooks is the "bad" sibling who
steals money to play the horses
and tries to steal her sister's beau
(Lawrence Gray).

PANDORA'S BOX

(1928) Nero-Film
German director G. W. Pabst's
most celebrated work, a silent film
starring Brooks as a hedonistic
dancer named Lulu who turns to
prostitution after alienating her
associates in Weimar, Germany. This
is the vehicle that would transform
Brooks from a pretty Hollywood
ingenue into an icon of the Jazz Age.

DIARY OF A LOST GIRL

(1929) Hom Film/Pabst Film
Brooks's reunion with G. W. Pabst
after *Pandora's Box*, another silent
study of a troubled young woman
that would in time gain cult status.
Brooks is Thymiane, an innocent
who is impregnated by a chemist
and, after working as a prostitute,
marries a wealthy older man.

MISS EUROPE

(1930) Sofar-Film
A French film, released in both
silent and sound versions and titled
Prix de Beaute in its native land.
Brooks plays a Parisian typist who
wins a beauty contest and a movie
contract, only to have her brush
with fame lead to tragedy.

CIRCA 1926

STYLE NOTES

Louise's trademark bob was so popular during the 1920s that Parisian coiffeur Antoine established a "bobbing salon" at Saks on Fifth Avenue. Her famous haircut was talked about in every film and fashion magazine, and countless women copied it.

Louise loved glamour and her sense of style quickly made her a Hollywood trendsetter. "When I went to Hollywood in 1927, the girls were wearing lumpy sweaters and skirts . . . I was wearing sleek suits and half-naked beaded gowns and piles and piles of furs."

In Louise's words, "a well-dressed woman, even though her purse is painfully empty, can conquer the world."

Along with bobbed hair, other fashion innovations Brooks helped popularize were the cloche hat (the perfect complement for bobbed hair) and ankle watches. The latter hasn't quite survived the era.

LOVE 'EM AND LEAVE 'EM, 1926

behind the scenes

AT THE HEIGHT OF HER POPULARITY, LOUISE BROOKS WAS THE INSPIRATION FOR THE GERSHWIN MUSICAL *SHOW GIRL*. THAT PLAY, IN TURN, INSPIRED THE COMIC STRIP *DIXIE DUGAN*, WHOSE HEROINE SPORTED LOUISE'S TRADEMARK BLACK BOB.

G. W. PABST NEARLY SIGNED MARLENE DIETRICH FOR *PANDORA'S BOX*, ALTHOUGH HE GREATLY PREFERRED LOUISE (THIS WAS TWO YEARS BEFORE *THE BLUE ANGEL* MADE MARLENE A STAR). ACCORDING TO PABST, MARLENE WAS IN HIS OFFICE WAITING TO SIGN THE CONTRACT WHEN A CABLE CAME FROM PARAMOUNT SAYING THAT LOUISE WAS WILLING TO PLAY THE ROLE.

HER FILM CAREER ALMOST OVER, LOUISE WAS ACTING ON STAGE UNDER AN ASSUMED NAME, LINDA CARTER, WHEN A TALENT SCOUT FROM 20TH CENTURY-FOX DISCOVERED HER AND OFFERED HER A SCREEN TEST.

DURING HER YEARS OF OBSCURITY AFTER LEAVING HOLLYWOOD, LOUISE PERFORMED A VARIETY OF JOBS, INCLUDING A $40-A-WEEK GIG AS A SALES CLERK AT SAKS. SOME BIOGRAPHERS HAVE SUGGESTED SHE ALSO TURNED TO PROSTITUTION.

PANDORA'S BOX, 1928

She had true grace and class and radiated European chic, but it was her spunk and clever wit that made her accessible to all.

CLAUDETTE
COLBERT

Claudette Colbert was born French but quickly became the ultimate modern American woman after her family moved to the United States when she was three. She debuted on Broadway at the age of twenty and soon became a reliable leading lady. Claudette made her screen debut in the 1927 silent film *For the Love of Mike,* but she didn't care for the movies. She only returned to the screen when the Depression led to a decline in theatrical production. She caught on in her first few pictures, but her career didn't really take off until a picture she hated, *It Happened One Night* (1934), became a surprise hit and brought her an Oscar. The following year, Claudette found happiness off screen with a well-respected surgeon, and this stable relationship allowed her to focus on, as she put it, "being Claudette Colbert." That meant building a solid fan following in romances like *Imitation of Life* (1934), historical adventures like *Drums Along the Mohawk* (1939), and, best of all, comedies. Whether helping John Barrymore win back his philandering wife in *Midnight* (1939) or trying to land a rich husband in *The Palm Beach Story* (1942), Colbert had the charisma and flair to get laughs without straining. Her natural style also made her a perfect choice to embody America's homeland spirit during World War II in *Since You Went Away* (1944). When she injured her back filming the prison camp drama *Three Came Home* (1950), it cost her one of the great roles of all time, Margo Channing in *All About Eve* (1950). By the early 1950s, Claudette's film career had begun to fade, but she moved easily to the stage and television. She made her last Hollywood film, *Parrish* (1961), to help pay for an estate she wanted to buy in Barbados. In her later years that Barbados hideaway welcomed high society, old Hollywood, and even royalty with tea on the terrace and formal dinners every night. Claudette aged gracefully, with a perennially youthful look that was part genes and part sheer will. She made one final television appearance, as Ann-Margret's glamorous mother-in-law in *The Two Mrs. Grenvilles* (1982), which won her a Golden Globe.

Born
Lily Claudette Chauchoin
September, 13, 1903
Paris, France

Died
July 30, 1996
Speightstown, Barbados,
after a series of strokes

Star Sign
Virgo

Height
5'4 ½"

Husbands
Actor-director Norman Foster
(1928–35, divorced)

Dr. Joel Pressman
(1935–68, his death)

Essential
CLAUDETTE COLBERT Films

THE SIGN OF THE CROSS

(1932) Paramount
Cecil B. DeMille's first sound hit, set in ancient Rome, with Colbert as the lascivious Empress Poppaea, Fredric March as the military leader who is the object of her lust, and Charles Laughton as Nero. Colbert's most celebrated scene has her bathing in a pool of milk.

IT HAPPENED ONE NIGHT

(1934) Columbia
Frank Capra's charming romantic comedy won Oscars in all major categories including Best Actress for Colbert as the runaway heiress who meets up with a wisecracking reporter (Clark Gable) on the hunt for a good story. The film is full of memorable moments, including Colbert's famous hitchhiking scene in which she flashes some leg to stop a speeding car in its tracks.

MIDNIGHT

(1939) Paramount
A screwball picture that hints at the later, darker comedies of cowriter Billy Wilder, with Colbert as a cynical Cinderella who finds love despite herself. With Don Ameche and John Barrymore as costars, she plays an American showgirl posing as a Hungarian countess in Paris.

THE PALM BEACH STORY

(1942) Paramount
One more example of Colbert's skills as a farceur, this time working under director Preston Sturges. As the wife of an impoverished inventor (Joel McCrea), Colbert boards a train to Palm Beach in search of a second husband wealthy enough to support her man's crackpot schemes.

SINCE YOU WENT AWAY

(1944) United Artists
The other side of Colbert's screen image—the loyal, courageous wife. It was considered daring at the time for an actress in her late thirties to play the mother of grown children, as Colbert does in this story of a family serving on the home front during World War II.

IT HAPPENED ONE NIGHT, 1934

STYLENOTES

Claudette was obsessed with how she was photographed. She even preferred to do her own hair and makeup. She considered her left side her best and only rarely allowed full face or right profile shots; an injury to her nose had created a bump on the right. Once an entire set had to be rebuilt so she wouldn't have to show her right side. Film crews dubbed her right profile "the dark side of the moon."

Claudette had trouble working with Travis Banton, Edith Head, and other studio costume designers at Paramount. The daughter of a dressmaker, she was very critical of others' designs for her. Eventually Sophie Gimbel, her offscreen designer, became her on-screen designer as well.

Claudette's trademark fluffy bangs were first fashioned by Hollywood hairstylist Sydney Guilaroff to bring out what he called her "French and American elegance." She wore them for more than sixty years.

behindthescenes

FOUR MAJOR ACTRESSES PASSED ON *IT HAPPENED ONE NIGHT.* HARDLY SUSPECTING IT WOULD BECOME HER MOST MEMORABLE FILM, CLAUDETTE LONGED TO PASS AS WELL, ONLY AGREEING TO STAR IF THEY COULD WRAP HER ROLE UP IN TIME FOR A MUCH-ANTICIPATED CHRISTMAS WITH FRIENDS. CLAUDETTE'S ASSESSMENT OF THE FILM DURING THAT CHRISTMASTIME? "I'M GLAD I GOT HERE; I JUST FINISHED THE WORST PICTURE OF THE YEAR."

THE VILLAINESS CLAUDETTE COLBERT PLAYED IN *THE SIGN OF THE CROSS* BATHED IN MILK, REQUIRING HER TO SIT UNDER BRIGHT LIGHTS IN THE SMELLY, SPOILED LIQUID. SHOOTING WAS CONTINUALLY HALTED AS THE MILK RECEDED BELOW THE LEVEL OF CLAUDETTE'S BREASTS , AND THE STENCH REACHED SUCH A STATE THAT CLAUDETTE PRONOUNCED, "WELL, IT'S SUPPOSED TO BE A CHEESECAKE SHOT, ISN'T IT?" ONE WOMAN'S SUFFERING TURNED OUT TO BE MANY WOMEN'S TREAT: THE SCENE INSPIRED THE INVENTION OF BUBBLE BATH, GIVING REGULAR WOMEN A TOUCH OF MOVIE LUXURY.

CLAUDETTE KEPT HER PRIVATE LIFE SOMEWHAT PRIVATE, YET SHE DID ADMIT TO A DALLIANCE WITH CLARK GABLE DURING THE FILMING OF *IT HAPPENED ONE NIGHT,* PRIMARILY TO DISPROVE UNFLATTERING RUMORS ABOUT HIS VIRILITY.

THE SIGN OF THE CROSS, 1932

From flappers to self-sacrificing mothers to horror film divas, she kept her career going for half a century thanks to her ability to change with the times, but off screen her devotion to Hollywood glamour and the demands of stardom never wavered.

JOAN
CRAWFORD

Born
Lucille Fay LeSueur
March 23, 1904
San Antonio, Texas

Died
May 10, 1977
New York, New York,
of pancreatic cancer

Star Sign
Aries

Height
5'4"

Husbands and Children
James Welton (1923–24, divorced)

Actor Douglas Fairbanks Jr.
(1929–33, divorced)

Actor Franchot Tone
(1935–39, divorced)

adopted daughter, Christina Crawford

Actor Phillip Terry
(1942–46, divorced)

adopted son, Christopher Crawford

two adopted daughters, Cathy and
Cynthia Crawford

Pepsi magnate Alfred Steele
(1955–59, his death)

Joan Crawford spent much of her early movie career playing shopgirls short on cash but long on moxie who talked and occasionally danced their way to a better life. These were characters near but not dear to her heart; her own divorced mother had toiled as a maid and a laundress, and living behind the laundry gave the future star her legendary drive. Winning an amateur dance contest in 1923 led to chorus work, which in turn brought her to MGM, where her wild Charleston in 1928's *Our Dancing Daughters* made her a star. Joan quickly adjusted to talking films, building a solid fan base in a series of rags-to-riches stories opposite such stars as Robert Montgomery, Clark Gable, and Spencer Tracy (she had affairs with the latter two). Despite her hits, however, Joan soon realized that she would never be the top star at MGM. She bitterly resented losing roles to Norma Shearer, wife of production chief Irving Thalberg, and seeing new actresses like Greer Garson quickly rise above her. With her box office diminishing in the early 1940s, she left MGM after eighteen years. Joan was wise enough to wait for just the right comeback vehicle, which she found at Warner Bros. in *Mildred Pierce* (1945). As the long-suffering mother who builds a restaurant empire for her rotten daughter, she brought her fans back into theaters and captured an Oscar. After her reign as Warner's resident soap opera queen, she reinvented herself again at RKO in 1952 as a playwright trapped in a murderous marriage in *Sudden Fear*. But her biggest comeback would come in 1962, when she and rival Bette Davis teamed up as a pair of faded stars playing psychological war games in *What Ever Happened to Baby Jane?* As a horror-film queen, Joan kept her career going for another decade. Along the way, she toured the globe as a goodwill ambassador for Pepsi-Cola, a deal worked out with her last husband, a top executive for the company. Through it all, she was determined to show the world what a Hollywood star was. As she told one interviewer, "If you're going to be a star, you have to look like a star, and I never go out unless I look like Joan Crawford the movie star. If you want to see the girl next door, go next door."

Essential
JOANCRAWFORDFilms

ACADEMY AWARDS

Won Best Actress
Mildred Pierce

Nominated for Best Actress
Possessed
Sudden Fear

GRAND HOTEL
(1932) MGM
As a stenographer torn between
a wealthy, corrupt industrialist
(Wallace Beery) and a dying clerk
(Lionel Barrymore), Joan Crawford
radiated both innocence and
sexuality, and almost stole the
picture from its all-star cast.

RAIN
(1932) United Artists
Crawford's go at Sadie Thompson,
the W. Somerset Maugham character
also played on film by Gloria
Swanson and Rita Hayworth. Walter
Huston is the fiery, hypocritical
preacher who clashes with good-
time girl Sadie in the South Seas.

MILDRED PIERCE
(1946) Warner Bros.
Crawford's victorious Warner Bros.
comeback after being dismissed
by MGM, for which she won a
Best Actress Oscar. In the James
M. Cain murder melodrama, she
plays a waitress who becomes a
successful businesswoman, only to
be betrayed by her ungrateful,
vindictive daughter (Ann Blyth).

POSSESSED
(1947) Warner Bros.
A tale of a nurse, played by
Crawford, whose unfulfilled passion
for architect Van Heflin leads her
to madness and possibly murder.
Raymond Massey costars as
Crawford's employer, whom she
marries after the apparent suicide
of his wife.

WHAT EVER HAPPENED TO
BABY JANE?
(1962) Warner Bros.
Grand Guignol thriller with Crawford
and Bette Davis as sisters sharing
a warped life in a decaying Los
Angeles house. Crawford is Blanche,
a former movie star who was
crippled in a mysterious automobile
accident; Davis, in grotesque
makeup, is Baby Jane, the faded
vaudeville star who delights in
tormenting her.

GRAND HOTEL, 1932

STYLENOTES

MGM costume designer Adrian played a huge role in the Joan Crawford look, nixing frilly ensembles in favor of tailored clothes with take-no-prisoner shoulder pads. From 1929 to 1943, Adrian created everything Joan wore on screen, and much of what she wore in her private life as well.

When Joan moved out of flapper roles and began playing shopgirls on the rise, she demanded a new look with bigger lips. Max Factor ran a smear of color across her mouth to create her trademark look. He called it "the smear," but the official industry name was "Hunter's Bow Lips." The look is credited with selling lipstick to a public who had formerly preferred subtler lips.

After Joan appeared in *Letty Lynton* (1932) wearing a white organdy gown designed for her by Adrian, Macy's department store alone sold five hundred thousand copies of it.

behind the scenes

SHE BECAME KNOWN AS JOAN CRAWFORD AFTER A MAGAZINE HELD A CONTEST TO RENAME THE STARLET. HER STUDIO BOSSES THOUGHT HER REAL SURNAME, LUCILLE LESUEUR, SOUNDED TOO MUCH LIKE "SEWER." SHE ALWAYS HATED HER SCREEN NAME, HOWEVER, CLAIMING IT SOUNDED LIKE "CRAWFISH."

SHE WAS OBSESSIVE ABOUT KNITTING, CLEANING, AND ANSWERING HER FAN MAIL PERSONALLY. THE ONLY LETTERS SHE DID NOT ANSWER WERE FROM FORMER CLASSMATES AT STEPHENS COLLEGE, WHERE SHE FELT SHE HAD BEEN TREATED HORRIBLY BECAUSE OF HER LOWER-CLASS BACKGROUND.

WHEN CAROLE LOMBARD DIED IN A PLANE CRASH, JOAN TOOK HER ROLE IN *THEY ALL KISSED THE BRIDE* (1942), DONATING HER SALARY IN LOMBARD'S NAME TO WAR RELIEF. WHEN JOAN'S AGENT STILL INSISTED ON GETTING HIS 10 PERCENT, SHE FIRED HIM.

GREAT HOLLYWOOD CATFIGHTS: JOAN CRAWFORD WOULD GO HEAD-TO-HEAD WITH ANYONE TO KEEP HER STAR STATUS, BUT SHE MET HER MATCH IN BETTE DAVIS WHEN THE LONGTIME RIVALS WERE CAST AS ABUSIVE SISTERS IN *WHAT EVER HAPPENED TO BABY JANE?* (1962). BETTE KICKED JOAN IN THE HEAD SO HARD DURING A FIGHT SCENE THAT SHE REQUIRED STITCHES. WHEN BETTE HAD TO DRAG JOAN ACROSS A ROOM, JOAN LOADED HER POCKETS WITH WEIGHTS, CAUSING AN INJURY TO BETTE'S BACK THAT LASTED FOR DAYS. *BABY JANE* WAS A HIT, AND THE TWO WERE PAIRED AGAIN FOR *HUSH . . . HUSH, SWEET CHARLOTTE* (1964), BUT AFTER THREE WEEKS OF THE REMATCH, JOAN THREW IN THE TOWEL AND QUIT THE FILM.

AS JOAN LAY DYING, HER LAST WORDS TO A PRAYING COMPANION WERE, "DAMN IT, DON'T YOU DARE ASK GOD TO HELP ME."

For years overshadowed by her love affair with tycoon William Randolph Hearst, her magnificent gifts as a comedienne are finally earning the accolades they deserve.

MARION
DAVIES

Marion Davies was raised by her mother to delight audiences with her beauty and talent and catch the eye of a man who could give her the good life. Neither woman could have imagined, however, that William Randolph Hearst, a newspaper magnate thirty-four years Marion's senior, would catch her in the chorus of a 1918 stage musical and never let her go. Even though Marion's producer brother-in-law had already helped her make the transition from stage to films, Hearst decided that she should be a superstar and turned a Harlem casino into a movie studio for her. The Hearst media machine began the publicity parade, yet the dull movies Hearst chose for his charismatic lady friend were ignored by audiences and lost money time after time. Hearst loved to see Marion in costume dramas, but it was as a comedienne, in films like 1928's *Show People*, that she truly lit up the screen. Despite disappointing box office, Hearst had no trouble getting MGM to release his films. They were only too glad to benefit from favorable treatment in his papers. As protected as Marion was by Hearst, however, he couldn't always get her the top roles she wanted. Both *The Barretts of Wimpole Street* (1935) and *Marie Antoinette* (1938) went to Norma Shearer, wife of MGM production chief Irving Thalberg, prompting Hearst to move his production unit (Cosmopolitan) to Warner Bros. After a few flops there, Marion happily retired from the movies in 1937, at the age of forty. Four years later, her fans were shocked at the scathing fictional portrayal of their relationship in the Orson Welles classic *Citizen Kane*. The shrill, talentless opera singer representing Marion was a cruelly inaccurate view of a woman who possessed beauty, talent, generosity, charm, and a gift for living life to the fullest. She may have lived in a lavish, princess-like manner, but Marion also used her extraordinary wealth to help friends and acquaintances who were struggling financially—even Hearst himself, who fell into debt in the 1930s while Marion, through clever real estate investments, became rich.

Born
Marion Cecilia Douras
January 3, 1897
Brooklyn, New York

Died
September 22, 1961
Hollywood, California,
of cancer

Star Sign
Capricorn

Height
5'5"

Husband
Former naval officer and
stuntman Captain Horace Brown
(1951–61, her death)

Significant Other
Publishing tycoon
William Randolph Hearst
(1918–51, his death)

Essential
MARIONDAVIESFilms

ENCHANTMENT

(1921) Cosmopolitan/Paramount
One of the silent films elaborately
produced for Davies by William
Randolph Hearst through his
company, Cosmopolitan, and
released through Paramount.
Davies, as the spoiled daughter of
a millionaire, is cast in an amateur
production of *Sleeping Beauty*
opposite a virile actor who will
brook no nonsense.

CIRCA 1927

JANICE MEREDITH

(1924) Cosmopolitan/MGM
A silent epic about the American
Revolution, with Davies's title
character torn between her wealthy
Tory family and her lover, a servant
who fights on the side of George
Washington.

QUALITY STREET

(1927) Cosmopolitan/MGM
Another Davies-Hearst silent film,
based on the James M. Barrie
comedy of manners about a woman
who pretends to be her teenage
niece in order to win back a lover
who has been away at war and now
looks upon his former sweetheart
as an old maid.

SHOW PEOPLE

(1928) Cosmopolitan/MGM
An inside look at the world of
Hollywood filmmaking in the 1920s,
with Davies as a character loosely
based on Gloria Swanson. She is
Georgia-born Peggy Pepper, who
arrives at MGM determined to
become a dramatic actress but
instead emerges as the star of
slapstick comedies.

THE PATSY

(1928) Cosmopolitan/MGM
The screen version of a hit
Broadway comedy, with Davies
as a Cinderella type who secretly
loves her beautiful sister's
boy-friend but bemoans her own
lack of "personality." Known
as a wicked mimic, Davies here
offers her impersonations of
fellow stars Lillian Gish, Mae
Murray, and Pola Negri.

STYLE NOTES

Marion used very little makeup—just a little greasepaint, powder, and lipstick, which she would apply in the car on the way to the studio. Only her hair would be fixed on set.

Costume designer Adrian convinced MGM to sponsor a style contest in conjunction with Marion's period film *The Florodora Girl*. Hearst newspapers across the country ran pictures of Davies in her costumes from the film accompanied by the following caption, "Do you like Marion's costume? Do you wish to see these styles return?" MGM received thousands of letters and Marion's outfits caused a renewed interest in vintage fashion.

Marion was the ultimate party hostess at William Hearst's "castle," San Simeon. Her laid-back, fun-filled soirees stood in refreshing contrast to the over-the-top elegance of the home itself. The table may have been seventeenth-century Italian, but Marion was happy to cover it with condiment jars for these down-home dinners.

---

behind the scenes

WHEN HEARST FIRST SAW MARION IN THE CHORUS OF A STAGE MUSICAL, HE WAS SO STRICKEN THAT HE ATTENDED EVERY PERFORMANCE FOR THE NEXT EIGHT WEEKS, BUYING TWO TICKETS—ONE FOR HIMSELF AND ONE FOR HIS HAT.

AN INCORRIGIBLE PRACTICAL JOKER, MARION ONCE GOT PRESIDENT CALVIN COOLIDGE DRUNK BY FEEDING HIM WINE AND TELLING HIM IT WAS FRUIT JUICE.

AS DEVOTED AS MARION WAS TO HEARST, SHE WAS NOT ABOVE ENGAGING IN A LITTLE HANKY-PANKY WHEN HIS BACK WAS TURNED. HOLLYWOOD LEGEND CLAIMS THAT HER AFFAIR WITH CHARLES CHAPLIN LED TO A SHOOT-OUT ON THE HEARST YACHT WHEN HE CAUGHT THEM TOGETHER. WHILE MAKING *PAGE MISS GLORY* (1935), SHE DEVELOPED A CRUSH ON LEADING MAN DICK POWELL, WHO AVOIDED HER FOR FEAR OF ANGERING HER POWERFUL LOVER.

CITIZEN KANE WAS FILLED WITH INSIDE REFERENCES TO HEARST AND MARION. ONE OF THE CRUELEST CAME IN THE SCENE IN WHICH KANE'S WIFE LEAVES HIM, AND HE TEARS APART HER BEDROOM, UNCOVERING A HIDDEN CACHE OF LIQUOR. MOST PEOPLE IN HOLLYWOOD KNEW THAT MARION WAS A SECRET DRINKER, FORCED TO HIDE HER TIPPLING FROM THE TEETOTALING HEARST.

PAGE MISS GLORY, 1935

She famously gave a "bumpy ride" to directors, costars, and studio executives alike, bringing audiences a new kind of screen heroine, as tough as any man.

BETTE
DAVIS

Bette Davis was shocked when Hollywood first came calling. She had never thought a world that worshipped beauties like Jean Harlow would take an interest in her. Yet her confidence grew with each picture until, insecure about her talent no longer, she was like a boxer, going rounds with costars and directors, scriptwriters and studio executives. She was so tough, in fact, that her boss at Warner Bros., Jack Warner, was afraid of her. Ironically, her career took off when Warner reluctantly loaned her out to RKO to make *Of Human Bondage* (1934). He cautioned that playing the totally unsympathetic role of a seductive waitress would sink her career, but when critics hailed the performance as the best in screen history, he had to admit he had been wrong. Yet he was still slow to capitalize on her talents, working her tirelessly in numerous thankless parts for each decent role. She tried to walk out on her contract but was forced back by the courts. When Hal Wallis took over production, Warner Bros. started making glossier productions, including the kinds of moody dramas and unconventional romances that best suited Bette's keen intelligence and captivating manner. *Jezebel* (1938); *Dark Victory* (1939); *The Letter* (1940); *Now, Voyager* (1942)—in each film she shattered the stereotype of the helpless female, so popular on screen at the time. Instead, she brought audiences spirited women with inner resources and unwavering standards, not unlike the American women who had survived the Depression to man the home front during World War II. Bette made two comebacks in her decades-long career. When age and declining box office led to her departure from Warner Bros., she scored the role of aging actress Margo Channing in *All About Eve* (1950) at 20th Century-Fox, a part planned for Claudette Colbert until she injured her back. Facing career doldrums again more than a decade later, she took a chance on horror in 1962's *What Ever Happened to Baby Jane?* Joining forces with offscreen rival Joan Crawford, she created a juicy camp fest and paved the way for other aging actresses in search of interesting roles.

Born
Ruth Elizabeth Davis
April 5, 1908
Lowell, Massachusetts

Died
October 6, 1989
Neuilly, France,
of failing health due to
breast cancer and a stroke

Star Sign
Aries

Height
5'3"

Husbands and Children
Musician Harmon Nelson
(1932–39, divorced)

Innkeeper Arthur Farnsworth
(1940–43, his death)

Boxer-painter-masseur
William Grant Sherry
(1945–50, divorced)
daughter, Barbara Davis ("B.D.")

Actor Gary Merrill
(1950–60, divorced)
two adopted children,
Margot and Michael

Essential
BETTEDAVISFilms

JEZEBEL

(1938) Warner Bros.
Davis's consolation prize for not getting the role of Scarlett O'Hara, which she turned into an Oscar-winning triumph. She plays Julie Marsden, a Southern belle of the 1850s whose love for the wrong man (Henry Fonda) leads to much tempestuous suffering and causes her Aunt Belle (Fay Bainter) to brand her a "jezebel."

DARK VICTORY

(1939) Warner Bros.
Classic tearjerker with Davis as Judith Traherne, a Long Island heiress who is told that she has a brain tumor. She marries the kindly doctor (George Brent) who sees her through surgery—only to discover that the tumor has returned.

THE LETTER

(1940) Warner Bros.
W. Somerset Maugham's melodramatic novel, transferred to the screen by director William Wyler, with Davis in one of her signature roles as an unfaithful wife who coldly murders her lover and uses her sexual wiles to escape a murder conviction.

NOW, VOYAGER

(1942) Warner Bros.
The tale of a dowdy, repressed spinster (Davis) who manages to break free from a domineering mother in search of love, self-fulfillment, and fashion. Adapted from Olive Higgins Prouty's novel, the film costars Paul Henreid as the married man who shares his heart—and, memorably, his cigarettes—with Davis.

ALL ABOUT EVE

(1950) 20th Century-Fox
A revitalization of Davis's career after many years at Warner Bros., courtesy of writer-director Joseph L. Mankiewicz and his stinging comedy about the world of theater. As aging actress Margo Channing, Davis bites off the best lines, including the endlessly quoted "Fasten your seat belts—it's going to be a bumpy night!"

JEZEBEL, 1938

STYLENOTES

Bette told designer Edith Head that her costumes had to be comfortable: "If clothes don't move with me, I can't wear them." Head herself once said admiringly, "No one can drop a mink more elegantly than Bette Davis."

Bette was unique among actresses of her generation in her willingness to sacrifice beauty for realism. She promoted wigs, costumes, and makeup that would distinguish her from the typical young movie star and emphasize her image as a serious actress. What mattered most to Bette was not how she looked but how her look brought the audience into the story.

Bette was known for her remarkable eyes, "the best feature I had to offer the camera." In 1981, the pop song "Bette Davis Eyes," sung by Kim Carnes, stayed at the top of the charts for nine weeks, thrilling the actress.

NOW, VOYAGER, 1942

behindthe**scenes**

BETTE DAVIS WAS FURIOUS AT WARNER BROS. FOR CONTINUING TO PUT HER IN B-PICTURES, SO SHE BROKE HER CONTRACT WITH THE STUDIO AND HEADED TO EUROPE TO MAKE MOVIES WITH BRITISH FILM MOGUL LUDOVICO TOEPLITZ. WARNER PROMPTLY SERVED HER WITH AN INJUNCTION. MUCH TO HER SURPRISE, THE COURT TRIAL ONLY INCREASED HER VALUE IN THE STUDIO'S EYES. WHEN SHE GOT BACK, THEY STARTED GIVING HER BETTER ROLES. "IN A WAY," BETTE RECALLED LATER, "MY DEFEAT WAS A VICTORY."

IN *MARKED WOMAN* (1937), BETTE PLAYED A WOMAN SCARRED BY THE MOB. FOR THE HOSPITAL SCENE AFTER THE ATTACK, SHE WAS ASKED TO WEAR A FANCY GAUZE CONTRAPTION THAT LOOKED MORE LIKE AN EASTER BONNET THAN A BANDAGE. SHE LEFT THE SET, FOUND A DOCTOR TO BANDAGE HER AS THOUGH SHE HAD SURVIVED A KNIFE ATTACK, AND THEN WENT BACK TO THE SET AND TOLD THEM THEY WOULD FILM HER THAT WAY OR NOT AT ALL.

IN 1941 BETTE SERVED AS THE FIRST FEMALE PRESIDENT OF THE ACADEMY OF MOTION PICTURE ARTS AND SCIENCES.

BETTE CONTRIBUTED TO THE WAR EFFORT BY HELPING TO ORGANIZE THE HOLLY-WOOD CANTEEN FOR SOLDIERS PASSING THROUGH LOS ANGELES. SHE TOOK A ONCE-ABANDONED NIGHTCLUB AND TURNED IT INTO A TOP-NOTCH ENTERTAINMENT FACILITY. IN 1980, SHE WAS AWARDED THE DISTINGUISHED CIVILIAN SERVICE MEDAL FOR THAT EFFORT, WHICH SHE DEEMED ONE OF THE "FEW ACCOMPLISHMENTS IN MY LIFE THAT I AM SINCERELY PROUD OF."

ON BETTE'S TOMBSTONE IS WRITTEN, "SHE DID IT THE HARD WAY."

PERHAPS NO ACTRESS IS MORE IDENTIFIED WITH SMOKING THAN BETTE, A FIVE-PACK-A-DAY PUFFER WHO SEEMED TO PUNCTUATE EVERY MOVEMENT AND THOUGHT WITH A DRAG ON A LIT CIGARETTE. YET BETTE CLAIMED SHE NEVER INHALED: "I JUST BLOW THE SMOKE OUT OF MY MOUTH."

The girl next door of every man's dreams and the woman every girl dreamed of befriending, her trademark chic and feisty career-woman characters helped Rock Hudson take the romantic sex comedy to penthouse heights.

DORIS
DAY

Doris Day started out as a dancer and even won a dancing contest in her native Cincinnati. She used her winnings for a trip to Hollywood, but on the drive back she shattered her leg in a car accident. While recovering, she discovered she could sing, so she changed vocations, eventually winning a gig with the Les Brown Band, with whom she recorded the hit "Sentimental Journey." In 1948, director Michael Curtiz signed her to a personal contract (later sold to Warner Bros.) and gave her the lead in his next film, *Romance on the High Seas* (1948). There she introduced another of her signature songs, "It's Magic." Warner kept her mostly in lighthearted musicals, though some of them, like *Calamity Jane* (1953), were among Hollywood's best. They also loaned her to MGM for a rare dramatic turn as singer Ruth Etting in *Love Me or Leave Me* (1954). She even got to be one of director Alfred Hitchcock's trademark blondes in *The Man Who Knew Too Much* (1956), in which she introduced the song that would become her trademark, "Que Sera, Sera (Whatever Will Be, Will Be)." When Hollywood started cutting back on musicals in the late 1950s, Doris effortlessly switched to sex comedies with *Pillow Talk* (1959), the first of three films she made with Rock Hudson and Tony Randall. Their success made her the nation's top box-office star. Although she rued the "eternal virgin" typecasting these films brought her, her heroines were assertive, honest, and unmistakably modern career women. When Doris's husband and manager, Martin Melcher, died in 1968, she discovered that he had lost most of her fortune and signed her for a CBS television series without her knowledge. Although she initially did not want to do the show, it turned out to be very popular and made her a great deal of money during its five-year run (1968–73). After *The Doris Day Show* went off the air, she retired from show business to devote herself to animal rights activism.

Born
Doris Mary Ann Von Kappelhoff
April 3, 1924
Cincinnati, Ohio

Star Sign
Aries

Height
5'7"

Husbands and Child
Trombonist Al Jorden
(1941–43, divorced)
son, Terry

Saxophonist George Weidler
(1946–49, divorced)

Manager-producer Martin Melcher
(1951–68, his death)

Restaurant manager Barry Comden
(1976–81, divorced)

Essential
DORISDAYFilms

ACADEMY AWARDS

Nominated for Best Actress

Pillow Talk

CALAMITY JANE

(1953) Warner Bros.
A rowdy musical, Warner's answer to *Annie Get Your Gun,* with Day as the rambunctious Calamity Jane and Howard Keel as the apple of her eye, Wild Bill Hickok. Day's songs include one of her biggest hits, "Secret Love."

LOVE ME OR LEAVE ME

(1955) MGM
Gutsy film biography with Day as 1930s torch singer Ruth Etting and James Cagney as her shady manager and husband Martin Snyder.

THE MAN WHO KNEW TOO MUCH

(1956) Paramount
Unfamiliar territory for Day—an Alfred Hitchcock thriller in which she and James Stewart play the anguished parents of a kidnapped boy. The most important song of Day's career, "Que Sera, Sera (Whatever Will Be, Will Be")," provides an important plot point.

THE PAJAMA GAME

(1957) Warner Bros.
Lively screen re-creation of the hit Broadway musical, complete with exuberant Bob Fosse choreography. As a union leader bargaining for a 7 ½-cent raise at a pajama factory, Day steps in as star with most of the original stage cast intact, including John Raitt as the management representative who falls for her.

PILLOW TALK

(1959) Universal
Doris Day plays a chic and modern interior decorator forced to share a telephone party line with a handsome composer-playboy (Rock Hudson). Much to Day's annoyance, their calls always seem to overlap at the worst possible moments; however, once Hudson gets a glance at his telephone sparring partner, he sets out to add her to his list of conquests. This is the first of three films Day made with Rock Hudson and Tony Randall.

***PILLOW TALK*, 1959**

Fashion designer Micheal Kors said, "Day was always someone very interesting to look at on film because she really wore the clothes, the clothes never wore her, she can make glamorous look sort of approachable . . . Day was never the sort of a woman on a pedestal, she's a woman you want to know, she's the girl next door . . ."

The bouffant Day developed after her move to romantic comedy became a beauty shop trend, yet she always thought she looked best in a Dutch-boy bob.

THE UPROARIOUS MOVIE FROM THE BIG BEST-SELLER!

METRO-GOLDWYN-MAYER presents

DORIS DAY
DAVID NIVEN

in A EUTERPE PRODUCTION
in COLOR!

PLEASE DON'T EAT THE DAISIES

Co-Starring
JANIS PAIGE · SPRING BYINGTON
RICHARD HAYDN

Screen Play by ISOBEL LENNART · Associate Producer MARTIN MELCHER · Directed by CHARLES WALTERS
Produced by JOE PASTERNAK · CinemaScope and METROCOLOR

PLEASE DON'T EAT THE DAISIES, 1960

behind the scenes

AFTER THE MANSON MURDERS IN 1969, IT WAS DISCOVERED THAT THEIR INTENDED VICTIM WAS NEITHER ILL-FATED ACTRESS SHARON TATE NOR ANY OF HER FRIENDS BUT DORIS'S SON TERRY MELCHER. A RECORD PRODUCER AT THE TIME, HE HAD TURNED DOWN ASPIRING SINGER-SONGWRITER CHARLES MANSON. THE MIXUP? MELCHER AND GIRLFRIEND CANDICE BERGEN HAD PREVIOUSLY LIVED IN THE HOUSE WHERE MANSON'S FOLLOWERS ENACTED THEIR GRUESOME REVENGE.

DORIS, A VEGETARIAN WHO CAN'T BELIEVE SHE USED TO WEAR FUR, BECAME AN ANIMAL LOVER AFTER WITNESSING THE TREATMENT OF ANIMALS ON THE SET DURING LOCATION SHOOTING FOR *THE MAN WHO KNEW TOO MUCH* (1956). SHE FOUNDED THE DORIS DAY ANIMAL LEAGUE IN 1987.

DORIS'S NICKNAME, CLARA BIXBY, WAS GIVEN TO HER BY COMEDIAN BILLY DE WOLFE. ONE DAY ON THE SET OF *TEA FOR TWO* (1952), HE TOLD HER SHE DIDN'T LOOK LIKE A DORIS DAY BUT RATHER LIKE A CLARA BIXBY. HER CLOSEST FRIENDS STILL CALL HER THAT.

IN RECENT YEARS, DORIS HAS REFUSED ALL OFFERED ROLES. ALTHOUGH SHE HAS RECORDED SOME INTERVIEWS, HER LAST NATIONAL APPEARANCE WAS WHEN SHE ACCEPTED THE HOLLYWOOD FOREIGN PRESS ASSOCIATION'S CECIL B. DEMILLE AWARD FOR CAREER ACHIEVEMENT AT THE 1989 GOLDEN GLOBES PRESENTATION. SHE ONLY AGREED TO APPEAR AFTER A PERSONAL APPEAL FROM FRIEND AND NEIGHBOR CLINT EASTWOOD.

THE THRILL OF IT ALL, 1963

The original steel magnolia, her Melanie in *Gone with the Wind* reflected both her beauty and her strength, but when she sued Warner Bros. to be freed from her contract and won, she changed the studio system forever.

OLIVIA DE HAVILLAND

Some young women try in vain to get into the movies; Olivia de Havilland fell into movie stardom almost against her will, and this ambivalence echoed throughout her remarkable career. An unlikely series of events led her from a community college production of *A Midsummer's Night's Dream* to famed director Max Reinhardt's version at the Hollywood Bowl. When Warner Bros. decided to make a film version of the production, they were anxious to sign the talented and lovely Olivia. Against her better judgment, she joined the Warner Bros. family. Soon enough, Olivia found herself rushing through productions in which the bottom line was money, not art, and she was quite overwhelmed. Stardom arrived when the studio teamed her with Errol Flynn in *Captain Blood* (1935) and seven more films, most of them historical adventures. But she soon chafed at this typecasting, yearning for dramatic roles that would reveal her true dimensions. Realizing she was best when cast in good-girl roles, Olivia was one of the few *Gone with the Wind*-obsessed actresses who dreamt of playing Melanie rather than Scarlett. But even with that film's groundbreaking success, Olivia continued to be underused by Warner Bros. After a protracted battle to free herself from her contract there, she became a free agent. Her second film with Paramount, 1946's *To Each His Own,* finally showed the world what a natural and gifted actress she was, and Olivia received two great gifts: critical acclaim and Oscar gold. She expanded her range further by playing an asylum inmate in *The Snake Pit* (1948) and the embittered spinster in *The Heiress* (1949). At the start of the 1950s, Olivia changed her focus to home and family. Marriage to a *Paris Match* editor found her raising her children in France, far from the Hollywood film factory. She continued to act occasionally for many years afterward, even taking a stab at horror films (*Hush . . . Hush, Sweet Charlotte,* 1964), disaster flicks (*Airport '77,* 1977), and the occasional television movie (most notably *Anastasia: The Mystery of Anna,* 1986).

Born
Olivia Mary de Havilland
July 1, 1916
Tokyo, Japan

Star Sign
Cancer

Height
5'3"

Husbands and Children
Writer Marcus Goodrich
(1946–53, divorced)
son, Benjamin

Paris Match editor Pierre Galante
(1955–79, divorced)
daughter, Gisele

Essential
OLIVIA DE HAVILLAND Films

ACADEMY AWARDS

Won Best Actress
To Each His Own
The Heiress

Nominated for Best Actress
Hold Back the Dawn
The Snake Pit

**Nominated for
Best Supporting Actress**
Gone with the Wind

THE ADVENTURES OF ROBIN HOOD

(1938) Warner Bros.
A quintessential swashbuckler film, one of the eight films in which de Havilland costarred with Errol Flynn. She is Maid Marian to his Robin Hood in a story that follows the outlaw's exploits from the capture of Richard the Lionhearted (Ian Hunter) to Richard's triumphant return to England.

GONE WITH THE WIND

(1939) MGM
The movie milestone—producer David O. Selznick's film treatment of Margaret Mitchell's novel about the Old South, with de Havilland representing the gentler side of Southern womanhood. Melanie Wilkes is everything Scarlett O'Hara is not: gracious, kind, loyal, and self-sacrificing.

TO EACH HIS OWN

(1946) Paramount
De Havilland's Oscar-winning performance as an unwed mother who gives up her baby for adoption during World War I, only to rediscover him as an adult as World War II rages. John Lund does double duty as lover and son.

THE SNAKE PIT

(1948) 20th Century-Fox
De Havilland's brave and unglamorous portrayal of a woman who must endure the overcrowded "snake pit" of a mental institution. The film, directed by Anatole Litvak, was considered a breakthrough in its day for addressing the subject of mental illness.

THE HEIRESS

(1949) Paramount
Director William Wyler's film version of the Henry James story about a young woman who is "taught by masters" to excel in cruelty. De Havilland's Catherine Sloper learns her lessons from a domineering father (Ralph Richardson) and a handsome fortune hunter (Montgomery Clift).

THE ADVENTURES OF ROBIN HOOD, 1938

STYLENOTES

Olivia was somewhat overweight when she first came to Paramount, yet Edith Head was able to design costumes with a slimming effect. In one scene, Edith put Olivia in a pale blue dress next to a white-clad Paulette Goddard, causing the women to appear identical in size.

For *The Heiress,* Edith Head made clothes that didn't fit right, in keeping with the insecure character. Olivia felt suitably uncomfortable in the outfits.

GONE WITH THE WIND,
1939

behind the scenes

OLIVIA DE HAVILLAND WAS RELIEVED WHEN HER SEVEN-YEAR CONTRACT WITH WARNER BROS. FINALLY ENDED. YET WHEN SHE PREPARED TO SEVER TIES, JACK WARNER HIT HER WITH A CHILLING REALITY: SHE HAD ACCUMULATED SIX MONTHS OF SUSPENSION TIME FOR REFUSING SCRIPTS, AND THAT TIME WOULD BE ADDED TO THE END OF HER CONTRACT. FED UP WITH WHAT SHE SAW AS SERVITUDE TO THE STUDIO, OLIVIA FOUGHT BACK WITH ALL SHE HAD. WHEN THE LOWER COURTS RULED IN HER FAVOR, WARNER SENT OUT A LETTER TO THE OTHER STUDIOS THAT VIRTUALLY BLACKLISTED HER, BUT WHEN THE CASE WAS HEARD BY THE CALIFORNIA SUPREME COURT, OLIVIA WON. UNDER THE DE HAVILLAND DECISION, STUDIO CONTRACTS COULD NOT BE ENFORCED PAST A SEVEN-YEAR LIMIT.

OLIVIA AND FREQUENT COSTAR ERROL FLYNN FIRST MET WHEN SHE TESTED FOR THE FEMALE LEAD IN *CAPTAIN BLOOD* (1935), AND IT WAS LOVE AT FIRST SIGHT. SHE WAS THE ONLY ACTRESS HE ACTUALLY LOOKED AT DURING THE TESTS. HER FONDNESS FOR HIM SHONE THROUGH IN ALL OF THEIR EIGHT FILMS TOGETHER, BUT SHE REALIZED EARLY ON THAT HE WAS TOO LACKADAISICAL IN HIS APPROACH TO ACTING AND LIVING TO BE AN IDEAL REAL-LIFE ROMANTIC MATCH FOR HER.

OLIVIA'S SISTER, JOAN FONTAINE, WAS ALSO A WELL-KNOWN STAR, BUT THEIR RELATIONSHIP SUFFERED FROM PERIODIC RIVALRY. THEIR CONFLICT SURFACED PUBLICLY AT THE 1946 OSCARS, WHEN OLIVIA TURNED AWAY FROM HER SISTER'S OUTSTRETCHED HAND, STILL MIFFED FROM A SNIDE COMMENT JOAN HAD MADE ABOUT OLIVIA'S HUSBAND. OBSERVERS ALSO SUGGESTED THAT OLIVIA'S BITTERNESS STEMMED FROM THE FACT THAT JOAN HAD BEEN THE FIRST OF THE TWO TO WIN AN OSCAR.

ONE OF OLIVIA'S BIGGEST CAREER MISTAKES WAS TO TURN DOWN THE ROLE OF BLANCHE DUBOIS IN *A STREETCAR NAMED DESIRE* (1951). SHE STATED THAT "A LADY JUST DOESN'T DO OR SAY THOSE THINGS ON THE SCREEN."

DURING THE PRODUCTION OF *GONE WITH THE WIND,* THE CREW PLAYED A PRANK ON CLARK GABLE BY SEWING SEVENTY POUNDS OF LEAD WEIGHT INTO DE HAVILLAND'S COSTUME JUST BEFORE A SCENE WHEN RHETT (GABLE) HAD TO LIFT A FRAIL MELANIE (DE HAVILLAND) FROM HER BED AND CARRY HER DOWN A FLIGHT OF STAIRS.

Famously androgynous and eternally exotic, this leggy German beauty dazzled audiences on screen and off with her carefully contrived and controlled image as an icon of forbidden passions and daring love.

MARLENE
DIETRICH

Arriving in the United States in 1930, Marlene Dietrich was Paramount's answer to Greta Garbo. No wide-eyed ingenue from the hinterlands, the leggy German beauty had already become a minor legend in her homeland. A major turning point in her career came after years of stage and screen work in Germany, when director Josef von Sternberg saw her perform. Struck not just by her beauty but also by her "remarkable vitality," he cast her in *Der Blaue Engel* ("The Blue Angel"). For the next five years, von Sternberg and his muse collaborated on a number of films in a unique relationship that some assumed was a simple affair. Others called von Sternberg "Svengali Joe," observing Marlene's acquiescence to his many strong opinions. Yet in reality Marlene brought to the set a keen intuition and vast technical knowledge that von Sternberg found invaluable. *Shanghai Express* (1932) is a favorite Dietrich–von Sternberg collaboration of many fans, smitten with Marlene's glamorous look and the erotic charge she brings to scenes that might seem merely campy in lesser hands. Stunning as she was on screen, Marlene dazzled audiences off screen as well. Fashionable women donned her daring pantsuits and read avidly of her dizzying social life. Eventually, however, fans tired of her manufactured exoticism. Von Sternberg left Paramount, and Marlene found herself labeled "box office poison." But she bounced back as the raucous, owner of a Wild West saloon in *Destry Rides Again* (1939), which put her back on top. As the years went by, Marlene's penchant for reinvention and a thorough understanding of her appeal gave her staying power in a fickle business. She even demonstrated solid dramatic chops as the cheating wife in *Witness for the Prosecution* (1957) and a German general's widow in *Judgment at Nuremberg* (1961). Whether entertaining World War II troops in artfully tailored fatigues or taking an eclectic cabaret act from Las Vegas to Russia, Marlene Dietrich remained a universal elixir: part sophistication, part personal magnetism, wrapped in a package of unadulterated glamour—all of it real, yet calculated at the same time.

Born
Marie Magdalene Dietrich
December 27, 1901
Schöneberg, Germany

Died
May 6, 1992
Paris, France,
of kidney failure

Star Sign
Capricorn

Height
5'5"

Husband and Child
Producer-turned-chicken-farmer
Rudolf Sieber
(1924–76, his death)
daughter, Maria Riva

Essential
MARLENE DIETRICH Films

ACADEMY AWARDS

Nominated for Best Actress
Morocco

THE BLUE ANGEL
(1930) UFA
The creation of a legend, with Dietrich playing temptress Lola, the cabaret performer who brings staid professor (Emil Jannings) to ruin. Dietrich's mentor Josef von Sternberg directs, and the new star sings "Falling in Love Again"—which would become her trademark song.

MOROCCO
(1930) Paramount
An exotic and erotic Josef von Sternberg–Marlene Dietrich film in which Dietrich plays a seductive tuxedo-clad cabaret performer in Morocco and forms a romantic triangle with a Foreign Legionnaire (Gary Cooper) and a wealthy businessman (Adolphe Menjou).

SHANGHAI EXPRESS
(1932) Paramount
Another of her seven collaborations with von Sternberg, this one with Dietrich as Shanghai Lily, who travels from man to man through the Far East. To rescue her true love (Clive Brook), she gives herself to a Eurasian rebel (Warner Oland).

DESTRY RIDES AGAIN
(1939) Universal
Western satire with Dietrich resuscitating her career by playing on her own image, portraying a dance hall hostess who uses her wiles on a shy sheriff (James Stewart). Memorably, she warbles the song "See What the Boys in the Back Room Will Have."

WITNESS FOR THE PROSECUTION
(1957) United Artists
Agatha Christie's courtroom thriller, with Dietrich as the wife of an accused murderer (Tyrone Power). Billy Wilder directs a cast that also includes Charles Laughton.

MOROCCO, 1930

STYLENOTES

Marlene's clothes matched her persona, a melding of masculine and feminine attributes. Designer Travis Banton created most of her trademark masculine suits, cutting them to highlight, not hide, her shapeliness. She believed that when you put on men's clothing, you also put on their privileges.

Marlene managed her appearance with scientific precision. To keep her mouth taut in close-ups, she sucked on lemons right before filming. Gold powder made her hair look paler; white liner enlarged her eyes. Her lovely legs, shown with artful precision, deflected, she felt, from her less-than-perfect breasts.

When Marlene was asked to be a presenter at the 1951 Academy Awards, she had a gown designed with a slit that fell to the side in a revealing fashion as she walked up the steps. Marlene went so far as to go to test the gown at the theater before the event, ensuring that it revealed a devastating amount of leg as she strutted across the stage. The planning paid off; her stroll to the podium elicited a standing ovation.

CIRCA 1947

behind**the**scenes

MARLENE DIETRICH WAS DISINCLINED TO VIEW MONOGAMY AS IMPORTANT. "IT DOESN'T MATTER IF YOU'RE A MAN OR A WOMAN," SHE PRONOUNCED, "I'LL MAKE LOVE WITH ANYONE I FIND ATTRACTIVE." GIVEN SUCH AN ATTITUDE, IT'S NO SURPRISE THAT HER MARRIAGE TO RUDI SIEBER QUICKLY BECAME PLATONIC IN NATURE. IN LATER LIFE SHE EVEN SUPPORTED HIM AND HIS MISTRESS. YET THEIR ALLIANCE WAS A REAL ONE, AND HE REMAINED, THROUGH THE YEARS, A TRUSTED ADVISER.

NOT ONLY DID MARLENE REFUSE TO WORK FOR THE FILM INDUSTRY UNDER HITLER, SHE REFUSED THE LEADER HIMSELF AFTER A NAZI OFFICER MADE SEXUAL REQUESTS ON THE FÜHRER'S BEHALF. INSTEAD, SHE DEVOTED HERSELF TO HER NEW HOMELAND AND THE USO IN WORLD WAR II, PERFORMING TIRELESSLY FOR THREE YEARS UNDER PUNISHING CONDITIONS. BECOMING THE FIRST WOMAN TO EARN THE MEDAL OF FREEDOM, DIETRICH EXPLAINED, "I DID WHAT I COULD TO SHOW THOSE GIS THERE WERE GOOD GERMANS TOO."

MARLENE ONCE DECLINED AN OFFER TO MEET ENGLAND'S PRINCESS MARGARET, SAYING, "I'M A QUEEN. I SHOULD STAY UP FOR A PRINCESS?"

A classically trained singer with great versatility, her lyrical inflections and subtle charms added a unique spark to all of her roles.

IRENE
DUNNE

Irene Dunne was a gifted child with a solid ambition to either teach music or become an opera singer. Her famous versatility showed up early in her career as she developed her acting chops in a number of musicals, often replacing performers who had to leave the show. An early *New York Post* review described Irene in terms that fit throughout her career: ". . . a bright, guileless clarity which was not without dignity, too." She caught Hollywood's attention when she starred in the touring company of the classic musical *Show Boat,* which she would film at Universal in 1936. RKO thought of Irene for their musical comedies, yet in only her second picture she found herself in the epic Western *Cimarron* (1931), in which film audiences first caught sight of the dark-haired beauty. Her classic and delicate face, well-modulated voice, and gracious manner were well suited to the women's pictures so popular in the 1930s, and she made two of the genre's most famous, *Back Street* (1932) and *Magnificent Obsession* (1935). Yet just a year after the latter her career took on a new dimension. Columbia cast her as a prim small-town woman who secretly writes torrid romances in the screwball comedy *Theodora Goes Wild,* and many were pleasantly surprised that this queen of the tearjerkers could also clown around with the best of them. *The Awful Truth* (1937) and *My Favorite Wife* (1940), both costarring her good friend Cary Grant, demonstrate that Irene's fame as a screwball comedienne was a reflection of her uniqueness. She played it small where others might have played it big, and straight where others might have done zany. She continued scoring hits through the late 1940s, particularly as the Norwegian immigrant mother in *I Remember Mama* (1948). After retiring from acting in the early 1950s, Irene continued to lead the rich, rewarding life she had always led, enjoying a stable marriage to her husband of many years and continuing her political and philanthropic efforts.

Born
Irene Marie Dunn
December 20, 1898
Louisville, Kentucky

Died
September 4, 1990
Los Angeles, California,
of heart failure

Star Sign
Sagittarius

Height
5'5"

Husband and Child
Dr. Frank Griffin
(1928–65, his death)
adopted daughter, Mary Frances

Essential
IRENEDUNNEFilms

SHOW BOAT
(1936) Universal
The first of three movie versions of the landmark Jerome Kern–Oscar Hammerstein II stage musical, with Dunne as Magnolia, the sweet songbird who is swept off her feet by gambler Gaylor Ravenal (Allan Jones). Dunne does her own singing, holding her own with such legendary performers as Paul Robeson and Helen Morgan.

THE AWFUL TRUTH
(1937) Columbia
Archetypal screwball comedy, with Dunne and Cary Grant as a quarreling married couple who agree to a trial divorce only to find themselves jealously attempting to foil each other's plans for remarriage.

LOVE AFFAIR
(1939) RKO
The original version of the tale of two strangers (Dunne and Charles Boyer) who fall in love during an ocean voyage and vow to meet again six months later atop the Empire State Building. Plans go awry, of course, in this bittersweet comedy-drama from writer-director Leo McCarey.

LIFE WITH FATHER
(1947) Warner Bros.
Broadway's longest-running nonmusical, faithfully adapted for the screen, with William Powell as stern but loving patriarch Clarence Day and Dunne as Vinnie, the wife who seems flighty but actually runs the household.

I REMEMBER MAMA
(1948) RKO
Director George Stevens's film version of Kathryn Forbes's collection of short stories entitled *Mama's Bank Account,* in which Forbes recalled how her Norwegian-immigrant mother coped with raising her family in turn-of-the-century San Francisco. Irene Dunne and Barbara Bel Geddes play the title matriarch and her daughter.

LOVE AFFAIR, 1939

STYLE NOTES

From the beginning, Irene was fanatical about matching costume with character. When the budding movie actress didn't like a hat that RKO designed for her to wear, she insisted on trading it for the toque hat that one of the seamstresses had on her own head.

"I love beautiful things," Irene told The *New York Times*, "but a woman who considers herself best dressed usually spends all of her time at it."

Irene claimed that always getting enough sleep kept her looking young. Her studio contracts allowed her to start work as late as 10:00 A.M. and leave by 6:00 P.M.

HIGH, WIDE, AND HANDSOME, 1937

behindthescenes

IN A BUSINESS WHERE MARRIAGE IS OFTEN A CASUALTY, IRENE DUNNE ENJOYED A LONG AND STABLE RELATIONSHIP WITH FRANK GRIFFIN, A DENTIST TURNED BUSINESSMAN WHO HADN'T PLANNED ON HAVING A WORKING WIFE BUT REFUSED TO STAND IN THE WAY OF HER SUCCESS. "WE WERE BOTH DETERMINED TO MAKE THE MARRIAGE WORK," HE ONCE EXPLAINED, AND, INDEED, THE RELATIONSHIP THRIVED, FROM THEIR MEETING IN 1924 UNTIL HIS DEATH IN 1965.

IRENE WAS HAPPY WHEN COLUMBIA FOUND A COMEDY FOR HER, BUT AFTER LOOKING AT THE PLOT OF THEODORA GOES WILD SHE GREW ALARMED AND WENT OFF ON A LONG EUROPEAN VACATION WITH FRANK, HOPING THE STUDIO WOULD FIND SOMEONE ELSE. THE TALE OF A PRIM TEACHER WHO WRITES A DARING NOVEL AND THEN ATTEMPTS TO LIVE UP TO HER NEW IMAGE STRUCK IRENE AS BRASH AND A BIT OF AN ATTACK ON HER OWN SOLID ROOTS. NONETHELESS, IRENE EVENTUALLY PLAYED THE PART, AND WITH GUSTO—AND SHE RECEIVED AN OSCAR NOMINATION FOR THE PERFORMANCE.

A LONGTIME REPUBLICAN, IRENE WAS NAMED AN ALTERNATE DELEGATE TO THE UNITED NATIONS BY PRESIDENT EISENHOWER IN 1959.

CARY GRANT RECALLED IRENE TO BE THE "SWEETEST-SMELLING ACTRESS" HE HAD EVER WORKED WITH.

One of the most flawless faces and intense women in movie history, with a whiskey-and-cigarettes voice and a mysterious, elusive quality captured forever in her famous line from *Grand Hotel*, "I vant to be alone."

GRETA
GARBO

When Swedish film director Mauritz Stiller was brought to the United States by MGM, he insisted on bringing along his protégée, the young Greta Garbo. In the 1926 film *Torrent*, the nineteen-year-old Garbo dazzled audiences with her beauty and complex emotions. Her films with silent screen star John Gilbert (and their offscreen romance) made for big box office as well, and by the end of the silent era she was Hollywood royalty. Yet the life of a famous movie star was challenging to Garbo. She was homesick for her beloved Sweden, visiting when she could, and valued her privacy like no other star of her magnitude. As photographer Cecil Beaton, her devoted friend, once noted dryly, "She would make a secret out of whether she had an egg for breakfast." Garbo had many lovers, both men and women. Yet after breaking an early engagement to Gilbert, she stated that she would never marry and kept that promise. Her varied romantic life added to the eroticism of her screen presence, as though Greta contained a passion unbound by contemporary standards. With the advent of talkies, her career continued to rise; Greta's throaty, accented voice only added to her provocative persona, and she triumphed in a series of movies: *Anna Christie* (1930), *Grand Hotel* (1932), *Anna Karenina* (1935), and *Camille* (1937). She was the "pained lady," wrapped in mysterious desire and lovely agony until director Ernst Lubitsch cast her in his mirthful *Ninotchka* (1939). "Garbo laughs!" the ads proclaimed, as though she had never chuckled in a film before, yet the ploy worked—theaters filled with fans wanting to witness the miracle. When her follow-up comedy *Two-Faced Woman* (1941) turned into a humiliating debacle, Garbo decided not to make another movie until everything was just right. That day never came, and Greta Garbo spent the second half of her life rejecting film roles, visiting with friends, traveling the globe, and, eventually, holing up in her New York apartment, to be seen only during her solitary walks. Although she stayed in the United States, even becoming a citizen in 1951, Garbo belonged to no one: no country, no man, no woman.

Born
Greta Lovisa Gustafson
September 18, 1905
Stockholm, Sweden

Died
April 15, 1990
New York, New York,
of pneumonia

Star Sign
Virgo

Height
5'7 ½"

Essential
GRETA GARBO Films

ACADEMY AWARDS

Nominated for Best Actress

Anna Christie
Romance
Camille
Ninotchka

Honorary Award in 1955 for her "unforgettable screen performances"

FLESH AND THE DEVIL

(1926) MGM

One of Garbo's early Hollywood silents, and one of her most provocative pairings with John Gilbert. She is the irresistible seductress who comes between Gilbert and his lifelong friend (Lars Hanson).

GRAND HOTEL

(1932) MGM

One of MGM's all-star dramas, this one based on the Vicki Baum novel and featuring Garbo as the ballerina who "vants to be alone." Also on hand: Wallace Beery, Joan Crawford, and two Barrymores, John and Lionel.

QUEEN CHRISTINA

(1933) MGM

Garbo assumes the role of a seventeenth-century Swedish queen who relinquishes her crown for her ill-fated lover, a Spanish envoy (John Gilbert).

CAMILLE

(1936) MGM

Director George Cukor's adaptation of the Alexandre Dumas tragedy, with Garbo as the courtesan who sacrifices everything for her lover (Robert Taylor).

NINOTCHKA

(1939) MGM

A rare comedy role for Garbo, that of a frosty Russian agent who thaws in Paris with the help of bon vivant Melvyn Douglas. The movie featured a famous ad line: "Garbo laughs!"

FLESH AND THE DEVIL, 1926

TYLENOTES

Plastic surgeons have extolled Greta Garbo's features as flawless. Off screen, she used just a bit of eyebrow pencil, lipstick, dusting powder, and mascara to look her best.

Greta favored tweeds and trousers—oversized clothes that hid her figure but were comfortable. Adrian was the first designer to understand that she looked best when one worked with her style. He put her in high-necked clothes and trench coats, which only underscored her classic beauty.

QUEEN CHRISTINA, 1933

behindthe**scenes**

GRETA GARBO'S ROMANCE WITH JOHN GILBERT WAS AS DRAMATIC AS ANY OF THE FILMS THEY STARRED IN TOGETHER. AT VARIOUS TIMES HE CLIMBED HER BALCONY, STORMED INTO HER HOTEL ROOM WITH A REVOLVER, NAMED HIS LAVISH YACHT *THE TEMPTRESS* IN HER HONOR, AND PERSUADED HER TO ELOPE WITH HIM (THOUGH AT THE LAST MINUTE SHE HID IN THE LAVATORY, ENDING THE NUPTIAL PLAN).

GRETA'S TECHNIQUE WAS IMPRESSIVE. USUALLY WORD-PERFECT ON THE FIRST TAKE, SHE MADE HER FILMS QUICKLY. TO ACHIEVE THIS RESULT, THE VERY PRIVATE ACTRESS OFTEN BANISHED CREW MEMBERS AND EVEN THE DIRECTOR FROM HER RANGE OF SIGHT. VISITORS ON HER SETS WERE STRICTLY FORBIDDEN.

AT THE PREMIERE OF HER FILM *THE TEMPTRESS*, THE ANNOUNCER INTRODUCED THE STAR BY SAYING, "THIS IS MISS GRETA GARBO, FROM STOCKHOLM. MISS GARBO DOESN'T SPEAK A WORD OF ENGLISH." ANXIOUS TO UNDERSCORE THIS POINT, GARBO CHIMED IN WITH A FIRM "NO, NOT VON VORD!" THE ENSUING LAUGHTER SO EMBARRASSED HER THAT SHE NEVER ATTENDED ANOTHER PREMIERE.

GRETA WAS HORRIFIED WHEN THE SCRIPT OF *NINOTCHKA* REQUIRED HER TO PLAY DRUNK. SHE NEVER DRANK TO EXCESS AND THOUGHT IT WOULD MAKE HER LOOK CHEAP. DIRECTOR ERNST LUBITSCH WORKED HARD TO CONVINCE GARBO TO PLAY THE ROLE, EVEN SITTING IN HER CAR FOR A TWO-HOUR MEETING WHEN SHE REFUSED TO COME INTO THE STUDIO. IN THE END, SHE COMPROMISED BY PRIVATELY FILMING TWO SHOTS WITH COSTAR MELVYN DOUGLAS. THESE WERE LATER INTERCUT WITH GROUP SCENES OF NIGHTCLUB REVELERS.

AN AVID ART COLLECTOR, GRETA LOVED TO BE SURROUNDED BY BEAUTY. SHE AMASSED AN INTERNATIONALLY RENOWNED ART COLLECTION DURING HER LIFETIME, LINING THE WALLS OF HER POSH MANHATTAN APARTMENT WITH MASTERPIECES BY RENOIR, BONNARD, AND OTHERS.

Exotic and exuding raw sex appeal, she was pure sensuality wrapped in the form of an earthy goddess, an intoxicating mix of vitality and vulnerability.

AVA
GARDNER

Ava Gardner was born to a family of tobacco pickers living in a tar-paper shack, far from the glamorous world of Hollywood. She had never wanted to be an actress. Her loftiest dream had been to land a secretarial job in New York. Her film career came about purely by accident. Ava's brother-in-law ran a photo studio in New York and placed a picture of her at age eighteen in the window. An MGM errand boy spotted the photo and brought it to his bosses. When studio head Louis B. Mayer saw the young beauty's screen test, he said, "She can't act, she can't talk. She's terrific." For years, she was little more than a decoration in the studio's films, best known for her brief marriages to Mickey Rooney and Artie Shaw. But a pair of films she made while on loan-outs to Universal for sultry roles in *Whistle Stop* and *The Killers* (both 1946) revealed her star potential. After trying her out in a supporting role opposite Clark Gable in *The Hucksters* (1947), MGM finally started promoting her. Even then, she rarely got the best roles at her home studio. Only the African adventure *Mogambo* (1953) and the exotic *Bhowani Junction* (1957) gave a sense that there was more to Gardner than her beauty. She didn't care that much about her career anyway. Gardner loved the nightlife: going out with friends or alone suited her just fine, as long as there was live music, plenty of booze, and a party that lasted until dawn. And through it all, she never lost her country roots. When Humphrey Bogart teased her about being a "little hillbilly girl," she took it in stride, saying, "That's what attracts them, honey." In the 1960s, she gradually started moving into mature roles, showing how good an actress she could be in two 1964 hits, *Seven Days in May* and *The Night of the Iguana*. By then, she had fled MGM and Hollywood for life abroad, first in Spain, then in England. She only worked when she needed money. Nonetheless, Fans were eager to see her in *Earthquake* (1974), in which she surprised the director by insisting on doing her own stunts, and the prime-time soap *Knots Landing* (1985).

Born
Ava Lavinia Gardner
December 24, 1922
Grabtown, North Carolina

Died
January 25, 1990
London, England,
of pneumonia

Star Sign
Capricorn

Height
5'6"

Husbands
Mickey Rooney
(1942–43, divorced)

Artie Shaw
(1945–46, divorced)

Frank Sinatra
(1951–57, divorced)

Essential
AVAGARDNERFilms

ACADEMY AWARDS

Nominated for Best Actress
Mogambo

THE KILLERS

(1946) Universal
A star-making vehicle for both
Gardner and Burt Lancaster, based
on an Ernest Hemingway story
about the murder of an ex-fighter.
Gardner is the two-faced beauty
whose treachery helps to seal
Lancaster's fate.

SHOW BOAT

(1951) MGM
MGM's remake of the musical about
life on the Mississippi in the 1800s
and riverboat entertainers who
find love, laughs, and hardships
as they sail along "Old Man River."
Gardner performs famous torch
songs, including "Bill," with Annette
Warren's voice.

MOGAMBO

(1953) MGM
A remake of *Red Dust* for which
Gardner received her only Oscar
nomination, in honor of her
performance in the part originally
played by Jean Harlow. Clark
Gable reprises his role as the hero
of the romantic adventure, now
set in Africa, with Gardner as
wisecracking HoneyBear Kelly.

THE BAREFOOT CONTESSA

(1954) United Artists
Director, producer, and screenwriter
Joseph L. Mankiewicz's rags-to-
riches story of a Spanish dancer
(Gardner) who becomes an international star but still longs for the
simplicity of her youth. The film is
rumored to be loosely based on
Rita Hayworth's rise to stardom.

THE NIGHT OF THE IGUANA

(1964) MGM
A steamy Tennessee Williams
drama set in Mexico, with
Gardner as Maxine Falk, the salty
proprietress of a run-down resort.
Gardner is teamed with fellow
acting heavyweights Richard
Burton and Deborah Kerr.

THE KILLERS, 1946

STYLENOTES

Ava resisted the studio's elaborate makeover process, refusing to thin her eyebrows and fill in a dimple with plastic surgery.

Ava's tolerance for both liquor and late nights was the stuff of Hollywood legends. When fellow revelers had to drag themselves home at dawn after an evening of clubbing and late-night parties, Ava still looked terrific.

The sultry, appraising gaze that Ava often gives on camera is really a squint— she needed glasses but couldn't wear them in her pictures.

Ava learned the Flamenco for *The Barefoot Contessa* and it became a favorite pastime. Needing little sleep, she would put on a flouncing skirt and dance all night.

behindthescenes

GARDNER OFTEN DISMISSED HER OWN TALENT AND AMBITION, WHILE OTHERS DID NOT. WRITER ERNEST HEMINGWAY LOVED THE MIX OF SEXUALITY AND VULNERABILITY SHE DISPLAYED ON SCREEN. HE HIMSELF CHOSE HER FOR THE ROLE OF CYNTHIA IN *THE SNOWS OF KILIMANJARO* (1952), A CHARACTER NOT IN THE ORIGINAL STORY BUT CLEARLY INSPIRED BY THE LEADING LADY IN HIS CLASSIC *A FAREWELL TO ARMS*.

AVA'S MOST NOTORIOUS MARRIAGE WAS WITH ACTOR-CROONER FRANK SINATRA. THE WORLD WATCHED AS THE COUPLE, DUBBED "THE BATTLING SINATRAS," SPENT SEVERAL YEARS IN AN INCREDIBLY PUBLIC, STORMY ROMANCE THAT BEGAN WITH A TORRID AFFAIR. DESPITE THEIR BATTLES, HOWEVER, SINATRA CAME TO HER RESCUE WHEN HER HEALTH DETERIORATED, PAYING FOR ALL OF HER MEDICAL EXPENSES AFTER HER 1989 STROKE.

AVA AGREED TO MAKE *SHOW BOAT* (1951) ON THE CONDITION THAT SHE SING HER OWN SONGS. SHE RECORDED ALL OF THEM, BUT AT THE LAST MINUTE THE STUDIO DUBBED IN A MORE COMMERCIAL-SOUNDING VOICE, EVEN THOUGH THEIR DIALECTS DIDN'T MATCH. HOWEVER, HER VOICE DID REMAIN ON THE SOUNDTRACK ALBUM AND FOR THE REST OF HER LIFE SHE RECEIVED ROYALTY CHECKS FOR THE RECORD'S SALES.

CIRCA 1951

The combination of her incomparable voice and emotional fragility could turn even a lighthearted musical into a powerful work of art.

JUDY GARLAND

Born
Frances Ethel Gumm
June 10, 1922
Grand Rapids, Michigan

Died
June 22, 1969
London, England,
of an accidental
barbiturate overdose

Star Sign
Gemini

Height
4'11"

Husbands and Children
Musician David Rose
(1941-45, divorced)

Director Vincente Minnelli
(1945-51, divorced)
daughter, Liza

Producer Sidney Luft
(1952-65, divorced)
two children, Lorna and Joseph

Actor Mark Herron
(1965-66, divorced)

Nightclub manager Mickey Deans
(1969-her death)

Born into a hard-driving vaudeville family, Baby Frances was the youngest of the performing Gumm sisters (later, the Garland sisters)—and easily the most talented. Judy stepped on stage for the first time at age two, and by age ten she had gotten a positive notice in *Variety* for her "pip of a lowdown voice." In 1935, MGM finally signed the spunky child they'd been eyeing for over a year. A born entertainer, she could do it all—sing, dance, and act with such verve that her portrayal of Dorothy in *The Wizard of Oz* (1939) elevated a children's film into a complex physical and emotional experience. After *Oz*, Judy gamely continued her good-sport teen persona in a series of highly successful "backyard musicals" with Mickey Rooney. Judy's personal struggles with addiction began during those years, but they didn't detract from the enormous presence she brought to the screen. At age twenty-one, she appeared in *Meet Me in St. Louis* (1944), a huge hit for MGM, which introduced her to her second husband, director Vincente Minnelli. Over the next few years, Judy lent her charisma to a number of films, belting out an Oscar-winning song in *The Harvey Girls* (1946), making magic with Fred Astaire in *Easter Parade* (1948), and imbuing "Get Happy" in *Summer Stock* (1950) with edgy exuberance. By that time her personal problems had begun interfering with her work, and after *Summer Stock* MGM let her go. She bounced back with sellout performances at New York's Palace Theater and the London Palladium. The concerts helped Judy regain some footing in Hollywood, and she returned to make *A Star Is Born* (1954). Production delays, many caused by her continuing insecurities, made it almost impossible for the expensive film to turn a profit, and plans for follow-up pictures fell through. Instead, she went back to the concert stage, which Garland really preferred—nothing but her, the music, and the audience. She attempted to bring that sensibility to a CBS variety series in 1963–64, but, although it became a cult classic, network interference and bad scheduling did the show in. Her final years were filled with extreme difficulty, and in 1969 she succumbed to her addictions with a fatal overdose of sleeping pills. Nonetheless, Judy Garland's inner demons, however great, cannot overshadow the enormous talent she shared in her award-winning movies and musical performances.

Essential
JUDYGARLANDFilms

ACADEMY AWARDS

Nominated for Best Actress
A Star Is Born
Judgment at Nuremberg

Special Oscar in 1940 for "Outstanding Performance as a Screen Juvenile"

THE WIZARD OF OZ
(1939) MGM

Garland's star-making role as Dorothy Gale, the L. Frank Baum heroine who dreams herself into the magical land of Oz, where her quest to return home is aided by a Scarecrow (Ray Bolger), a Tin Man (Jack Haley), and a Cowardly Lion (Bert Lahr). The songs include Garland's rendition of the Oscar-winning "Over the Rainbow."

BABES IN ARMS
(1939) MGM

A Garland–Mickey Rooney "let's-put-on-a-show" musical, with Mickey and Judy in a gang of vaudeville kids who try to avoid being sent to a state-run school by staging their own musical revue. One of eight films the pair made as a team, this one was inspired by the Rodgers and Hart Broadway musical of the same name.

MEET ME IN ST. LOUIS
(1944) MGM

Young love and childish fears in a year in the life of a turn-of-the-century family. Directed by husband-to-be Vincente Minnelli, Judy sings several classics, including "The Trolley Song."

SUMMER STOCK
(1950) MGM

Garland's last MGM film, a musical costarring Gene Kelly, about a theater group taking over a farm to put on a show. Garland lights up the screen with several songs, including her legendary "Get Happy."

A STAR IS BORN
(1954) Warner Bros.

Director George Cukor's musical remake of the 1937 classic with Garland as a rising star who marries an alcoholic has-been actor, played by James Mason. The film marked Judy's triumphant return to the screen after a four-year hiatus.

A STAR IS BORN, 1954

78

STYLENOTES

MGM was obsessed with molding Judy into their image of a star. Finding fault with many aspects of her appearance, she was immediately put on a diet at MGM, which her mother supplemented with diet pills. When the pills kept her from sleeping, an MGM physician gave her sleeping pills. Thus began her substance abuse problems.

When Judy played Dorothy at the age of sixteen, she was a curvaceous adolescent playing an eleven-year-old. Yet when she wore an Adrian-designed smock and long braids pulled forward, few doubted her childlike innocence.

Garland took a break from shooting to lose more than twenty pounds for her *Summer Stock* sequence, where she showed off her shapely legs in that famous black evening jacket and fedora.

behindthescenes

JUDY GARLAND SANG "YOU MADE ME LOVE YOU" SO BEAUTIFULLY AT CLARK GABLE'S THIRTY-SIXTH BIRTHDAY PARTY THAT MGM HEAD LOUIS B. MAYER PUT HER IN *BROADWAY MELODY OF 1938* SINGING IN THE SAME STYLE TO A PHOTOGRAPH OF GABLE. JUDY LATER ADMITTED SHE WISHED SHE COULD HAVE SUNG TO A PHOTO OF HER REAL IDOL AT THE TIME, ACTOR ROBERT DONAT.

A HOLLYWOOD FAVORITE OF JUDY'S WAS THE ACTRESS MARILYN MONROE, OF WHOM JUDY SAID, "I BARELY KNEW HER BUT IT'S LIKE WE SHARED A SOUL."

BOTH OF JUDY'S DAUGHTERS BECAME PERFORMERS AS WELL. LIZA MINNELLI ACHIEVED GREATER FAME, YET LORNA LUFT HAS ALSO HAD HER SHARE OF RAPTUROUS FANS. "PEOPLE COME UP TO ME AND TELL ME THEY SAW MY MOTHER ON STAGE WITH ME AS I SANG," SHE RECOUNTED. "I TRY TO KEEP A SENSE OF HUMOR ABOUT IT AND WISECRACK, 'WAS SHE UP THERE? YOU NEVER COULD GET MOTHER OFF A STAGE.'"

THE DAY JUDY DIED, KANSAS WAS HIT WITH A TORNADO.

THE WIZARD OF OZ, 1939

A beautiful redhead with emerald eyes, she inspired legions of fans during World War II with quietly selfless, always relatable home-front heroines who kept their heads during the perils of war.

GREER
GARSON

MGM claimed for years that red-haired Greer Garson was Irish-born, yet in truth Garson was as properly British as many of the celebrated parts she played. She dreamt of being an actress, but as the only child of a widowed mother, she planned a more practical future. Post-college work with the Birmingham Repertory Theater, however, soon made Garson a popular star of London's West End, where her lovely appearance and elegant demeanor earned her the nickname "the Duchess of Garson." MGM head Louis B. Mayer was scouting talent in London when he saw her and, some say, fell in love. Yet once Garson landed in Hollywood, she was largely ignored, finally landing a part—ironically—in a film being made back home, the poignant *Goodbye, Mr. Chips* (1939). As the main character's ill-fated wife, Garson was only on screen for twenty minutes, but she made the most of it, receiving a Best Actress Oscar nomination for her memorable portrayal. After making such a splash, Garson was no longer relegated to second-class status. The actress seemed an ideal vision of womanhood, sparring with Laurence Olivier in *Pride and Prejudice* (1940) and finding her perfect cinema counterpart in Walter Pidgeon, with whom she made eight films. Their *Mrs. Miniver* (1942) was her triumph; she moved audiences to tears as a brave wife and mother trying to keep her family hopeful amidst the perils of war. Garson's captivating performance was capped with an Oscar for Best Actress. The same year, she added luster to her star as the wife of amnesiac Ronald Colman in *Random Harvest*. Lauded for her self-sacrificing heroines, Garson was eventually handicapped by such typecasting when audience tastes turned to more complicated females. After five straight years of receiving Oscar nominations, Garson found herself less popular in the postwar years. She finally retired in 1966, content with her long, stable marriage to a wealthy Texan who let her focus on the pleasures of ranching and philanthropy, including making generous contributions to young people studying theater.

Born
Eileen Evelyn Greer Garson
September 29, 1904
London, England

Died
April 6, 1996
Dallas, Texas,
of heart failure

Star Sign
Libra

Height
5'6"

Husbands
Civil servant Edwin A. Snelson
(1933–37, divorced)

Actor Richard Ney
(1943–47, divorced)

Texas businessman E. E. Fogelson
(1949–87, his death)

Essential
GREER **GARSON** Films

PRIDE AND PREJUDICE
(1940) MGM
Jane Austen's comedy of manners about a family with five marriageable daughters in nineteenth-century England, transferred to the screen in grand style by MGM. Garson is Elizabeth, the most independent daughter, and Laurence Olivier is her unlikely romantic partner, the boorish Mr. Darcy.

MRS. MINIVER
(1942) MGM
Director William Wyler's morale-boosting account of family life in England during World War II, with Garson as the courageous, warm-hearted matriarch. The film won six Oscars, including awards for Best Picture and Actress (Garson).

RANDOM HARVEST
(1942) MGM
Sentimental drama with Garson as a music-hall entertainer who helps World War I veteran Ronald Colman cope with amnesia. After they are happily married, the poor chap loses his memory once again and forgets her (temporarily).

MRS. PARKINGTON
(1944) MGM
A reteaming of MGM favorites Garson and Walter Pidgeon in novelist Louis Bromfield's romantic family saga about a maid who marries an oilman and financier who pushes her into high society.

JULIA MISBEHAVES
(1948) MGM
Garson and Walter Pidgeon together again, this time in a comedy about a showgirl who returns to her stuffy estranged husband when their daughter (Elizabeth Taylor) becomes engaged.

MRS. MINIVER, 1942

STYLENOTES

Greer Garson defied the accepted rules governing what redheads could and could not wear. In an article entitled "Rules for Redheads" she advised, "Experiment—don't be content to stay faithful to one safe color scheme." Nonetheless, Greer followed the green-is-good rule for redheads in one respect: her living room was decorated in emerald green to better show off her hair.

The legendary redhead made headlines when she went brunette for *Mrs. Parkington.* She joked that so many girls were going red for Technicolor movies that "they're putting me out of business."

DESIRE ME, 1947

behindthescenes

LOUIS B. MAYER'S DISCOVERY OF GREER GARSON WAS QUITE ACCIDENTAL: WHEN HE ATTENDED THE PLAY *OLD MUSIC,* THE STORY DIDN'T THRILL HIM—BUT THE STUNNING RED-HAIRED ACTRESS WITH THE ELEGANT BEARING DID.

GREER WAS VERY RELUCTANT TO JOIN THE CAST OF *MRS. MINIVER,* FEARING THAT PLAYING A WOMAN WITH A GROWN SON WOULD AGE HER TOO MUCH. PRESSURED INTO THE ROLE BY MAYER, SHE FOUND COMPENSATION IN A SECRET ROMANCE WITH RICHARD NEY, THE ACTOR WHO PLAYED HER SON. WHEN MAYER GOT WORD OF THE RELATIONSHIP, HE PERSUADED THE COUPLE NOT TO MARRY UNTIL AFTER THE FILM'S GENERAL RELEASE.

WITH BETTE DAVIS , GREER HOLDS THE RECORD FOR THE MOST CONSECUTIVE OSCAR NOMINATIONS: FIVE IN A ROW FROM 1941 TO 1945.

GREER'S IMPECCABLE SCREEN IMAGE MADE HER AN EASY TARGET. AMONG THE MANY SPOOFING HER WAS JUDY GARLAND IN *ZIEGFELD FOLLIES* (1946), IN A NUMBER ORIGINALLY PLANNED FOR GREER HERSELF. ALTHOUGH SHE REFUSED TO DO THE TAKEOFF ON HER GREAT LADY ROLES, SHE WRYLY ACKNOWLEDGED HER POSITION AS "METRO'S GLORIFIED MOTHER," ALL THE WHILE MINDFUL OF HER GOOD FORTUNE. AS SHE WOULD SAY, "THERE ARE WORSE IMAGES."

GREER DONATED MILLIONS FOR THE CONSTRUCTION OF THE GREER GARSON THEATER AT THE UNIVERSITY OF SANTA FE ON THREE CONDITIONS: 1) THAT THE STAGE BE CIRCULAR, 2) THAT THE PREMIERE PRODUCTION BE WILLIAM SHAKESPEARE'S *A MIDSUMMER NIGHT'S DREAM,* AND 3) THAT IT HAVE LARGE LADIES' ROOMS.

One of the matriarchs of cinema, she virtually invented Method acting on film by using her ethereal beauty to reveal complex internal struggles with simple, subtle gestures and expressions.

LILLIAN
GISH

Lillian Gish's childhood in the theater mirrored the trials of her vulnerable yet spunky heroines. She began acting to support her struggling family, touring the country as a small girl with scarcely any adult supervision. Child welfare agents occasionally took custody of her until her mother could retrieve her. But though the advice to "speak loud and clear" was the only acting training she received, Lillian would develop a talent and passion for performing that influences film acting to this day. The turning point in her life came in 1912 when she and her sister, Dorothy, visited their old friend Gladys Smith (rechristened Mary Pickford for the screen) at New York's Biograph Studios. There, after an impromptu audition, director D. W. Griffith quickly hired the sisters each to play a small part in one of his films. Both continued to make films with Griffith, but it was Lillian with whom he developed a unique professional chemistry. Griffith's silent films often featured angelic-looking women facing unbearable situations, and the delicate, determined Lillian intuitively knew how to get to the core of such roles. Lillian never rested on her innate talent but instead worked hard every day to perfect her craft. At Griffith's urging, she visited prizefights and insane asylums to better understand the range of human experience. Lillian became a star in what is often called the first film of modern cinema, *The Birth of a Nation* (1915). Her relationship with Griffith flourished until 1921, when a financial disagreement finally severed their ties. She then became the darling of MGM, where she exercised unprecedented artistic control over films like *La Bohème, The Scarlet Letter* (both 1926), and *The Wind* (1928). After the introduction of sound, her innocent image seemed dated. When her contract expired, Lillian returned to the stage for many years, devoted herself to her mother's care, and went on the college lecture circuit, offering a firsthand account of film's origins and advocating for film preservation. Eventually she returned to the screen as a character actress, giving memorable performances in *Duel in the Sun* (1945), *The Night of the Hunter* (1955), and her last film, *The Whales of August* (1987).

Born
Lillian Diana de Guiche
October 14, 1893
Springfield, Ohio

Died
February 27, 1993
New York, New York,
of heart failure

Star Sign
Libra

Height
5'5"

Essential
LILLIANGISHFilms

ACADEMY AWARDS

**Nominated for
Best Supporting Actress**
Duel in the Sun

Honorary Award in 1971
for "superlative artistry
and for distinguished
contribution to the progress
of motion pictures"

BROKEN BLOSSOMS

(1919) United Artists
The story of a delicate young
woman (Gish) who is abused by
her brutal father (Donald Crisp),
with Richard Barthelmess as
her would-be rescuer, a young
Chinese aristocrat.

ORPHANS OF THE STORM

(1922) United Artists
Two orphans, one blind, who are
separated, then reunited, during
the French Revolution. Gish plays
the sighted sister , and her real-
life sister, Dorothy Gish, plays the
blind one.

LA BOHÈME

(1926) MGM
Gish's first film under an MGM
contract that gave her control over
her productions. In this film version
of the same novel that inspired the
Puccini opera, Gish is Mimi, the
seamstress who sacrifices herself
for an aspiring artist (John Gilbert).

THE SCARLET LETTER

(1926) MGM
The Nathaniel Hawthorne classic,
put on film by Gish herself as part
of her MGM contract. She plays
Hester Prynne, the young woman
who is branded an adulteress
in colonial Massachusetts after
becoming pregnant by a man who
is not her husband.

THE WIND

(1928) MGM
Director Victor Sjostrom's
American film about a sheltered
girl from the East who adapts to
the turbulent life of the Wild West.

THE SCARLET LETTER, 1926

STYLENOTES

In 1925, Lillian offended costume designer Erté by redesigning the costumes he had made for *La Bohème*. (She found his calico dresses to be "offensive," too opulent for her impoverished character, and too stiff to walk in.) Instead, Lillian had her costumes made of worn silk. Erté subsequently left MGM and went back to Paris (it was director Cecil B. DeMille who coaxed him back four years later to design for *Madame Satan*).

In the 1930s, Lillian spent her summers at European health spas. Beginning in 1940, she added the use of a "slanting board" to her daily regime. She believed that she was fighting gravity "by lying upside down on the slant board each morning at seven o'clock."

Lillian never once had a haircut (her tresses fell well below her waist all her life).

behindthe**scenes**

LILLIAN OFTEN PUT HERSELF IN DANGER FOR A PART, BUT FEW SCENES REQUIRED MORE OF HER THAN ONE IN *WAY DOWN EAST* (1920), WHERE FOR TAKE AFTER TAKE SHE FLOATED DOWN AN ICY RIVER. ALTHOUGH HER ADDED GESTURE OF TRAILING A FEW FINGERS IN THE WATER RESULTED IN PERMANENT NERVE DAMAGE, SHE STILL FELT THAT ANOTHER TAKE MIGHT HAVE MADE THE SCENE EVEN BETTER.

WHEN THE GISH SISTERS VISITED THEIR FRIEND MARY PICKFORD AT BIOGRAPH STUDIOS, DIRECTOR D. W. GRIFFITH SUDDENLY DREW A PROP GUN OUT AND STARTED SHOOTING IT, CHASING THEM AROUND THE STUDIO. THEIR TERRIFIED EXPRESSIONS PLEASED HIM, AND HE HIRED THEM ON THE SPOT.

LILLIAN HAD A MAJOR RUN-IN WITH LOUIS B. MAYER AT MGM WHEN HE INSISTED ON CONCOCTING A SCANDAL TO GIVE HER ADDED SEX APPEAL IN THE ERA OF NAUGHTY, CAREFREE FLAPPERS. LILLIAN STOOD HER GROUND, AND MAYER MADE LIFE QUITE DIFFICULT FOR HER UNTIL THEY PARTED WAYS.

THE ROCK GROUP SMASHING PUMPKINS NAMED THEIR FIRST ALBUM GISH IN HER HONOR.

MILDRED HARRIS CHAPLIN, MARY PICKFORD, LILLIAN GISH, AND DOROTHY GISH, 1919

When an overzealous hairdresser dyed her hair platinum, the Blonde Bombshell was born, but it was her smarts and sass that made her a star during a tragically short, but legendary, career.

JEAN
HARLOW

Born
Harlean Harlow Carpenter
March 3, 1911
Kansas City, Missouri

Died
June 7, 1937
Los Angeles, California,
of uremic poisoning

Star Sign
Pisces

Height
5'2"

Husbands
Chicago socialite
Charles McGrew III
(1927–29, divorced)

MGM executive Paul Bern
(1932–32, his death)

Cameraman Harold Rosson
(1933–35, divorced)

Jean Harlow got into the movies on a dare. She was a dentist's daughter from a well-off family when she eloped with a Chicago socialite at the age of sixteen. After the couple moved to Los Angeles, some friends wagered that she didn't have the nerve to try out for a film. She proved that she did—and won the part. After her first marriage broke up, Jean continued playing small roles until eccentric tycoon Howard Hughes signed her for a contract that included the female lead in his groundbreaking aviation drama *Hell's Angels* (1930). Hughes then loaned her to other studios, capitalizing on her sexual image (she was the first woman called a "slut" in a talking picture). Executive Paul Bern convinced MGM's bosses to buy out her contract with Hughes and give her a chance to be more than a sexy trifle in *Red-Headed Woman* (1932), a film whose steamy plot was tempered by Jean's high spirits. Bern also married her, but when he committed suicide two months later under mysterious circumstances (years later it was revealed that he had been confronted by a common-law wife he'd deserted), the scandal almost ruined her. Fortunately for Jean, Bern had gotten her another meaty role, opposite Clark Gable in the tropical romance *Red Dust* (1932). Jean plunged back into work and scored again. When she stole *Dinner at Eight* (1933) from such accomplished screen actors as Marie Dressler, Wallace Beery, and John Barrymore, the studio knew they had a star on their hands. Even the arrival of stricter film censorship in 1934 couldn't dim her luster. She simply changed her hair color to a more reserved "brownette" and played more virtuous versions of her earlier, earthy roles. Scoring one of her biggest hits as Spencer Tracy's jilted fiancée in *Libeled Lady* (1936), she got the chance to work with her new love, actor William Powell. She dreamed of marrying him, but while shooting *Saratoga* (1937) Jean fell ill, dying ten days later at the age of twenty-six. Mystery surrounded her sudden death, but research eventually revealed that she had suffered from kidney disease since her teens.

Essential
JEANHARLOWFilms

RED-HEADED WOMAN
(1932) MGM
A racy tale with Harlow as a gold digger from the wrong side of the tracks who seduces her way into society but falls for a French chauffeur (Charles Boyer).

RED DUST
(1932) MGM
The potent combo of Harlow and Clark Gable, in an early, naughtier version of *Mogambo* (1953). The story is set in Indochina, with Gable as a rubber-plantation overseer, Harlow as a prostitute who enjoys bathing in a barrel, and Mary Astor as an adulteress and the third part of an erotic triangle.

BOMBSHELL
(1933) MGM
A dissatisfied Hollywood "bombshell" named Lola (Jean Harlow) finds herself fed up with her leeching relatives, overly demanding studio bosses, and a press agent who works overtime planting lurid stories about her. The film is allegedly based on actress Clara Bow's life and career.

DINNER AT EIGHT
(1933) MGM
MGM's all-star version of the George S. Kaufman–Edna Ferber stage hit, with the standout Harlow as the faithless wife of crooked businessman Wallace Beery. George Cukor directed a cast that also included John and Lionel Barrymore, Billie Burke, and Marie Dressler.

LIBELED LADY
(1936) MGM
A screwball comedy with a cast headed by Harlow, Spencer Tracy, Myrna Loy, and William Powell. A newspaper managing editor (Tracy) enlists his long-suffering fiancée (Harlow) in a plot to foil a wealthy socialite's plans to sue his newspaper.

RED DUST, 1932

STYLENOTES

Jean spent her Sundays having her ash-blonde hair bleached platinum with a mixture of peroxide, ammonia, Clorox, and Lux flakes. The painful procedure wreaked such havoc on her hair that she was eventually forced to don a wig.

Jean is mostly remembered for her Adrian-designed satin gowns—so form fitting that they had foundation garments built into them—yet it was her day-wear costumes—clinging bias-cut dresses—that were copied by adoring fans.

She refused to wear a bra and panties and liked to sleep in the nude. Despite her glamorous look on screen, the real Jean Harlow loved to throw on sweaters and slacks, referring to her personal wardrobe as "far from elaborate."

William Powell gave Jean an eighty-five-carat star sapphire ring, which she hoped signified their engagement. However, he said nothing to confirm this, so she wore it on her right hand and rarely took it off, even wearing it in her 1937 comedy *Personal Property*.

DINNER AT EIGHT, 1933

behindthescenes

JEAN HARLOW'S BRASSY, BAD-GIRL ROLES CAUSED PEOPLE TO ASSUME THAT SHE CAME FROM THE WRONG SIDE OF THE TRACKS. IN TRUTH, SHE CAME FROM MONEY.

JEAN, WHO HAD ONE OF THE PUSHIEST STAGE MOTHERS IN THE BUSINESS, TOOK HER MOTHER'S NAME PROFESSIONALLY. FOR YEARS JEAN HAD TO SUPPORT NOT JUST HER MOTHER BUT ALSO THE WOMAN'S SECOND HUSBAND, A WOULD-BE ENTREPRENEUR WHOSE BUSINESS DEALS WERE A HUGE DRAIN ON JEAN'S FINANCES.

WHEN CLARA BOW FIRST SPOTTED JEAN ON THE SET OF *THE SATURDAY NIGHT KID* (1929), SHE WAS COWED BY THE YOUNG GIRL'S BEAUTY AND WANTED HER KICKED OFF THE LOT. SOON, HOWEVER, THEY BECAME GREAT FRIENDS.

AN AVID READER, JEAN ALSO LOVED TO WRITE; SHE COAUTHORED THE NOVEL *TODAY IS TONIGHT* (WHICH HER MOTHER PUBLISHED IN 1964).

JEAN MAY HAVE FOUND HER GREATEST HAPPINESS WITH ACTOR WILLIAM POWELL. HE ADORED HER TOO, BUT HE WAS DISCLINED TO MARRY, EXPLAINING, "NO MAN CAN COPE WITH BEING MARRIED TO THE WORLD'S SEX SYMBOL . . . I DON'T WANT IN MY DECLINING YEARS TO BE MARRIED TO A GIRL MEN KILL THEMSELVES OVER." JEAN'S DEATH AT THE TENDER AGE OF TWENTY-SIX DEVASTATED HIM, AND FOR YEARS POWELL SENT FRESH FLOWERS TO HER GRAVE EVERY DAY.

This flame-haired Brooklyn beauty, part hard-boiled sex goddess and part tenacious workhorse, set fire to 1950s cinema with her gutsy portrayals of women way over the edge.

SUSAN
HAYWARD

"I learned at a very early age that life is a battle," Susan Hayward once said—or maybe she said it a hundred times—for this was a woman unafraid to speak up. Her fair-skinned, sultry beauty got her out of the slums of Brooklyn and into the *Saturday Evening Post.* The magazine's photo of Susan so impressed producer David O. Selznick that he brought her out to Hollywood in 1937 to join the growing pool of starlets vying to play Scarlett O'Hara. Susan's audition was such a wash that Selznick himself suggested she head back home, but her reply was typical of her borough-bred moxie: "I like oranges. I think I'll stay." After some lean years at Warner Bros., Susan flourished in a variety of roles at Paramount. Still feeling held back, in 1946 she signed with producer Walter Wanger, claiming that at last she had found an advocate who understood her. Their collaboration resulted in a Best Actress Oscar nomination for *Smash Up: The Story of a Woman* (1947), in which she played an alcoholic singer with full-out bravado. A contract with 20th Century-Fox provided the comfort that her rocky marriage to actor Jess Barker could not, and Susan toiled as though the soundstage were her only home. Soon she was Fox's first lady, angling for challenging roles that put her at the forefront, whether as a noble heroine or a man-eating seductress. In 1952 the Hollywood Foreign Press Association named Susan and John Wayne the year's most popular film stars. 1955's biopic of alcoholic entertainer Lillian Roth, *I'll Cry Tomorrow,* got her an Academy Award nomination, but Susan didn't win her longed-for Oscar until she reteamed with Wanger to play convicted murderess Barbara Graham in 1958's *I Want to Live!* That high point in her career was followed by an inevitable decline, partly fueled by Susan's offscreen happiness in her second marriage. By the 1960s, she had slowed down considerably, though she did replace Judy Garland as a tough Broadway star in *Valley of the Dolls* (1967) and headline the Las Vegas production of *Mame.* She was still very much a star when, after a two-year struggle, brain cancer took her life in 1975.

Born
Edythe Marrener
June 30, 1917
Brooklyn, New York

Died
March 14, 1975
Hollywood, California,
of brain cancer

Star Sign
Cancer

Height
5'3"

Husbands and Children
Actor Jess Barker
(1944–54, divorced)
twin sons, Timothy and Gregory

Businessman Floyd Eaton Chalkley
(1957–66, his death)

Essential
SUSANHAYWARDFilms

ACADEMY AWARDS

Won Best Actress
I Want to Live!

Nominated for Best Actress
Smash-Up: The Story of a Woman
My Foolish Heart
With a Song in My Heart
I'll Cry Tomorrow

SMASH-UP: THE STORY OF A WOMAN
(1947) Universal
Hayward's depiction of a singer who falls prey to alcoholism. Lee Bowman plays her husband for whom the ambitious singer gives up her career, with disastrous results.

MY FOOLISH HEART
(1949) RKO
The only J. D. Salinger story ever transferred to the screen. Hayward plays a woman who becomes pregnant by a soldier who is killed in the war and then marries another man in order to give her child a name.

WITH A SONG IN MY HEART
(1952) 20th Century-Fox
Film biography of singer Jane Froman, who made a stirring comeback after becoming paralyzed from the waist down in an airplane accident. Using Froman's voice, Hayward mimed the musical numbers.

I'LL CRY TOMORROW
(1955) MGM
Another musical bio, with Hayward as singer-actress Lillian Roth, who climbed back after hitting bottom as an alcoholic. This time Hayward sang her own songs.

I WANT TO LIVE!
(1958) United Artists
Hayward's portrayal of accused murderess Barbara Graham. This real-life story takes Graham from her days as a "B-girl" who shilled for crooked card players to her involvement in a killing for which she faced the gas chamber.

I'LL CRY TOMORROW, 1955

STYLE NOTES

Dubbed "the sexiest hair" in movies, Susan's tresses were her primary physical asset and she refused to endorse hair coloring products. "No, I am a natural redhead" was always her firm response to such requests.

Nolan Miller designed the spectacular green-sequined gown that Susan wore for her triumphant appearance at the 1974 Academy Awards to present the Best Actress Oscar. When Susan passed away a year later, she was buried in the dress.

I'LL CRY TOMORROW, 1955

behind the scenes

SUSAN HAYWARD LANDED AN AGENT BY LITERALLY LANDING ON HIS FRONT LAWN. A BIKE ACCIDENT CAUSED HER TO CRASH ON THE PROPERTY OF AGENT BENNY MEDFORD. HE HELPED HER UP AND THEN HELPED HER CAREER, GIVING HER A NEW NAME AND GETTING HER A CONTRACT WITH WARNER BROS.

YOU CAN TAKE THE GIRL OUT OF BROOKLYN, BUT HER GUMPTION IS SURE TO LAST A LIFETIME. SUSAN DEMONSTRATED THIS EARLY IN HER CAREER, WHEN AT A PARAMOUNT SALES CONVENTION IN 1941 THE NEOPHYTE ACTRESS USED HER CHEESECAKE MOMENT ON STAGE TO ASK PRODUCTION CHIEF WILLIAM LEBARON TO PUT HER IN MORE MOVIES, SAYING, IN EFFECT, "HOW ABOUT IT, MR. LEBARON?" THE GREATLY AMUSED AND CHEERING SALES FORCE GAVE HER THEIR APPROVAL— AS DID THE STUDIO, WHICH QUICKLY STARTED PUTTING HER INTO BETTER ROLES.

ACCORDING TO HOLLYWOOD LEGEND, SUSAN'S CANCER WAS THE RESULT OF RADIOACTIVE FALLOUT THAT ALLEGEDLY LANDED ON THE UTAH LOCATION SET OF *THE CONQUEROR* (1956). THE LEGEND GREW BECAUSE A LARGE NUMBER OF CAST AND CREW MEMBERS—INCLUDING ACTORS JOHN WAYNE, AGNES MOOREHEAD, AND JOHN HOYT, AND DIRECTOR DICK POWELL—DIED OF CANCER.

SUSAN'S BRAVERY AS AN ACTRESS TOOK A MORE POIGNANT TURN WHEN SHE PRESENTED AN AWARD AT THE 1974 OSCARS. UNBEKNOWNST TO MANY, SHE WAS SUFFERING FROM BRAIN CANCER. SHE GAMELY TOOK SOME PAINKILLERS, GOT A COMPLETE TRANSFORMATION FROM A SKILLED MAKEUP ARTIST, AND MADE A BRIEF BUT MEMORABLE APPEARANCE ON JOHN WAYNE'S ARM.

Forever immortalized as *Gilda* doing a mock striptease in a black strapless satin gown, she was christened "the Love Goddess" by the press, and World War II soldiers made her their pinup queen.

RITA
HAYWORTH

Born
Margarita Carmen Cansino
October 17, 1918
Brooklyn, New York

Died
May 14, 1987
New York, New York,
of Alzheimer's disease

Star Sign
Libra

Height
5'6"

Husbands and Children
Salesman Edward C. Judson
(1937–43, divorced)

Orson Welles
(1943–48, divorced)
daughter, Rebecca

Prince Aly Khan
(1949–53, divorced)
daughter, Yasmin

Singer Dick Haymes
(1953–55, divorced)

Producer James Hill
(1958–61, divorced)

Rita Hayworth was born to dance. The child of a Spanish dancer and a Ziegfeld chorus girl, she had a lot of talent and little choice in the matter. "Instead of a rattle," she once said, "I had castanets." "The Dancing Cansinos" became a father-daughter team when Rita was still a girl, entertaining on gambling boats and in Mexican nightclubs. One night the head of Fox Studios, Winfield Sheehan, saw the teen beauty and brought her to Hollywood for screen tests. Incredibly shy off camera, Rita nonetheless wanted to make it in the movies, partly to break away from her domineering father. To accomplish that feat, the eighteen-year-old Rita married another father figure, Edward C. Judson, beginning a series of failed relationships with men who loved her sexual image but couldn't deal with the real woman underneath. After a brief period at Fox, Rita began a twenty-year relationship with Columbia Pictures. Studio head Harry Cohn blew hot and cold on Rita; his frequent disdain struck many as frustrated desire. Still, he supervised the sometimes-painful process that transformed her from Latin dancer Margarita Cansino into love goddess Rita Hayworth. He also nursed her through a series of roles, including a strategic loan-out to Warner Bros. for *The Strawberry Blonde* (1941) and her two musicals with Fred Astaire, that made her a star. Rita reached the height of her popularity as the sultry femme fatale in *Gilda* (1946), doing a mock striptease while singing "Put the Blame on Mame." Husband Orson Welles saw her dramatic potential and put it on screen in *The Lady from Shanghai* (1948). Off screen, she yearned for a happy family life, even retiring temporarily when she married Prince Aly Khan. When that marriage ended, she returned to the screen, but by then her star was fading and Cohn was more interested in a new sex symbol, Kim Novak. Any chance of a comeback was cut short by the discovery that Rita was suffering from Alzheimer's disease. She retired from the screen after the 1972 Western *The Wrath of God*. Yet to the legions of fans who continue to adore her, Rita Hayworth's star still shines. A goddess on the screen, the real Rita was probably closer to the high-spirited dancers she played in her films with Fred Astaire. As she would say late in her life, "Whatever you write about me, don't make it sad."

Essential
RITAHAYWORTHFilms

YOU WERE NEVER LOVELIER
(1942) Columbia
The second of two Hayworth and Fred Astaire musicals, this one set in Argentina. Hayworth is the daughter of a wealthy nightclub owner (Adolphe Menjou) and refuses to seriously consider marriage. While her father is hot on the trail of proper son-in-law prospects, she falls for an American dancer (Astaire), much to his disapproval.

COVER GIRL
(1944) Columbia
A Technicolor musical with a score by Jerome Kern, Ira Gershwin, and Yip Harburg that tells of the romance between a nightclub owner (Gene Kelly) and a chorus girl (Hayworth) who gets a shot at stardom by appearing on magazine covers.

GILDA
(1946) Columbia
Hayworth's Gilda is the tempestuous wife of a South American casino owner who, in between clinches with her ex-lover (Glenn Ford), memorably performs "Put the Blame on Mame," a mock striptease number that solidified Hayworth's "love goddess" image.

THE LADY FROM SHANGHAI
(1948) Columbia
Hayworth's collaboration with then-husband Orson Welles, a noir thriller with a celebrated "hall of mirrors" finale. Blonde in the noir tradition, Hayworth is the femme fatale of the film.

PAL JOEY
(1957) Columbia
A Rodgers-Hart musical with Frank Sinatra in the title role as lovable louse Joey and Hayworth as his wealthy benefactress, a former stripper who sings "Zip" and "Bewitched, Bothered and Bewildered." Kim Novak costars as the chorus girl who captures Joey's heart.

GILDA, 1946

STYLENOTES

The process that changed Margarita Cansino into Rita Hayworth was elaborate: it included, among other things, a strict diet and electrolysis to raise her hairline. The painful procedure took two years to complete and made a subtle difference that Rita felt was truly worth the trouble.

The strapless black gown Rita wore in *Gilda*, created by Parisian designer Jean Louis, became a fashion favorite.

When Orson Welles dared to make Rita's hair both short and platinum blonde for *The Lady from Shanghai*, the public outcry was deafening. "The public became as angry with me over Rita's hair as the Hearst family had been about *Citizen Kane*," he recalled.

behindthescenes

RITA HAYWORTH'S MOST FAMOUS PUBLICITY POSE, WHICH HAD HER PERCHED ON HER OWN BED IN A SHEER LACE NIGHTGOWN, INSPIRED WORLD WAR II SOLDIERS SO MUCH THAT THEY PASTED IT ON THE ATOMIC BOMB THAT WAS DROPPED ON BIKINI ATOLL.

IN THE KIND OF IRONY THAT DOMINATED RITA'S LIFE, *LIFE* MAGAZINE DUBBED HER "THE LOVE GODDESS" IN AN ISSUE THAT CAME OUT JUST AS HER DIVORCE FROM ORSON WELLES BECAME FINAL.

EXASPERATED BY THE DISCREPANCY BETWEEN THE MONEY SHE MADE FOR COLUMBIA AND HER TAKE-HOME PAY, RITA FORMED BECKWORTH CORPORATION, GIVING HER A SIGNIFICANT PERCENTAGE OF THE PROFITS FROM HER FUTURE FILMS.

ALTHOUGH BEST REMEMBERED FOR HIS PAIRINGS WITH GINGER ROGERS, FRED ASTAIRE ONCE CLAIMED THAT RITA HAYWORTH WAS HIS FAVORITE DANCING PARTNER.

THE LADY FROM SHANGHAI, 1948

Elegant and angelic, she has enchanted generations. Whether she played a princess, a nun, or an iconic Manhattanite, she infused each of her characters with a bit of her own humanity and charm.

AUDREY
HEPBURN

Born
Audrey Kathleen Hepburn-Ruston
May 4, 1929
Brussels, Belgium

Died
January 20, 1993
Tolochenaz, Switzerland,
of stomach cancer

Star Sign
Taurus

Height
5'7"

Husbands and Children
Actor-director Mel Ferrer
(1954–68, divorced)
son, Sean

Italian psychoanalyst
Dr. Andrea Dotti
(1969–82, divorced)
son, Luca

Significant Other
Actor Robert Wolders
(1981–93, her death)

Audrey Hepburn grew up in Holland during World War II and began life with great uncertainty—not knowing when she would see her estranged father, where her next meal would come from, or even whether she would survive the war. Dance was her refuge and it brought her to the movies, where she quickly rose to stardom. After small roles in a few British features, she found herself cast opposite Gregory Peck in *Roman Holiday* (1953) and helped to make the film a critical and commercial triumph. At just twenty-four, Audrey won an Academy Award, followed later that year by a Tony for her Broadway role in *Ondine*. A string of romantic comedies followed—*Sabrina* (1954), *Funny Face* (1957), *Breakfast at Tiffany's* (1961)—and the fans' romance with Audrey continued as well. Both men and women were drawn to this slender, doe-eyed beauty, so different from the blonde bombshells of the day. Yet she was also attracted to films that explored life's hidden dramas. *The Nun's Story* (1959), *The Children's Hour* (1962), and *Wait Until Dark* (1967) expanded on her ingenue image. In pictures like *Love in the Afternoon* (1957) and *Two for the Road* (1967), she took a fresh approach to contemporary female characters, which may have been closer to her own life. She struggled to balance career and family, while also dealing with men who resisted becoming "Mr. Audrey Hepburn." Audrey tried twice to retire from the screen, but each time she attempted to focus on her private life, she found herself wooed back by an admiring director. One such director, Richard Lester, brought her back after nine years to costar with Sean Connery in *Robin and Marian* (1976), while Steven Spielberg coaxed her back for her last film, *Always* (1989). Yet her true passions seemed to lie outside conventional marriage and Hollywood. Domestic contentment came with her last partner, fellow Dutch actor Robert Wolders, and true fulfillment arrived when she signed on as a goodwill ambassador for UNICEF. Her own war-torn childhood was never far from her mind, prompting a serious commitment to the starving children of the world. Audrey Hepburn truly knew what mattered most, and when this very private woman bravely used her fame to mother the world, she stole our hearts all over again.

Essential
AUDREY HEPBURN Films

ROMAN HOLIDAY
(1953) Paramount
Audrey Hepburn's star debut, as a runaway princess touring Rome who shares a fleeting romance with an American reporter, played by Gregory Peck.

SABRINA
(1954) Paramount
The Broadway comedy *Sabrina Fair*, refashioned as a film vehicle for fresh new star Hepburn. She plays a chauffeur's daughter who spends two years in Paris, changing from an awkward girl to an elegant young woman, and captivates wealthy brothers Humphrey Bogart and William Holden.

FUNNY FACE
(1957) Paramount
A buoyant musical set in Paris, starring Hepburn as a bookstore clerk and Fred Astaire as the photographer who turns her into a top fashion model.

BREAKFAST AT TIFFANY'S
(1961) Paramount
Hepburn as Holly Golightly, the Truman Capote heroine who transforms from country girl to chic, daffy Manhattanite. A well-paid escort to rich, older men, she falls in love with another jaded innocent (George Peppard), a writer who's being kept by a wealthy socialite (Patricia Neal).

CHARADE
(1963) Universal
Hepburn's only movie with Cary Grant, a Hitchcock-influenced caper, where a mystery man (Grant) wants to help a recently widowed socialite (Hepburn) recover a fortune left behind by her murdered husband. Or does he?

BREAKFAST AT TIFFANY'S, 1961

STYLENOTES

The Hepburn look blends simple chic with European flair: oversized turtlenecks and sweaters, sleek cigarette-cut pants, and stylish flats. "The perfect American look," proclaimed designer Isaac Mizrahi, noting that it represents the "feminine edge of androgyny."

Although Head received an Oscar for *Sabrina,* many of Audrey's costumes in that film came from fledgling French designer Hubert de Givenchy, beginning a forty-year partnership that would revolutionize fashion. Audrey's trust in Givenchy was such that she hated to use any other designer. She once said, "I depend on Givenchy in the same way that American women depend on their psychiatrists."

The sleek black dress that Givenchy designed for Audrey in *Breakfast at Tiffany's* changed the "little black dress" into an Everywoman wardrobe staple.

behindthe**scenes**

WHILE FILMING HER SOLE WESTERN, *THE UNFORGIVEN* (1960), HEPBURN WAS INJURED IN A FALL FROM A HORSE. THE NURSE WHO SHOWED UP TO CARE FOR HER DURING AN EXTENDED RECOVERY WAS LATER REVEALED TO BE THE WOMAN AUDREY HAD PLAYED IN *THE NUN'S STORY.* THIS WASN'T THE ONLY MEDICAL COINCIDENCE IN AUDREY'S LIFE. DURING WORLD WAR II, SHE TENDED WOUNDED SOLDIERS IN HER FATHER'S HOSPITAL. ONE OF HER PATIENTS WAS FUTURE DIRECTOR TERENCE YOUNG, WITH WHOM SHE WOULD LATER WORK ON *WAIT UNTIL DARK.*

INITIALLY, GREGORY PECK TURNED DOWN THE MALE LEAD IN *ROMAN HOLIDAY* (1953) BECAUSE HE DIDN'T WANT TO PLAY SECOND FIDDLE TO AN UNKNOWN ACTRESS. DIRECTOR WILLIAM WYLER PERSUADED HIM TO TAKE THE ROLE, YET WHEN PECK REALIZED HOW WONDERFUL AUDREY WAS GOING TO BE IN THE PART, HE INSISTED THAT THE STUDIO GIVE HER BILLING EQUAL TO HIS. THEY BECAME LIFELONG FRIENDS.

AUDREY'S CAREER IS OFTEN DESCRIBED AS A PURE SUCCESS STORY, BUT THERE WERE STUMBLING BLOCKS: TRUMAN CAPOTE VEHEMENTLY DISAGREED WITH THE CHOICE OF AUDREY FOR THE FILM ADAPTATION OF HIS *BREAKFAST AT TIFFANY'S*—HE WANTED MARILYN MONROE—AND JULIE ANDREWS'S FANS WERE OUTRAGED WHEN AUDREY SNAGGED THE ROLE OF LIZA DOOLITTLE IN *MY FAIR LADY* (1964), WHICH ANDREWS HAD CREATED ON BROADWAY.

Her dramatic depths and independent spirit were the constants of her career, starting with her insistence on playing tough, hard-headed women. She became the ultimate "battle of the sexes" heroine.

KATHARINE
HEPBURN

Broadway producers thought Katharine Hepburn was too much the individual to achieve stardom, but she caught the eye of director George Cukor, who offered her the lead in *A Bill of Divorcement* (1932). Despite her early success in that film and in *Morning Glory* (1933), by decade's end exhibitors had labeled her box office poison. She made her comeback through the stage door when playwright Philip Barry wrote *The Philadelphia Story* to mirror her personality. With help from former beau Howard Hughes, she bought the play's film rights, and its success put her right back on top. Her professional and personal life both benefited from her MGM contract, particularly when she fell in love with costar Spencer Tracy while making *Woman of the Year* (1942), their first of nine films together. Blessed with a strong bone structure, Katharine aged gracefully in a series of mature roles in the 1950s. Her film work kept her a star despite frequent breaks to pursue theatrical projects and care for Tracy as his health declined. She put her salary on the line so he could play opposite her in his last film, *Guess Who's Coming to Dinner* (1967). He died seventeen days after filming was complete. Katharine won an Oscar for the film, but she said she could never watch it because the memories were too painful. On her own, Katharine continued to triumph as the imprisoned Queen Eleanor of Aquitaine in *The Lion in Winter* (1968) and Henry Fonda's supportive wife in *On Golden Pond* (1982), the latter bringing her a record fourth Oscar for Best Actress. Katharine also turned to television, first as Amanda in an acclaimed production of Tennessee Williams's *The Glass Menagerie* (1973) and then in an Emmy-winning performance opposite Laurence Olivier in the romantic comedy *Love Among the Ruins* (1975). Late in life, Katharine wrote a best-selling memoir, *Me: Stories of My Life* and appeared in the television documentary *Katharine Hepburn: All About Me* (1993). Katharine Hepburn lived life on her own terms at all times and was loved for it.

Born
Katharine Houghton Hepburn
May 12, 1907
Hartford, Connecticut

Died
June 29, 2003
Old Saybrook, Connecticut,
of natural causes

Star Sign
Taurus

Height
5'7"

Husband
Philadelphia businessman
Ludlow Ogden Smith
(1928–34, divorced)

Significant Other
Spencer Tracy
(1941–67, his death)

Essential
KATHARINE HEPBURN Films

BRINGING UP BABY
(1938) RKO
The definitive screwball comedy, with Hepburn as a scatterbrained socialite whose pet leopard plays havoc with the life of paleontologist Cary Grant.

THE PHILADELPHIA STORY
(1940) MGM
Hepburn's major movie comeback after starring in the stage version of this Philip Barry comedy of manners. She plays Tracy Lord, an imperious socialite who has second thoughts about her impending marriage after encounters with her ex-husband (Cary Grant) and a charming magazine writer (James Stewart).

WOMAN OF THE YEAR
(1942) MGM
Hepburn's first of nine films with partner Spencer Tracy. She's a political columnist, he's a sports reporter, and sparks fly as their two worlds collide.

THE AFRICAN QUEEN
(1951) United Artists
Stirring film version of the C. S. Forester novel, with spinster missionary Hepburn joining hard-drinking boat captain Humphrey Bogart on a perilous river journey in Africa during World War I.

THE LION IN WINTER
(1968) AVCO Embassy
The film treatment of the James Goldman play, featuring Hepburn's fierce Eleanor of Aquitaine, for which she won her third of four Oscars. Peter O'Toole is King Henry II of England, Eleanor's estranged and embattled husband.

THE PHILADELPHIA STORY, 1940

STYLENOTES

Her offhand chic earned her the 1985 Council of Fashion Designers of America's Lifetime Achievement Award. Katharine seemed amazed to be chosen: "We're in a serious spot when the original bag lady wins a prize for the way she dresses," she said. Calvin Klein called her "the epitome of style . . . everything that's modern."

Katharine's deliberately slouchy style didn't impress Hollywood at first. Executives at RKO threatened to steal her "dungarees" (jeans) if she didn't stop wearing them.

PAT AND MIKE, 1952

behindthe**scenes**

KATHARINE WAS COLDLY SHOT DOWN IN HER BID TO PLAY SCARLETT O'HARA BY PRODUCER DAVID O. SELZNICK: "I JUST CAN'T IMAGINE CLARK GABLE CHASING YOU FOR TEN YEARS." KATHARINE'S ICY REPLY WAS TYPICAL OF HER MOXIE: "I MAY NOT APPEAL TO YOU, DAVID, BUT THERE ARE MEN WITH DIFFERENT TASTES!"

THROUGHOUT THEIR LONG LOVE AFFAIR, SPENCER TRACY STAYED MARRIED TO ANOTHER WOMAN, PARTLY BECAUSE OF HIS CATHOLIC UPBRINGING, AND PARTLY OUT OF RESPECT FOR HER POSITION AS AN ADVOCATE FOR THE DEAF (HIS OLDER CHILD, JOHN, HAD BEEN BORN DEAF). IT IS DOUBTFUL THAT KATHARINE MINDED; SHE ONCE CALLED MARRIAGE "AN ARTIFICIAL RELATIONSHIP BECAUSE YOU HAVE TO SIGN A CONTRACT."

ANTHONY HOPKINS, WHO PLAYED KATHARINE'S SON IN *THE LION IN WINTER,* LATER MODELED THE VOICE OF HANNIBAL LECTER IN *THE SILENCE OF THE LAMBS* (1991) AFTER HERS.

KATHARINE PAINTED AND SCULPTED IN HER SPARE TIME. AT SOTHEBY'S AUCTION OF HER PERSONAL BELONGINGS AFTER HER DEATH, HER ARTWORK DREW SURPRISINGLY HIGH BIDS. THE HIGHEST BID ON ANY ITEM WAS $316,000, FOR THE BRONZE BUST OF SPENCER TRACY THAT SHE MADE DURING THEIR LAST FILM TOGETHER, *GUESS WHO'S COMING TO DINNER.*

An earthy beauty and an incredible talent, she fought to overcome racial stereotypes and limitations and became Hollywood's first glamorous African American star.

LENA
HORNE

Lena Horne was born into the world of entertainment: her mother was a traveling stage performer who sometimes took Lena on the road. Young Lena knew she could sing and had found her way into Harlem's Cotton Club chorus by the time she was sixteen. Lena developed her chanteuse persona through years of singing on the road, despite rampant racial discrimination, and then scored a triumph at New York's Café Society Downtown, where intellectuals and activists of both races celebrated what seemed a step forward for America. Lena wanted to move forward in her career as well and in 1941 traveled to California. By the next year, she had a seven-year contract with MGM, making her the first African American woman to sign with the studio in more than twenty-five years. Yet MGM found itself in a quandary: Lena refused to play the stereotypical roles that were the bread and butter of many black actors. At the same time, the studio considered her too light to act opposite other African Americans yet too black for romantic scenes with white actors. In addition, local censors in the South routinely banned any film depicting people of color interacting with whites on an equal basis. MGM's solution was to place the glamorous singer in a series of isolated musical numbers that could be cut in the Southern states. Lena fared better in two all-black musicals: MGM's *Cabin in the Sky* (1943) featured her as a bewitching temptress, and 20th Century-Fox's *Stormy Weather* (1943) showcased her performance of the beautifully moody title song, a staple of cabaret acts to this day. After World War II, her movie work slowed as she refused to back down on civil rights issues or back off from her friendship with controversial black entertainer Paul Robeson. Eventually, Hollywood blacklisted her, which cost her the chance to play her dream role, Julie in *Show Boat* (1951). Through it all she continued her fight for racial equality, joining the March on Washington in 1963 and working tirelessly for the National Council for Negro Women. An ageless entertainer, she appreciates, more than most, the power of being understood and welcomed into the limelight.

Born
Lena Calhoun Horne
July 30, 1917
Brooklyn, New York

Star Sign
Leo

Height
5'5"

Husbands and Children
Family friend Louis Jones
(1937–44, divorced)
two children, Gail and Edwin
"Teddy"

Musician Lennie Hayton
(1947–71, his death)

Essential
LENAHORNEFilms

THE DUKE IS TOPS
(1938) Million Dollar Productions
Horne's screen debut in a low-budget
musical made for black audiences,
in which she plays a singer who
abandons her performing partner
(Ralph Cooper) when she gets a
chance to be in a Broadway show.
Her songs include a sensuous
rendition of "I Know You Remember."

CABIN IN THE SKY
(1943) MGM
An all-black musical, a radical
move for a major studio (MGM)
at the time, with Horne as the
seductive beauty who comes
between a shantytown resident
(Eddie "Rochester" Anderson) and
his faithful wife (Ethel Waters).

STORMY WEATHER
(1943) 20th Century-Fox
Another all-black musical, with
Horne leading an exceptional
company as a singer in love with
dancer Bill "Bojangles" Robinson.
Horne's delivery of the title tune
tops a total of fourteen songs
delivered by the likes of Fats
Waller, Cab Calloway, and the
Nicholas Brothers.

SWING FEVER
(1943) MGM
A showcase for bandleader Kay
Kyser, featuring Horne stopping the
show with "You're So Indifferent."
All too often, Horne's fate in MGM
musicals was to perform such
specialty numbers that could be cut
when the movie was shown in the
Deep South.

BROADWAY RHYTHM
(1944) MGM
An MGM musical that amounts
to a variety show, with Horne
performing three songs, including
Gershwin's "Somebody Loves Me."
The plot revolves around producer
George Murphy and his efforts to
stage a Broadway musical, oblivious
to the fact that his own family
and friends are among the most
talented performers around.

STORMY WEATHER, 1943

STYLENOTES

MGM called upon makeup legend Max Factor to create a shade for Lena Horne called "Light Egyptian." Ironically, the shade was also applied to white actresses—Hedy Lamarr used it to play a half-caste African native in *White Cargo* (1942) and Ava Gardner wore it while playing Lena's dream role, biracial singer Julie in *Show Boat* (1951). The color is still in use by African Americans.

At the time of her eightieth birthday, Lena gained a new set of fans when she brought her timeless, elegant look to a well-received Gap clothing ad.

CABIN IN THE SKY, 1943

behindthescenes

WHEN LENA HORNE WAS OFFERED A CONTRACT AT MGM, HER FATHER TOOK THE OPPORTUNITY TO TAKE LOUIS B. MAYER TO TASK FOR HOLLYWOOD'S BLACK STEREOTYPES. "I DON'T SEE WHAT THE MOVIES HAVE TO OFFER MY DAUGHTER," HE TOLD THE MOGUL. "I CAN HIRE A MAID FOR HER. WHY SHOULD SHE ACT AS ONE?" LENA'S REFUSAL TO PLAY DOMESTICS COST HER A ROLE OPPOSITE JEANETTE MACDONALD IN *CAIRO* (1942), BUT SHE HARDLY REGRETTED IT.

STARTING OUT IN THE BUSINESS, LENA REVERED SINGER-ACTRESS ETHEL WATERS. YET THEIR FRICTION ON THE SET OF *CABIN IN THE SKY* (1943) WAS LEGENDARY. THE FACT THAT LENA WAS DATING CABIN DIRECTOR VINCENTE MINNELLI WAS LIKELY A FACTOR CONTRIBUTING TO THE FEUD.

NEPOTISM WAS HIGHLY JUSTIFIED WHEN LENA'S SON-IN-LAW AT THE TIME, DIRECTOR SIDNEY LUMET, CAST HER AS GLINDA IN THE FILM VERSION OF THE HIT MUSICAL *THE WIZ* (1978).

CIRCA 1956

From high society to Hollywood stardom to royal life in Monaco, she was the ultimate blue-blood blonde, a fairy-tale princess who seemed born to her official title, "Her Serene Highness."

GRACE
KELLY

The daughter of a successful brick merchant and his wife, Grace Kelly was born into more money than social breeding. However, she came from fine old theater stock; her uncle, George Kelly, was a Pulitzer Prize–winning playwright (*Craig's Wife*, 1925). Grace aspired to be an actress from an early age and moved to New York when she was just eighteen. There, modeling led to Broadway and television roles, but that wasn't enough, so she moved west. The girl one photographer dismissively called "nice clean stuff" didn't blow Hollywood away with her sex appeal at first. She made her debut with a small role in 1951's *Fourteen Hours*, but then flunked a black-and-white screen test at Fox. Her role as Gary Cooper's Quaker bride in the Western *High Noon* (1952) was overshadowed by Katy Jurado's fiery portrayal of his rejected mistress. Still, when director John Ford was looking for someone to play the other woman opposite Clark Gable and Ava Gardner in the jungle adventure *Mogambo* (1953), he knew he had found that person in Grace. He insisted that MGM test her in color, and suddenly her porcelain perfection was catnip for the cameras. Her love scenes with Gable made her a star. MGM signed Grace to a seven-year contract that allowed for high-profile loan-outs to director Alfred Hitchcock to play the ultimate in cool blondes in *Dial M for Murder* (1954), *Rear Window* (1954), and *To Catch a Thief* (1955). While doing publicity at the Cannes Film Festival, Grace met Monaco's Prince Rainier. After having gone through a series of very public romances with everyone from Gable to fashion maven Oleg Cassini, she knew that this was the real thing. She gave up her film career to become Princess Grace of Monaco. Her last role was headstrong socialite Tracy Lord in *High Society* (1956), the musical version of *The Philadelphia Story*. Not only did she go out with a bang on screen, she even had a hit recording of Cole Porter's "True Love" with costar Bing Crosby. Princess Grace's work for a variety of charitable causes kept her in the public eye until her death after suffering a stroke behind the wheel of her car in 1982. She lives on through the handful of films she made and through the Princess Grace Foundation, which helps struggling artists early in their careers.

Born
Grace Patricia Kelly
November 12, 1929
Philadelphia, Pennsylvania

Died
September 14, 1982
Monacoville, Monaco,
from injuries suffered
in a car accident

Star Sign
Scorpio

Height
5'6"

Husband and Children
Prince Rainier of Monaco
(1956–82, her death)
three children,
Caroline, Albert, and Stephanie

Essential
GRACEKELLYFilms

ACADEMY AWARDS

Won Best Actress
The Country Girl

**Nominated for
Best Supporting Actress**
Mogambo

HIGH NOON
(1952) United Artists
Not Kelly's film debut but her first chance to attract major attention. She plays the Quaker bride of a sheriff (Gary Cooper) who stands alone against outlaws.

DIAL M FOR MURDER
(1954) Warner Bros.
This was Kelly's first of three films for director Alfred Hitchcock. In this adaptation of the Frederick Knott stage thriller, Kelly plays the intended murder victim of a plot hatched by her jealous husband (Ray Milland).

REAR WINDOW
(1954) Paramount
In Kelly's second Hitchcock film, she plays the ultraglamorous socialite fashion–model girlfriend of a wheelchair-bound photojournalist (James Stewart). When Stewart believes he has witnessed a murder in an apartment across the way, he enlists Kelly's help to piece together the mystery.

TO CATCH A THIEF
(1955) Paramount
The final Hitchcock film for Kelly, who shares romantic fireworks with Cary Grant in a jewel-thief caper set on the French Riviera. He's a retired cat burglar who is suspected of resuming his occupation, and she's a wealthy vacationer who finds him irresistible even though she thinks he's still a thief.

HIGH SOCIETY
(1956) MGM
Kelly's final film before she became the Princess of Monaco, a musical reworking of 1940's *The Philadelphia Story*. Kelly steps into Katharine Hepburn's role as icy socialite Tracy Lord, with Bing Crosby and Frank Sinatra as her suitors.

CIRCA 1954

STYLENOTES

While pregnant with Princess Caroline, Grace often used her Hermès bag to shield her belly from prying paparazzi. The company nicknamed that purse "the Kelly bag."

Grace's wedding gown was paid for by MGM and was the most expensive garment ever made by Oscar-winning designer Helen Rose, complete with 125-year-old lace from a French museum, twenty-five yards of silk taffeta, one hundred yards of silk net, and thousands of seed pearls sewn into the veil and headdress.

Grace had fashioned her blue-blood persona long before the studios got hold of her. She spent hours a day perfecting her voice until her nasal tone was replaced by an elegant, almost British inflection.

After seeing the large diamond engagement rings flaunted by her fellow stars, Prince Rainier called Cartier to upgrade Grace's would-be eternity band of rubies and diamonds to a twelve-carat diamond flanked by two baguettes. She wore the ring in her final film, *High Society* (1956).

REAR WINDOW, 1954

behindthescenes

GRACE KELLY CAME FROM A FAMILY OF ATHLETES; HER FATHER AND BROTHER BOTH EARNED OLYMPIC MEDALS IN SCULLERY. HER SKILL WITH A RIFLE HELPED HER WIN CLARK GABLE'S RESPECT AND AFFECTION WHEN THEY FILMED *MOGAMBO* (1953) IN AFRICA.

GRACE'S FIRST BIG ROLE IN *HIGH NOON* (1952) WASN'T INTENDED TO BE THAT MEMORABLE, BUT DIRECTOR FRED ZINNEMANN LIKED HER LOOK SO MUCH THAT HE FILMED MORE CLOSE-UPS OF HER THAN THE SCRIPT CALLED FOR.

ALFRED HITCHCOCK THOUGHT GRACE WAS JUST RIGHT FOR HIS PSYCHOLOGICALLY FRAUGHT MYSTERIES; HE CALLED HER A "SNOW-COVERED VOLCANO." SOME BIO-GRAPHERS HAVE SUGGESTED THAT HE WAS IN LOVE WITH HER AND TRIED TO MOLD FUTURE PROTÉGÉES VERA MILES AND TIPPI HEDREN IN HER IMAGE.

WHEN PRINCE RAINIER OF MONACO MET GRACE AT THE 1955 CANNES FILM FESTIVAL, HE WAS LOOKING FOR AN AMERICAN FILM-STAR WIFE TO BOOST HIS COUNTRY'S IMAGE. MARILYN MONROE HAD BRIEFLY BEEN CONSIDERED FOR THE POSITION, BUT GRACE WAS HIS DREAM GIRL.

AMONG THE ROLES GRACE LEFT BEHIND WHEN SHE MARRIED WAS MAGGIE IN *CAT ON A HOT TIN ROOF* (1958). ORIGINALLY, JAMES DEAN HAD BEEN SCHEDULED TO COSTAR. THE ROLES WENT TO ELIZABETH TAYLOR AND PAUL NEWMAN INSTEAD. OTHER LOST ROLES WERE THE FEMALE LEADS IN *GIANT* (1956, ALSO GIVEN TO TAYLOR), *THE COBWEB* (1955, GIVEN TO LAUREN BACALL), AND *DESIGNING WOMAN* (1957, ALSO GIVEN TO BACALL).

Delightfully proper on screen, with an engaging, ladylike voice, she had an impeccable grace and fair beauty that belied the discipline and the intense dedication she brought to her craft as an actress.

DEBORAH
KERR

Deborah Kerr spent her lonely Scottish childhood dreaming of a life filled with color and drama. She got her chance at age fifteen while studying dance and acting. Realizing her height would relegate her to the chorus line if she pursued dance, she soon set her sights on acting. Her featured debut in a British film version of Shaw's *Major Barbara* (1941) typed Deborah as a genteel lady. However, she managed to break through her typecasting and impress Hollywood with her portrayal of an arrogant nun in *Black Narcissus* (1947). MGM's Louis B. Mayer bought out Deborah's British film contract and offered her a seven-year deal that would eventually award her $7,000 a week. She and her husband bought a beautiful house in Los Angeles, started a family, and prepared to take America by storm. Yet despite her generous contract, MGM kept Deborah mostly in roles in which, as she recalled, "all I had to do was be high-minded, long-suffering, and decorative." The one exception, her role as Spencer Tracy's alcoholic wife in *Edward, My Son* (1949), brought Deborah her first Oscar nomination. As Mayer's reign came to an end, she saw a perfect opportunity to strike out for new territory. When Joan Crawford rejected the role of a promiscuous army wife in *From Here to Eternity* (1953), Deborah's agent convinced the film's producer that casting her against type would generate good publicity. She lost her British accent, her auburn hair color, and her inhibitions, rolling in the surf with Burt Lancaster in a scene that remains a classic depiction of unbridled passion. She continued to attract fans through the 1950s, particularly with two well-remembered films, the touching *An Affair to Remember* and, perhaps her best-loved role, the hit musical, *The King and I*. In 1959, Deborah burned up the gossip columns when she left her husband of fourteen years to marry writer Peter Viertel, but it did little to tarnish her star power. The changing movie climate of the 1960s was more damaging to her career, however. In 1969, Deborah left the screen for many years, only returning to take a few television roles in the 1980s. After receiving six nominations over the course of her career, she finally was awarded an honorary Oscar statuette in 1994 for her contributions to film. Deborah was deeply touched by the honor, a suitable reward for a woman whose excellent performances consistently touched audiences around the world.

Born
Deborah Jane Kerr-Trimmer
September 30, 1921
Helensburgh, Scotland

Star Sign
Libra

Height
5'7"

Husbands and Children
RAF officer Anthony Bartley
(1945–59, divorced)
two daughters,
Melanie Jane and Francesca Ann

Writer Peter Viertel
(1960–present)

Essential
DEBORAHKERRFilms

ACADEMY AWARDS

Nominated for Best Actress
Edward, My Son
From Here to Eternity
The King and I
Heaven Knows, Mr. Allison
Separate Tables
The Sundowners

Honorary Award in 1994 for being "an artist of impeccable grace and beauty, a dedicated actress whose motion picture career has always stood for perfection, discipline, and elegance"

BLACK NARCISSUS

(1947) Universal
British drama about a group of nuns struggling to establish a mission in a remote Himalayan outpost, based on the Rumer Godden novel. Kerr and Kathleen Byron, as the heads of an Anglican hospital and school, face many challenges—not the least of which is dealing with their own frustrated sexual desires, sparked by the presence of an attractive British agent (David Farrar).

FROM HERE TO ETERNITY

(1953) Columbia
A dramatic rendering of the James Jones novel set in Pearl Harbor at the time of the Japanese attacks, with a star-heavy cast headed by Kerr, Burt Lancaster, Montgomery Clift, Frank Sinatra, and Donna Reed. In an image-breaking role as an adulterous Army wife, Kerr shares a memorable seaside love scene with Lancaster.

THE KING AND I

(1956) 20th Century-Fox
Elaborate film version of the Rodgers and Hammerstein Broadway hit, with Kerr in her favorite role as "Mrs. Anna," the teacher who brings civility to the court of the King of Siam (Yul Brynner).

AN AFFAIR TO REMEMBER

(1957) 20th Century-Fox
The first remake of 1939's *Love Affair,* with original director Leo McCarey returning to guide Kerr and Cary Grant through the story of shipboard lovers whose plans to reunite at the Empire State Building go awry.

THE INNOCENTS

(1961) 20th Century-Fox
Jack Clayton directed and Truman Capote contributed to the screenplay of this film version of Henry James's chilling novella *The Turn of the Screw.* Kerr is a repressed Victorian governess who believes her young charges to be haunted by ghosts they refuse to acknowledge.

FROM HERE TO ETERNITY, 1953

STYLENOTES

British films often gave Deborah Kerr a glossy, very made-up look. Yet at MGM, ace makeup man Jack Dawn decided simplicity was the keynote with Deborah, feeling she was "admirably equipped to face the cameras with a minimum of embellishment."

For *From Here to Eternity*, Kerr didn't just dye her hair blonde; she transformed herself into the archetypical 1950s sex goddess. Marilyn Monroe was currently at her peak, and some of Deborah's publicity stills at the time bear such similarity to images of the legendary blonde actress that they could actually have been taken of Monroe herself.

Irene Sharaff's historically accurate gowns for Kerr in *The King and I* (1956) weighed 30 to 40 pounds each. Between the costumes and the lights, she sweated off 12 pounds making the film and referred to herself as "The Melting Miss Kerr."

behindthescenes

DEBORAH VISITED REX HARRISON AT HIS HOME IN DENHAM, ENGLAND, DURING WORLD WAR II, WHERE THEY THOUGHT LITTLE OF AN AIR-RAID ALERT UNTIL THEY HEARD THE UNMISTAKABLE SOUND OF GERMAN AIRCRAFT. WHEN A BOMB HIT IN THE GARDEN, THE COTTAGE WAS FILLED WITH BLACKNESS. ONLY SLIGHTLY HURT BUT BADLY SHAKEN, REX ANNOUNCED TO THE PARTY, "I THINK I NEED A LITTLE DRINK." ENGLISH TO THE CORE, DEBORAH COUNTERED WITH, "ALCOHOL IS VERY BAD WHEN YOU'VE HAD A SHOCK. WE MUST HAVE SOME TEA."

NEVER TEMPTED TO WRITE AN AUTOBIOGRAPHY, DEBORAH EXPLAINED, "ALL THE SAME RAGS-TO-RICHES, OR I-SLEPT-WITH-SO-AND-SO. DAMNED IF I'M GOING TO SAY THAT. ALL SUCCESSFUL PEOPLE THESE DAYS SEEM TO BE NEUROTIC. PERHAPS WE SHOULD STOP BEING SORRY FOR THEM AND START BEING SORRY FOR ME—FOR BEING SO CONFOUNDED NORMAL."

THE KING AND I, 1956

She once claimed, "Any girl can be glamorous, all you have to do is stand still and look stupid." But behind her beauty and glamorous exterior was a keen intelligence and a great inventive mind.

HEDY
LAMARR

Born
Hedwig Eva Maria Kiesler
November 9, 1913
Vienna, Austria

Died
January 19, 2000
Orlando, Florida,
of natural causes

Star Sign
Scorpio

Height
5'7"

Husbands and Children
Multimillionaire manufacturer
Fritz Mandl
(1933–37, divorced)

Screenwriter Gene Markey
(1939–40, divorced)
adopted son, James

Actor John Loder
(1943–47, divorced)
two children,
Denise Hedy and Anthony

Restaurateur Ted Stauffer
(1951–52, divorced)

Oil millionaire W. Howard Lee
(1953–60, divorced)

Attorney Lewis Boies
(1963–65, divorced)

Hedy Lamarr is the most successful actress to rise from erotic films to international stardom. Two years after dropping out of school to appear in movies, she achieved notoriety for her nude scene in the 1932 Czech-Austrian coproduction *Extase*. After a brief retirement during her first marriage, Hedy set out to find stardom, meeting MGM studio head Louis B. Mayer in London. Intrigued by her beauty but put off by her sensual image, he offered her a six-month contract at $125 a week. Instead of signing, she pulled strings to sail to back to the States with him, landing in New York with a seven-year contract starting at $500 a week. When Mayer didn't know what do to with her, she scored a meeting with independent producer Walter Wanger, who cast her as Charles Boyer's love interest in *Algiers* (1938). The film's success made her a star, and Mayer decided to produce her next vehicle personally. The result, *I Take This Woman* (1940), was a box office disaster, but Hedy was smart enough to fight for a sexy supporting role in *Boom Town* (1940), with Clark Gable, which put her back on top. She specialized in playing exotic temptresses who could shake up any man, most notably the jungle temptress in *White Cargo* (1942) and the independent business woman in *H. M. Pulham, Esq* (1941). Unfortunately, bad casting choices (she turned down *Laura* and *Gaslight*, among others) put her career in trouble. After leaving MGM she scored her biggest hit in director Cecil B. DeMille's *Samson and Delilah* (1949). She didn't like working with the director, however, and turned down a chance to costar in his next film, *The Greatest Show on Earth* (1952). Her career never recovered, and she retired from the screen a few years later. Hedy had trouble adjusting to life outside the limelight. Divorce, scandal, and even two shoplifting arrests clouded her image. When her best-selling tell-all, 1966's *Ecstasy and Me,* told too much, she sued the publisher, claiming that the book's ghostwriters had added salacious details without her permission. She also sued Mel Brooks for naming a character in *Blazing Saddles* (1974) "Hedley Lamarr," and a computer company for using an unauthorized portrait of her to sell software. Yet their use of her image, even without permission, attests to her timeless glamour.

Essential
HEDYLAMARRFilms

EXTASE

(1933) Ceskoslovensky Filmexport
Experimental Czechoslovakian film
that gained notoriety from a ten-
minute sequence in which Lamarr
(billed as Hedy Keisler) takes a
midnight swim while totally nude.
The movie brought the Viennese
beauty worldwide fame, and within
five years she was a Hollywood star.

EXTASE, 1933

H. M. PULHAM, ESQ.

(1941) MGM
The film version of the John P.
Marquand novel about a proper
Bostonian (Robert Young) whose
place in society has kept him from
tasting life fully. Lamarr, in her most
critically praised performance, is
the vibrant career woman who
persuades Pulham, at least briefly,
to turn his back on tradition.

TORTILLA FLAT

(1942) MGM
MGM's version of the John
Steinbeck novel about immigrants
in a California fishing village.
Lamarr plays the sexy Portuguese
cannery worker who is pursued by
both fisherman (John Garfield) and
idler (Spencer Tracy).

THE CONSPIRATORS

(1944) Warner Bros.
A romantic wartime drama often
compared to 1942's *Casablanca*,
with Paul Henreid elevated to
leading man and Lamarr playing
the enigmatic beauty he loves.
Henreid is a Dutch freedom fighter
caught in Lisbon along with fellow
Casablanca refugees Sydney
Greenstreet and Peter Lorre.

SAMSON AND DELILAH

(1949) Paramount
DeMille's extravagant account of
the Biblical strongman and the
temptress who brings him down by
clipping his hair, with Victor Mature
and Lamarr in the title roles.

STYLENOTES

During the 1940s, Hedy was the star most women wanted to look like, at least according to plastic surgeons, who reported that large numbers of female patients asked for her profile.

Edith Head created Hedy's peacock-feathered cape in *Samson and Delilah* from feathers that Cecil B. DeMille had hand-plucked from his own birds.

Hedy's hairstyle popularized the center part and influenced blondes like Joan Bennett to dye their hair brown. The change not only made Bennett a star but also put her in the running to play Scarlett O'Hara.

Lamarr was never impressed with her star status. When praised for her glamorous look, she responded, "Any girl can be glamorous. All you have to do is stand still and look stupid."

behindthe**scenes**

HEDY'S FIRST HUSBAND, MUNITIONS MANUFACTURER FRITZ MANDL, WAS SO JEALOUS THAT HE TRIED TO BUY UP AND DESTROY ALL EXISTING PRINTS OF *EXTASE*. THE FILM OWNERS AND FANS, INCLUDING ITALIAN DICTATOR BENITO MUSSOLINI, REFUSED TO PART WITH THEIR COPIES.

DURING HER OCEAN VOYAGE WITH MGM STUDIO HEAD LOUIS B. MAYER, SHE CONSENTED TO CHANGE HER NAME TO HEDY LAMARR. MAYER CHOSE HER LAST NAME IN HONOR OF THE WOMAN HE CONSIDERED HOLLYWOOD'S MOST BEAUTIFUL ACTRESS EVER, SILENT-SCREEN SIREN BARBARA LA MARR.

BEYOND ANY FILM SHE MADE, HEDY'S GREATEST ACCOMPLISHMENT WAS HER DEVELOPMENT OF A RADAR GUIDING SYSTEM FOR TORPEDOES THAT HELPED THE ALLIES WIN WORLD WAR II. WORKING WITH COMPOSER GEORGE ANTHEIL, SHE DREW ON IDEAS SHE'D GLEANED FROM HER FIRST HUSBAND, A MUNITIONS MANUFACTURER AND NAZI SYMPATHIZER. THE PRINCIPLE BEHIND THEIR INVENTION, FREQUENCY HOPPING, IS STILL IN USE.

The two most famous Southern belles in history (Scarlett O'Hara and Blanche DuBois) were played by a British actress whose black hair and catlike green eyes barely masked the determination she shared with her most memorable characters.

VIVIEN
LEIGH

Born
Vivien Mary Hartley
November 5, 1913
Darjeeling, West Bengal,
British India (now India)

Died
July 7, 1967
London, England,
of chronic tuberculosis

Star Sign
Scorpio

Height
5'3"

Husbands and Child
Herbert Leigh Holman
(1932–40, divorced)
daughter, Suzanne

Laurence Olivier
(1940–60, divorced)

Significant Other
John Merivale
(1959–67, her death)

Vivien Leigh's career was a product of indefatigable will, starting with that of her mother, who stared at the Himalayas for fifteen minutes every day of her pregnancy in the hopes that their beauty would pass to her child. After her idyllic early days in India, Vivien was sent to a convent school in England, where she fell in love with the stage the first time she saw a professional production. She married young, but fortunately her first husband supported her acting ambitions. When she heard of a leading role in *The Green Sash* that required more beauty than experience, she went for it, making her stage debut in 1935. By then, she had also started playing small screen roles. In 1937, while performing a supporting part in *Fire Over England,* she started a romance with costar Laurence Olivier. Vivien then set her sights on Hollywood and the coveted role of Scarlett O'Hara in *Gone with the Wind* (1939). She used a visit to Olivier in Hollywood, where he was filming *Wuthering Heights* (1939), to meet agent Myron Selznick, whose brother, David, was producing *Gone with the Wind.* With the role still uncast as filming started, Myron introduced her to his brother by saying, "Hey, genius, meet your Scarlett!" Four days after her screen test, she was cast in the role that would make her a legend. But though she won an Oscar and international acclaim, Vivien was now more interested in another role, that of Mrs. Laurence Olivier. They were finally married in 1940, returning to England shortly thereafter. While filming *Caesar and Cleopatra* in 1945, she fell ill as a result of tuberculosis. A few years later, her erratic mood swings were diagnosed as manic depression. These problems hindered her career, but she still managed to star in the London production of Tennessee Williams's *A Streetcar Named Desire,* directed by Olivier. That success helped her land the lead in the film version—and another Oscar for playing a Southern belle. It was to be her last great film role. Mental problems caused her to forgo more-demanding film projects and led to the dissolution of her marriage to Olivier. But through it all, Vivien continued her acclaimed stage work. She was rehearsing for a film version of Edward Albee's *A Delicate Balance* when she passed away in 1967.

Essential
VIVIENLEIGHFilms

GONE WITH THE WIND

(1939) MGM
Producer David O. Selznick's
screen version of the Civil War
romantic epic, one of the best-
selling books of all time. Leigh is
cast as the spoiled Southern
belle Scarlett O'Hara. Other
notable cast members included
Clark Gable, Olivia de Havilland,
and Leslie Howard.

WATERLOO BRIDGE

(1940) MGM
A cleaned-up remake of the 1931
film of Robert E. Sherwood's drama
about a prostitute's tragic love
affair with a soldier (Robert Taylor).
In this version, Leigh is a chaste
ballerina who takes to the streets
only after she believes Taylor has
been killed—but the sentimental
effect is the same.

A STREETCAR NAMED DESIRE

(1951) Warner Bros.
Kazan's film of the hit Broadway
drama, featuring Leigh as Tennessee
Williams's beleaguered heroine
Blanche DuBois. Flitting about the
New Orleans tenement home of her
sister (Kim Hunter), Blanche finds
conflict with her brutish brother-
in-law (Marlon Brando).

THE DEEP BLUE SEA

(1955) 20th Century-Fox
A Terence Rattigan stage drama,
brought to the screen by director
Anatole Litvak. As the troubled
wife of a London attorney (Emlyn
Williams), Leigh attempts suicide
after a stormy affair with an RAF
officer (Kenneth More).

SHIP OF FOOLS

(1965) Columbia
Stanley Kramer's film version of the
Katherine Anne Porter novel about
a German ocean liner traveling from
Mexico to Germany in the 1930s.
Among a cast that includes Oscar
nominees Simone Signoret and
Oscar Werner, Leigh is a standout
as an aging Southern coquette.

GONE WITH THE WIND, 1939

She was obsessed with hiding her large hands. Gloves were a favorite cover-up; she owned more than 150 pairs.

———

Promotional items released in conjunction with *Gone with the Wind* included Scarlett O'Hara cameos (available for fifteen cents and three Lux soap wrappers), perfume (Apple Blossom and Bittersweet), nail polish (three shades: Morning, Noon, and Night), and even morning glory seeds.

behindthescenes

SCARLETT O'HARA WASN'T THE FIRST AMERICAN FILM ROLE OFFERED TO VIVIEN LEIGH. WHEN LAURENCE OLIVIER WAS CAST AS HEATHCLIFF IN *WUTHERING HEIGHTS* (1939), SHE APPROACHED DIRECTOR WILLIAM WYLER ABOUT COSTARRING IN THE FILM. ACTRESS MERLE OBERON WAS ALREADY SET FOR THE LEAD PART, SO WYLER SUGGESTED THAT SHE TRY FOR A SUPPORTING ROLE. WHEN SHE TURNED HIM DOWN, HE UTTERED ONE OF THE LEAST PROPHETIC LINES IN HOLLYWOOD HISTORY: "YOU WILL NEVER GET A BETTER PART THAN ISABELLA FOR YOUR AMERICAN DEBUT."

VIVIEN CAMPAIGNED AS HARD AS MANY ACTRESSES DID FOR THE COVETED ROLE OF SCARLETT—YET HER CHALLENGES WERE EVEN GREATER. SELZNICK HAD ALREADY NARROWED THE SELECTION DOWN TO A FEW STARS OF THE DAY, THE FILM HAD ALREADY BEGUN SHOOTING, AND VIVIEN WAS JUST SOME ENGLISH ACTRESS SELZNICK HAD AGREED TO MEET BECAUSE HIS BROTHER WAS LAURENCE OLIVIER'S AGENT. YET SELZNICK LATER SAID OF MEETING HIS SCARLETT, "I'LL NEVER RECOVER FROM THAT FIRST LOOK."

FILMING *GONE WITH THE WIND* WAS A TERRIBLE EXPERIENCE FOR VIVIEN. SHE CONNECTED WELL WITH THE FILM'S FIRST DIRECTOR GEORGE CUKOR, BUT HE WAS FIRED AFTER A FEW WEEKS. VICTOR FLEMING, A GOOD FRIEND OF CLARK GABLE'S, TOOK OVER, AND VIVIEN FELT LIKE A SECOND-CLASS CITIZEN. FLEMING'S ONLY DIRECTION TO HER WAS "HAM IT UP!" SHE SECRETLY WENT TO CUKOR EACH SUNDAY TO WORK ON THE NEXT WEEK'S SCENES. ONE WEEK SHE ACCIDENTALLY RAN INTO OLIVIA DE HAVILLAND, WHO WAS PLAYING MELANIE. SHE WAS DOING THE SAME THING.

EVENTUALLY, VIVIEN NEEDED SHOCK THERAPY TO CONTROL HER MANIC DEPRESSION. SOMETIMES SHE WOULD GO ON STAGE JUST HOURS AFTER HER TREATMENTS, WITHOUT MISSING A BEAT IN HER PERFORMANCES.

FIRE OVER ENGLAND, 1937

A STREETCAR NAMED DESIRE, 1951

She brought a tomboy's enthusiasm and a vixen's curves to the screen, tools that captured the physicality and wit of screwball romantic comedy and made her one of the most beloved stars of the 1930s.

CAROLE
LOMBARD

Carole Lombard did more in just over thirty years than many people do in a life twice as long. With nonstop gusto, she dove into sports, moviemaking, party going, and party giving. Always the tomboy, Carole made her film debut in *A Perfect Crime* (1921) at the age of twelve after director Allan Dwan spotted her playing baseball with a bunch of boys. Within three years, she had dropped out of school to pursue acting full-time. A contract with comedy genius Hal Roach, for whom she starred in short films, started her on the road to the top. At Paramount, she started landing meaty roles, opposite future husband Clark Gable in *No Man of Her Own* (1932) and George Raft in the musical *Bolero* (1934). When the studio loaned her to Columbia to star opposite John Barrymore in one of the first screwball comedies, *Twentieth Century* (1934), the film made her a star. She followed this performance with a succession of portrayals of dizzy heroines in films like *My Man Godfrey* (1936), with former husband William Powell, and *Nothing Sacred* (1937), with Fredric March. By this time, she was living with the love of her life, Clark Gable, whose wife wouldn't grant him a divorce. The affair was one of Hollywood's worst-kept secrets, but everybody loved Carole so much that the press wouldn't have dared to turn it into a scandal. When Gable's wife finally set him free, they were married in 1939. Carole turned down the chance to star in director Orson Welles's first film, preferring to stick to comedy in Alfred Hitchcock's *Mr. and Mrs. Smith* (1941) and Ernst Lubitsch's *To Be or Not to Be* (1942). She had finished work on the latter when she set out on a wartime bond-selling tour. Eager to get home after her last stop, she decided to fly. The plane crashed into Table Rock Mountain in Nevada, killing all on board. Gable was shattered. His last two wives bore an uncanny resemblance to Carole, and he is now buried by her side. President Franklin Roosevelt awarded her the Medal of Freedom posthumously as the first woman to die in the line of duty during World War II.

Born
Jane Alice Peters
October 6, 1908
Fort Wayne, Indiana

Died
January 16, 1942
Table Rock Mountain,
Nevada, in a plane crash

Star Sign
Libra

Height
5'2"

Husbands
William Powell
(1931–33, divorced)

Clark Gable
(1939–42, her death)

Essential
CAROLELOMBARDFilms

NO MAN OF HER OWN
(1932) Paramount
The story of a small-town librarian (Lombard) and a crooked cardsharp on the lam (Clark Gable) who find romance and eventually marry, with complications arising as his past catches up with him. This was Lombard's only screen teaming with future husband Clark Gable (at the time of production both actors were married to other people).

TWENTIETH CENTURY
(1934) Columbia
A prototype of the screwball comedy and the movie that elevated Lombard to the rank of top comic actress. She plays Lily Garland, shopgirl turned diva, opposite John Barrymore's egomaniacal Broadway impresario Oscar Jaffe.

MY MAN GODFREY
(1936) Universal
A screwball classic with Lombard as a Depression-era society heiress who brings an erudite homeless man back to the family mansion as part of a scavenger hunt. William Powell (Lombard's real-life ex-husband) plays Godfrey, the supposed hobo who becomes her family's butler.

MR. AND MRS. SMITH
(1941) RKO
Alfred Hitchcock's only venture into the screwball genre, with Lombard and Robert Montgomery as a couple who separate after learning that their marriage isn't legal. Among the obstacles to a happy reunion is the fact that Mrs. Smith has taken a new beau (Gene Raymond).

TO BE OR NOT TO BE
(1942) United Artists
Lombard's final film before her untimely death, a World War II political satire from German expatriate director Ernst Lubitsch, who takes aim at Hitler and his fellow Nazis. Lombard and Jack Benny play a theatrical couple in Poland who find ingenious ways to support the Warsaw resistance.

MY MAN GODFREY, 1936

STYLENOTES

Costume designer Travis Banton once said, "You could toss a bolt of fabric at Carole Lombard, and however it would land on her she would look smart."

Carole arrived in Hollywood much plumper than stars of today. A crash diet took off the pounds before her first dramatic role and she never put them back on. Carole viewed the primping required to look great as just part of the job, yet also as something that all women should do with pride.

A 1925 car accident left Carole with a scar across her left cheek. Studying cinematography, Carole learned that a diffusing glass in the camera would hide the mark. Said cameraman Harry Stradling admiringly, "She knows as much about the tricks of the trade as I do!"

behindthescenes

WHILE STILL A SCHOOLGIRL, CAROLE LOMBARD TOOK BOXING LESSONS FROM A LIGHTWEIGHT CHAMP AND WON MEDALS FOR SPRINTING AND HIGH JUMPING. AS AN ADULT SHE PLAYED HOURS OF TENNIS EVERY DAY. TO PLEASE HUSBAND CLARK GABLE, SHE EVEN TOOK UP HUNTING AND SKEET SHOOTING, EVENTUALLY SURPASSING HIM AS A MARKSMAN.

LOMBARD'S INFAMOUS SWEARING WAS A CALCULATED MOVE ON HER PART. WHEN SHE SAW HOW WOMEN WERE USED, ABUSED, AND OFTEN IGNORED IN THE FILM INDUSTRY, SHE ASKED HER BROTHERS TO TEACH HER EVERY SWEAR WORD THEY KNEW. HER SALTY VOCABULARY NOT ONLY CAUGHT PEOPLE'S ATTENTION BUT ALSO TURNED THE STUDIO BOSSES INTO HER BUDDIES. WHEN COLUMBIA PICTURES HEAD HARRY COHN MADE A PASS AT HER, SHE TOLD HIM OFF SO COLORFULLY THAT HE HAD TO LAUGH.

FAMOUS FOR HER PARTIES, PRANKS, AND IMPISH BEHAVIOR, LOMBARD HAD SOME FUN WITH COSTAR BING CROSBY WHILE FILMING *WE'RE NOT DRESSING* (1943). ONE MORNING SHE HOLLERED ACROSS THE HOTEL BREAKFAST ROOM, "BY THE WAY, BING, I FORGOT MY NIGHTIE IN YOUR BEDROOM." SHE ALSO PULLED ONE ON DIRECTOR ALFRED HITCHCOCK (FAMOUS FOR HIS VIEW OF ACTORS AS CATTLE) WHEN SHE ARRANGED TO HAVE COWS GREET THE DIRECTOR ON THE SET OF *MR. AND MRS. SMITH* (1941).

A sensation when she hit the American screen, the voluptuous Italian goddess came to life with a feisty realism and regal sensuality that never seems to age.

SOPHIA
LOREN

Puberty can be kind or cruel to young women; to Sophia Loren, it was a blessing. Adolescence transformed the once-scrawny girl nicknamed "Toothpick" into a curvaceous and desirable woman. Her savvy mother realized Rome held more promise for lovely Sophia than their little village did, and she moved the family to a small apartment in the big city. Sophia supported the family with work as a film extra and model, finally catching the eye of producer Carlo Ponti. He shepherded her career with enthusiasm, and by the time she was eighteen they had begun what would become a lifelong love affair. Sophia went from bit parts to starring roles in more than a dozen films before *The Gold of Naples* (1954) made her a bona fide star. It was in this role that director Vittorio De Sica realized she was not only a woman of beauty but also a woman of character, which added significant depth to her image. Hollywood was the next stop, and after a stiff adjustment to a new language and country she began to bring an earthy, European realism to her parts, with plenty of sensuality to boot. Working under a four-year contract with Paramount, Sophia made herself a household name. In 1960, she drew upon her wartime childhood to play a beleaguered widow in De Sica's *Two Women*. She continued to make international films, most notably with De Sica and fellow Neapolitan Marcello Mastroianni. Their romantic and comic chemistry brought international acclaim to films like *Yesterday, Today and Tomorrow* (1963) and *Marriage, Italian Style* (1964). Sophia continued to work through the 1960s and beyond, yet the much-awaited birth of her two sons gave her a reason to slow down; she appeared only when it pleased her, in gems like *A Special Day* (1975), again with Mastroianni. They teamed up once more for Robert Altman's *Prêt-à-Porter* (1994), in which she re-created her classic strip scene from *Yesterday, Today and Tomorrow*. Her pairing with Walter Matthau in 1995's *Grumpier Old Men* demonstrates that even at sixty she can pull off the role of an Italian sexpot. Whether serving as a United Nations goodwill ambassador, promoting a movie, or just gracing an event with her presence, Sophia Loren appears in public as an ageless vision of beauty and style, brimming with a passion for life that seems irrepressibly *Italiano*.

Born
Sofia Villani Scicolone
September 20, 1934
Rome, Italy

Star Sign
Virgo

Height
5'8"

Husband and Children
Producer Carlo Ponti
(1957–62, annulled;
1966–present)
two sons,
Carlo Jr. and Edoardo

Essential
SOPHIALORENFilms

ACADEMY AWARDS

Won Best Actress
Two Women

Nominated for Best Actress
Marriage, Italian Style

**Honorary Award in 1991
"for a career rich with
memorable performances that
has added permanent
luster to our art form"**

HOUSEBOAT

(1958) Paramount
A domestic comedy with Cary
Grant, made the year Loren arrived
in Hollywood. She plays Grant's
housekeeper and governess,
eventually sharing a romance that
spilled over into their real lives.

TWO WOMEN

(1960) Embassy Pictures Corp.
Loren's return to Italian films, for
which she won a Best Actress
Oscar. Directed by Vittorio De Sica
in an earthy role originally intended
for Anna Magnani, Loren plays a
widow who suffers the ravages
of war with her young daughter
(Eleanor Brown).

EL CID

(1961) Allied Artists
Elaborate cinematic rendition
of the life of eleventh-century
Spanish hero Rodrigo Diaz de Bivar,
also known as "El Cid." Playing
opposite Charlton Heston in the
title role, Loren is Chimene, El Cid's
duplicitous wife.

YESTERDAY, TODAY AND TOMORROW

(1963) Embassy
Neorealist director Vittorio De
Sica's trilogy of short stories about
three different women and the
types of men they attract, starring
Loren and Marcello Mastroianni.

MARRIAGE, ITALIAN STYLE

(1964) Embassy
A reunion of Loren, Mastroianni, and
director De Sica, the story of a man
who finally marries his longtime
employee and mistress, thinking
she is on her deathbed—only to
have her "recover" and move in,
with three grown sons in tow. In
an Oscar-nominated performance,
Loren amusingly turns the tables on
her costar.

HOUSEBOAT, 1958

STYLENOTES

In Sophia's first screen test, she was deemed "impossible to photograph," and a nose job was suggested. Sophia declined the advice. "If you change your nose, you change your face," she said.

When Edith Head began her costume work on *Houseboat,* the leading lady had been written as an American, and Head envisioned dungarees and sweatshirts for the young woman. When Sophia first met with her, she was polite—but horrified. "I do not wear blue jeans," she said simply.

Sophia caused tongues to wag when she accidentally wore a tiara to a 1954 opening night with Queen Elizabeth in attendance—a royal no-no. The British press dubbed her "Queen Sophia."

Sophia's oversized eyeglass frames have become part of her sophisticated sex appeal. She even has her own eyeglass line, touting the look.

FIRE POWER, 1979

behindthescenes

AMERICA FELL IN LOVE WITH SOPHIA WHEN SHE ARRIVED IN HOLLYWOOD—AND SO, IT SEEMS, DID COSTAR CARY GRANT. PRODUCER CARLO PONTI, WHO WAS ALSO ROMANTICALLY INVOLVED WITH SOPHIA, WAS SO MOTIVATED BY GRANT'S FAWNING THAT HE GOT A MEXICAN DIVORCE THAT WOULD ENABLE HIM TO FINALLY MARRY HER. YEARS LATER THEY WERE FORCED TO HAVE THE MARRIAGE ANNULLED DUE TO CONTINUED PRESSURE FROM THE VATICAN. FINALLY, HOWEVER, PONTI, SOPHIA, AND HIS FIRST WIFE ALL OBTAINED FRENCH CITIZENSHIP SO THAT THE DIVORCE AND REMARRIAGE COULD NOT BE CONTESTED.

FOR SOPHIA'S FORTIETH BIRTHDAY, PONTI GAVE HER A CUSTOM-FITTED FOURTEEN-CARAT-GOLD TOILET SEAT.

IN THE 1980 TELEVISION MINISERIES *SOPHIA LOREN: HER OWN STORY,* SHE PLAYED THE ROLES OF HERSELF AND HER MOTHER. THE FILM ALSO FEATURED RIP TORN AS PONTI AND FUTURE U.S. AMBASSADOR TO MEXICO JOHN GAVIN AS CARY GRANT.

ARABESQUE, 1966

Confident, sophisticated, whip smart, and equipped with a wit as dry as the martinis she favored in her films, she had a gift for nuance and comedic timing.

MYRNA
LOY

Born
Myrna Adele Williams
August 2, 1905
Radersburg, Montana

Died
December 14, 1993
New York, New York,
from complications
during surgery

Star Sign
Leo

Height
5'6"

Husbands
Producer Arthur Hornblow Jr.
(1936–42, divorced)

Rental car magnate John Hertz Jr.
(1942–44, divorced)

Writer-producer Gene Markey
(1946–50, divorced)

Diplomat Howland H. Sergeant
(1951–60, divorced)

Myrna Loy was born in a small town in Montana but moved to Los Angeles with her family at the age of thirteen following her father's death. Loy caught the acting bug in high school and got a job in a chorus, which allowed her to help with the family bills. Her unusual look—Celtic red hair and freckles complemented by exotic almond eyes—caught the attention of Rudolph Valentino's wife, acclaimed designer Natasha Rambova. She helped Myrna break into the movies during the silent era, when she specialized in playing villainous vamps who showed more skin than subtlety. Myrna worked hard to develop the right voice for talkies. When she signed with MGM in 1933, she started to move away from exotic sirens to her trademark sophisticated women. As a society girl torn between gangster Clark Gable and slick lawyer William Powell in *Manhattan Melodrama* (1934), she convinced director Woody Van Dyke of her star potential. He fought MGM management to cast Loy and Powell as husband-and-wife detectives in *The Thin Man* (1934). Everybody else thought them typed as villains, but their witty banter and the obvious affection beneath it made the film a huge hit. The two stars would reteam twelve more times. Myrna had a string of hits in the 1930s, including several with Gable that further played up her image as a sophisticate who could hold her own with any man. In all of her films she displayed a subtle approach to character and nuance that was years ahead of its time. During World War II, Myrna spent more time working for the war effort than she did acting. Afterward, she came back to star in one of the 1940s' biggest hits, *The Best Years of Our Lives* (1946), in which she helps husband Fredric March adjust to civilian life after years at war. Despite more top assignments, Myrna began devoting more and more time to public service. But when she did appear on screen, as Doris Day's aunt in *Midnight Lace* (1960) or Alan King's secretary in *Just Tell Me What You Want* (1980), she lit up the screen. Even her last job—the television film *Summer Solstice* (1981), which was also the last for Henry Fonda—showed her to be an actress as fresh and contemporary as she had been fifty years earlier.

Essential
MYRNA LOY Films

THE THIN MAN

(1934) MGM
The first of a series of six films, in
which husband-and-wife detectives
Nick and Nora Charles (William
Powell and Myrna Loy) solve
murders with the aid of dog Asta
and a couple dozen martinis.

LIBELED LADY

(1936) MGM
A gruff newspaper editor (Spencer
Tracy) accidentally prints a story
about a wealthy socialite (Myrna
Loy) who has stolen another
woman's husband. Tracy enlists the
help of his fiancée (Jean Harlow)
and former employee (William
Powell) in a harebrained plan
to stop her libel suit against the
newspaper.

THE BEST YEARS OF OUR LIVES

(1946) RKO
A story of three soldiers facing
readjustment after returning
home from World War II. William
Wyler directs the Oscar-winning
production, costarring Fredric
March, Dana Andrews, Harold
Russell, and Teresa Wright.

THE BACHELOR AND THE BOBBY SOXER

(1947) RKO
Loy plays an uptight judge whose
teenage sister (Shirley Temple)
develops a crush on a debonair,
troublemaking artist (Cary Grant).
The judge decides that the best way
to curb her sister's crush is to
sentence the much-older playboy to
date her younger sister. Meanwhile,
Loy realizes that she is actually the
one who is love struck by Grant.

MR. BLANDINGS BUILDS HIS DREAM HOUSE

(1948) RKO
Loy's third and final teaming with
Grant as Mr. and Mrs. Blandings, a
couple with big suburban dreams.
Unfortunately, their fixer-upper
house turns into an anything-that-
can-go-wrong-will comedy of delays.

THE THIN MAN, 1934

STYLENOTES

Impressed by sixteen-year-old Myrna Williams's beauty, the head of the art department at Venice High School assigned her to model for a seminude statue that stands even today in the school's courtyard.

Although she appeared pale and raven-haired in movies, Myrna was a red-haired and freckle-faced woman who despised her "piano" legs. MGM producer David O. Selznick was more concerned with her prominent ears, forcing makeup artists to glue them to her head. Myrna briefly considered plastic surgery to deal with the issue, but she decided it was too dramatic a response.

EVELYN PRENTICE, 1934

behindthescenes

MYRNA ALWAYS FELT BAD THAT SHE WAS FAMED CRIMINAL JOHN DILLINGER'S FAVORITE ACTRESS: WHEN HE CAME OUT OF HIDING TO SEE HER IN *MANHATTAN MELODRAMA* (1934), HE WAS GUNNED DOWN BY THE FBI.

MYRNA WAS UNAFRAID TO GIVE AUTHORITY FIGURES A PIECE OF HER MIND. IN THE 1940S SHE REPORTEDLY HARANGUED STUDIO HEADS ABOUT THEIR DEPICTION OF AFRICAN AMERICANS: "WHY DOES EVERY NEGRO IN A FILM HAVE TO PLAY A SERVANT? WHAT ABOUT A BLACK PERSON WALKING UP THE STEPS OF A COURTHOUSE CARRYING A BRIEFCASE?"

MYRNA ONLY LIKED THE SPOTLIGHT WHEN THE CAMERAS WERE ROLLING, PREFERRING NIGHTS AT HOME WITH HER BROTHER AND MOTHER. DIRECTOR JOHN FORD JOKED, "WOULDN'T YOU KNOW, THE KID THEY PICK TO PLAY TRAMPS IS THE ONLY GOOD GIRL IN HOLLYWOOD."

She brought a unique hybrid image to the screen: part kooky comedienne, part natural dramatic actress. Her tender, funny performances built a bridge between 1950s repression and 1960s rebellion.

SHIRLEY
MACLAINE

If you were designing parents to produce a child with Shirley MacLaine's interests, you couldn't have done better than her own: a drama teacher married to a professor of psychology and philosophy who also played music. Part entertainer, part searcher, Shirley has always followed her passion, a journey that's taken her to Broadway, Hollywood, and points beyond. Talent and persistence brought her to the Broadway chorus line, where Cinderella-like success came at a young age. Her understudy role in *The Pajama Game* quickly turned into the lead, and producer Hal Wallis caught her performance. Wallis saw promise in the effervescent Shirley and shepherded her early career through Alfred Hitchcock's *The Trouble with Harry* (1955) and other films. In less than five years, she made it to the big time, running with the Rat Pack and going from $6,000 to $250,000 a picture. Shirley's gamine kookiness mixed with pathos allowed her to offer up subtle, honest portrayals of small-town girls (1958's *Some Came Running*) and big-city girls (1960's *The Apartment*) with a desperate need for love—often from the wrong guy. Shirley worked in films steadily through the 1960s, but in the 1970s she expanded to other media. For her film comeback she chose wisely: 1977's *The Turning Point* presented an older version of Shirley's pixie, a world-weary former ballerina wondering what might have been. Never afraid to look dowdy, manic, or unattractive, she was suited for older parts that emphasized character over physical perfection. The pinnacle of her later career was her creation of Aurora Greenway, the fiercely controlling mother in *Terms of Endearment* (1983), which brought her a long-overdue Oscar. In recent years, she has been involved in politics and New Age explorations of all kinds, written several best-selling books about her life and varied interests, and starred as herself in a miniseries based on her life, *Out on a Limb* (1987). Still active on the screen today, Shirley has sought standout character roles, including the temperamental piano teacher in *Madame Sousatzka* (1988), the belligerent town eccentric in *Steel Magnolias* (1989), a Hollywood diva in *Postcards from the Edge* (1990), and Endora in a film revival of the TV series *Bewitched* (2005).

Born
Shirley MacLean Beaty
April 24, 1934
Richmond, Virginia

Star Sign
Taurus

Height
5'6"

Husband and Child
Producer Steve Parker
(1954–82, divorced)
daughter, Sachi

Essential
SHIRLEY MACLAINE Films

SOME CAME RUNNING
(1958) MGM
MacLaine's breakthrough performance in director Vincente Minnelli's version of the James Jones novel. She plays a good-natured tart who meets a tragic end after following World War II veteran and would-be writer Frank Sinatra to his Indiana hometown.

THE APARTMENT
(1960) United Artists
A Best Picture Oscar winner, Billy Wilder's blend of comedy and drama that brought MacLaine her second Best Actress nomination. Jack Lemmon costars as the officer worker who allows company executives to use his apartment for romantic trysts—only to fall for his boss's mistress (MacLaine).

IRMA LA DOUCE
(1963) United Artists
MacLaine and Jack Lemmon reunited with director Billy Wilder in a comedy adapted from the stage musical of the same name. MacLaine has the title role as a highly successful Parisian prostitute, and Lemmon is the naive policeman who first tries to disrupt her work and then falls in love and becomes her pimp.

SWEET CHARITY
(1969) Universal
Bob Fosse's film version of his hit stage musical based on Federico Fellini's 1957 film *Nights of Cabiria*. MacLaine plays Charity, the hooker with a heart of gold, and, with costars Chita Rivera and Paula Kelly, dances up a storm to the Cy Coleman–Dorothy Fields score.

TERMS OF ENDEARMENT
(1983) Paramount
The winner of multiple Oscars, including Best Actress (MacLaine), directed by James L. Brooks and based on Larry McMurtry's novel. MacLaine plays Aurora Greenway, a widow who romances an astronaut (Jack Nicholson) and shares turbulent times with her daughter (Debra Winger).

THE APARTMENT, 1960

On the set of *Around the World in 80 Days* (1956), Marlene Dietrich taught Shirley how to light herself on camera, and how to give herself an "au naturel face lift" by using a gold chain and hair pins to pull her face taut.

Shirley claimed that on the set of *The Children's Hour* (1962), "Audrey Hepburn taught me how to dress, and I taught her how to cuss."

Paramount hairstylist Nellie Manley had instructions to help perpetuate Shirley's "kooky" stage persona. To that end, Nellie designed an impish pixie cut that flattered Paramount's fresh new face.

For her film debut in *The Trouble with Harry* (1955), MacLaine's costumes were pulled off the rack. By the time she made *What a Way to Go!* in 1964, she had a $500,000 Edith Head wardrobe featuring 72 costumes and $3.5 million in rented jewelry.

behind the scenes

BEFORE FILMING *IRMA LA DOUCE* (1963), JACK LEMMON AND SHIRLEY WENT TO *LES HALLES* DISTRICT IN PARIS AND, ACCORDING TO SHIRLEY, "SPENT TWO DAYS IN A HOUSE OF ILL REPUTE TO STUDY AND OBSERVE THE WORKING GIRLS." WHEN SHE WON THE GOLDEN GLOBE FOR BEST ACTRESS IN A COMEDY OR MUSICAL, SHE STARTED TO THANK THE WOMEN SHE'D RESEARCHED, AND THE NETWORK CUT TO A COMMERCIAL.

MACLAINE'S YOUNGER BROTHER IS THE ACTOR AND ONCE-INFAMOUS LOTHARIO WARREN BEATTY. THEIR COMPLEX RELATIONSHIP INCLUDES CLASSIC SIBLING TEASING, AS DISPLAYED DURING THE 1979 OSCARS, WHEN SHIRLEY USED HER TIME ON THE PODIUM TO SHORE UP OSCAR-LOSER WARREN WITH THESE WORDS: "I WANT TO TAKE THIS OPPORTUNITY TO SAY HOW PROUD I AM OF MY LITTLE BROTHER . . . JUST IMAGINE WHAT YOU COULD ACCOMPLISH IF YOU TRIED CELIBACY!"

SHIRLEY'S 1983 BOOK *OUT ON A LIMB* CREATED A SENSATION AND INCREASED INTEREST IN REINCARNATION. IN IT, SHE DETAILS HER MANY SESSIONS WITH MEDIUMS AND HER FIRM BELIEF IN PAST LIVES.

DURING THE FILMING OF SOME CAME RUNNING (1958), SHIRLEY BECAME THE UNOFFICIAL DEN MOTHER TO "THE CLAN," LATER KNOWN AS THE RAT PACK, A GROUP OF DRINKING BUDDIES ORIGINALLY ORGANIZED BY HUMPHREY BOGART AND LATER LED BY HER COSTAR FRANK SINATRA. OTHER MEMBERS INCLUDED DEAN MARTIN (ALSO IN THE FILM), SAMMY DAVIS JR., PETER LAWFORD, AND JOEY BISHOP. SHIRLEY CAMEOED AS A DRUNK IN THE FIRST OFFICIAL RAT PACK FILM, OCEAN'S ELEVEN (1960).

MACLAINE WAS THE INSPIRATION FOR FRANK SINATRA'S CLASSIC SONG "THE SECOND TIME AROUND." HIS ACCOMPANIST, JIMMY VAN HEUSEN, DESPERATELY WANTED HER TO LEAVE HER HUSBAND AND MARRY HIM.

SOME CAME RUNNING, 1958

Perhaps the greatest sex symbol of our time, with a blend of sexual confidence and childlike vulnerability that fired imaginations and inspired a worshipful protectiveness from generations of fans.

MARILYN
MONROE

Norma Jeane was Marilyn Monroe's name for the first two decades of her life. She never knew her father, saw her mother lapse into madness, and married in her teens with a desire to have a family of her own. Her first husband, Jim Dougherty, described his young wife as serious and religious, but when he was shipped overseas during World War II, all that changed. Norma Jeane went to work building planes and was discovered by photographers. By the time he returned from the war, Norma was on her way to becoming Marilyn Monroe, and the marriage was over. A major turning point in Marilyn's career came when agent Johnny Hyde suggested her to director John Huston for MGM's *The Asphalt Jungle* (1950). Soon 20th Century-Fox signed her to a seven-year contract, and films like *Gentlemen Prefer Blondes, How to Marry a Millionaire,* and *Niagara* (all 1953) helped her create a huge fan base. That same year *Photoplay* magazine voted Monroe "Best New Actress," and at twenty-seven years old she was the most beloved bombshell in Hollywood. Some mocked her dumb-blonde persona and breathy manner, but she was loved for her beauty and glamour. Her marriage to baseball superstar Joe DiMaggio played out on a worldwide stage, and its demise coincided with Marilyn's desperate need for respect as an actress. Walking out on her Fox contract, she moved to New York to study with Method acting teacher Lee Strasberg. When she returned to Hollywood for *Bus Stop* (1956), Marilyn showed an emotional depth that surprised her detractors. She then scored one of her biggest hits as the brokenhearted band singer in *Some Like It Hot* (1959), with Jack Lemmon and Tony Curtis. Marilyn's marriage to playwright Arthur Miller opened the door to an intellectual world she adored, yet her massive insecurities and inability to have children threatened her happiness. *The Misfits* (1961) would prove to be her last film, and in 1962, at thirty-six years old, she died of a drug overdose.

Born
Norma Jeane Mortenson
June 1, 1926
Los Angeles, California

Died
August 5, 1962
Los Angeles, California,
of a drug overdose

Star Sign
Gemini

Height
5'5"

Husbands
U.S. serviceman James Dougherty
(1942–46, divorced)

Baseball star Joe DiMaggio
(1954, divorced)

Playwright Arthur Miller
(1956–61, divorced)

Essential
MARILYN**MONROE**Films

GENTLEMEN PREFER BLONDES

(1953) 20th Century-Fox
Howard Hawks's sparkling film treatment of the stage musical, which was itself based on the Anita Loos novel, with Monroe as blonde gold digger Lorelei Lee and Jane Russell as her brunette, wisecracking best friend. A high point is Monroe singing "Diamonds Are a Girl's Best Friend."

HOW TO MARRY A MILLIONAIRE

(1953) 20th Century-Fox
A wide-screen farce with Monroe as one of a trio of models, with Betty Grable and Lauren Bacall, who pose as rich Manhattanites in order to snag wealthy husbands. Monroe is the comically nearsighted one who settles for a tax evader played by David Wayne.

THE SEVEN YEAR ITCH

(1955) 20th Century-Fox
Billy Wilder's film of the George Axelrod sex satire about a married New Yorker who fantasizes about the gorgeous girl next door (Monroe) while his wife is away on vacation. Posing on a subway grating with her white dress billowing about her, Monroe creates one of the film world's iconic images.

BUS STOP

(1956) 20th Century-Fox
The William Inge stage hit, with Monroe taking over for Kim Stanley as Cherie, a would-be chanteuse stranded by a snowstorm at a remote bus stop. Joshua Logan directs a cast that also includes Don Murray as the rodeo cowboy who kidnaps Cherie in hopes of making her his bride.

SOME LIKE IT HOT

(1959) United Artists
Billy Wilder's hilarious cross-dressing comedy, with Monroe as Sugar Kane, the lead singer in a 1920s band where two male musicians pose as females while on the lam from gangsters. Tony Curtis and Jack Lemmon are the guys in drag who pursue Sugar with something other than feminine friendship in mind.

SOME LIKE IT HOT, 1959

STYLENOTES

Marilyn lost her first modeling assignment because her incredible figure overshadowed the clothes. Photographers soon realized that she was more of a pinup than a clothes model.

Marilyn didn't want anything to distract from her curves, so she wore no underwear. Often she was sewn into her tight-fitting gowns.

Marilyn made even casual clothes look sexy. "Putting a girl in overalls is like having her work in tights, particularly if a girl knows how to wear them," she once explained. She was one of the first female stars to be photographed in jeans.

Jean Louis created the mesh silk souffle dress that Marilyn wore to President Kennedy's birthday celebration at Madison Square Garden. As the spotlights hit it, the dress was all but transparent. When the gown was auctioned by Christie's in 1999, it brought over $1 million.

behindthescenes

SOME STARS BECOME THEIR PERSONAE, BUT NORMA JEANE WAS ALWAYS AWARE WHEN SHE WAS "PUTTING ON" MARILYN MONROE. ONCE, WALKING DOWN A MANHATTAN STREET WITH ACTRESS SUSAN STRASBERG, SHE SAID, "HEY, YOU WANT TO SEE ME BE 'HER'?" AND SUDDENLY SWITCHED INTO DROP-DEAD-SEXY MARILYN MODE.

CERTAINLY SOME OF HER MARITAL DIFFICULTIES RESULTED FROM HER HUSBANDS' DISCOMFORT OVER THE CONSTANT ATTENTION SHE RECEIVED FROM MEN AROUND THE WORLD. JOE DIMAGGIO WAS PRESENT AND QUITE UNHAPPY DURING THE FILMING OF THE FAMOUS *SEVEN YEAR ITCH* SCENE IN WHICH MARILYN'S CLASSIC WHITE HALTER DRESS FLIES UP IN GUSTS FROM A SUBWAY GRATE. WHEN BILLBOARDS SEVERAL STORIES HIGH DUPLICATED THAT SHOT, IT WAS THE LAST STRAW IN THEIR MARRIAGE.

THOUGH FAMOUS FOR HER "DUMB-BLONDE" IMAGE, THE REAL MARILYN LOVED THE INTELLECTUAL WORLD. SHE WAS AN AVID READER, OPENING ACCOUNTS AT BOOKSTORES WHEREVER SHE LIVED. PLAYWRIGHT ARTHUR MILLER (HER THIRD HUSBAND), LEO TOLSTOY, AND THOMAS WOLFE WERE AMONG HER FAVORITE AUTHORS. WHEN SHE LEFT HOLLYWOOD TO STUDY ACTING, SHE MENTIONED THAT SHE WOULD LOVE TO STAR IN A PROJECTED SCREEN VERSION OF *THE BROTHERS KARAMAZOV*. ONE JOURNALIST SUGGESTED THAT THAT COULD ONLY HAPPEN IF THE BROTHERS WERE PLAYED BY GROUCHO, HARPO, AND CHICO.

CIRCA 1954

One of the most enigmatic sex symbols of the late 1950s and early 1960s, and one of the last studio-made stars, she was blonde and beautiful, all passionate heat blanketed with intellectual chilliness.

KIM NOVAK

The daughter of a traditional Midwestern couple, pretty young Marilyn Novak had dreams of stardom that intensified when she won a beauty contest sponsored by the Thor refrigerator company at age twenty. The new Miss Deepfreeze landed in Los Angeles, where a screen test caught the eye of Columbia's Harry Cohn. Cohn was looking for an actress to replace the older Rita Hayworth and compete with Marilyn Monroe. Yet from the start Cohn found Novak to be more than just a pretty piece of clay he could mold to his liking. She agreed to change her first name but, despite Cohn's protestations that "Novak" was too ethnic, she wouldn't drop her family name. What followed is the stuff of legends: an incredible trajectory that found Novak making six films in the next two years, from the broad comedy of *Phffft!* (1954) to the glamorous romance of *The Eddy Duchin Story* (1956). By 1956, she had become one of America's most popular movie stars. Her role as Madge in *Picnic* (1955) is often cited as a perfect example of the indefinable mystery that enhances Novak's performances. At one moment she's the confident sex goddess, the next, a lost small-town girl protesting, "I get so tired of just being told I'm pretty." Her ability to portray two very different kinds of women in the same movie soared to a new level in 1958's *Vertigo*, one of director Alfred Hitchcock's finest, in which Novak's glamorous look and chilly beauty magnified the director's trademark suspense. She worked with Frank Sinatra twice, happily in *The Man with the Golden Arm* (1955), and less happily in *Pal Joey* (1957), by which time she thought he was too much of a "hotshot,"—a tough experience softened by a friendship with her supposed rival, Rita Hayworth. In truth, Novak never found the experience of making movies to be a pure pleasure. Though her career continued beyond those glory years of the 1950s, she had the sense to leap off when she'd had enough. In the mid-1970s a marriage to a veterinarian gave her a second act as the mistress of a large ranch in Oregon, where no one—not her vast menagerie, friends, neighbors, or even her husband—seems to care that she was once a reigning Hollywood glamour queen. "I feel that it would be nice to be accepted as a total human being," she said, no doubt speaking for all the goddesses we create in our imaginations.

Born
Marilyn Pauline Novak
February 13, 1933
Chicago, Illinois

Star Sign
Aquarius

Height
5'6"

Husbands
Actor Richard Johnson
(1965–66, divorced)

Veterinarian Dr. Robert Malloy
(1976–present)

Essential
KIMNOVAKFilms

PICNIC
(1955) Columbia
The William Inge drama about a Labor Day celebration in a small Kansas town, with Novak as the local beauty who falls for an itinerant stud (William Holden). Joshua Logan directed, with the sexy "Moonglow" dance performed by Novak and Holden as a highlight.

THE MAN WITH THE GOLDEN ARM
(1955) United Artists
Novak plays the sympathetic girlfriend of addict Frank Sinatra, who is married to supposedly crippled Eleanor Parker, in a downbeat drama that broke the taboo against showing drug use in films. Otto Preminger directed the tale based on the Nelson Algren novel.

VERTIGO
(1958) Paramount
A gripping Hitchcock mystery, with Novak as the ethereal blonde who becomes an object of obsession by San Francisco detective James Stewart. Novak also appears as the unrefined redhead Stewart trains to replace his dream girl.

BELL, BOOK AND CANDLE
(1958) Columbia
A lighthearted Novak and Stewart reunion in a comedy based on John Van Druten's Broadway success. Novak plays a witch casting spells in contemporary Manhattan, until she falls for book publisher Stewart and loses her powers.

KISS ME, STUPID
(1964) Lopert
Novak's only film for writer-director Billy Wilder, a cynical comedy that was controversial in its day. Dean Martin is a playboy who gets head-aches without nightly sex, Ray Walston is a jealous husband, and Novak is a prostitute (called Polly the Pistol) who poses as Walston's wife.

THE MAN WITH THE GOLDEN ARM, 1955

STYLENOTES

Columbia's publicity department dubbed Novak a "lavender blonde," claiming that she only liked to wear shades of lavender. Her hair was tinted purple and her first Hollywood apartment was forcefully decorated entirely in shades of lavender.

Novak had a definitive sense of style. Louis Feraud outfits and Halston hats were favorites, which led to problems with Edith Head during the making of *Vertigo*. At their first meeting, she informed the famed costumer, "I don't wear suits and I don't wear gray." Kim wouldn't give in until Hitchcock bullied her into accepting his vision.

MIDDLE OF THE NIGHT, 1959

VERTIGO, 1958

behindthescenes

KIM'S FATHER NEVER APPROVED OF HER INVOLVEMENT IN THE MOVIE BUSINESS, PARTICULARLY WHEN HER 1964 SEX FARCE, *KISS ME, STUPID,* WAS CONDEMNED BY THE CATHOLIC CHURCH'S LEGION OF DECENCY. IT COST KIM AND HER PARENTS A VISIT WITH THE POPE, WHO TURNED DOWN HER REQUEST FOR AN AUDIENCE (YEARS LATER HE RELENTED, BUT MR. NOVAK WASN'T THERE TO SEE IT).

PLENTY OF MOVIE-WORTHY DRAMA SURROUNDED KIM'S RELATIONSHIP WITH AFRICAN AMERICAN ENTERTAINER SAMMY DAVIS JR. THEIR AFFAIR LITERALLY GAVE HARRY COHN NOT JUST ONE BUT TWO HEART ATTACKS. FINALLY, HE HAD MOB MEMBERS THREATEN SAMMY WITH CAREER RUIN—OR WORSE—IF HE DIDN'T STOP SEEING KIM. BROKENHEARTED BUT RESIGNED, KIM AND SAMMY WENT THEIR SEPARATE WAYS.

KIM ONCE CLAIMED THAT ALFRED HITCHCOCK SO RESENTED THE STUDIO'S INSISTENCE THAT HE USE HER IN *VERTIGO* THAT HE MADE HER REPEATEDLY JUMP INTO SAN FRANCISCO BAY WHILE FILMING HER CHARACTER'S ATTEMPTED SUICIDE. SOME DISPUTE THE STORY, YET HITCHCOCK CONFIDED TO A WRITER YEARS LATER, "AT LEAST I GOT THE CHANCE TO THROW HER INTO THE WATER."

Hollywood's ultimate Irish lass, she was a flame-haired beauty with a spirit that made her a match for her larger-than-life screen partners John Wayne and John Ford.

MAUREEN
O'HARA

Maureen O'Hara learned at age six that she loved an audience. Singing, dancing, and fencing lessons followed, and after a few years the lovely redhead started to win amateur acting competitions. She joined the prestigious Abbey Theater as soon as she was eligible, at just fourteen. Yet no sooner had she risen to leading roles than a screen test brought her to London, where, after a few minor films, she gained the attention of famed actor Charles Laughton. Maureen appeared with him in *Jamaica Inn* (1939), directed by Alfred Hitchcock, and when Laughton returned to America, he took his new protégée with him. Once in Hollywood, she started at the top, as Laughton's costar in the big-budget remake of *The Hunchback of Notre Dame* (1939). After struggling to establish an image, O'Hara played to her strengths as a Welsh coal-miner's daughter in *How Green Was My Valley* (1941), and her pairing with director John Ford was magical. She then dusted off her fencing skills and hitched up her skirts for a series of swashbucklers and other Technicolor adventures, working with actors like Tyrone Power, Cornel Wilde, and Anthony Quinn. But she also excelled in the dramatic romance *Sentimental Journey* (1946) and the holiday favorite *Miracle on 34th Street* (1947). A reunion with Ford brought her one of her best roles, in *Rio Grande* (1950), and a new favorite leading man, John Wayne. The three reunited for *The Quiet Man* (1952), a "silly, little Irish story" according to the studio, that scored big at the box office and with critics. Maureen made five films with Wayne altogether, finding in the Duke the perfect on-screen romantic partner. After two failed marriages, she finally found the love of her life in pilot Charles Blair and, in 1973, happily left acting to help him run an airline from their home in the Virgin Islands. Since Blair's death in a plane crash, Maureen has returned to the screen for *Only the Lonely* (1991) as John Candy's possessive mother, which marked a reunion with one-time costar Anthony Quinn, and has appeared in several television movies.

Born
Maureen FitzSimons
August 17, 1920
Ranelagh, Dublin, Ireland

Star Sign
Leo

Height
5'8"

Husbands and Child
Production assistant
George Hanley Brown
(1939–40, annulled)

Writer-director Will Price
(1941–53, divorced)
daughter, Bronwyn Brigid

General Charles F. Blair
(1968–78, his death)

Essential
MAUREEN O'HARA Films

THE HUNCHBACK OF NOTRE DAME

(1939) RKO
The nineteen-year-old Irish redhead's U.S. debut, in the second screen version of the much-filmed Victor Hugo classic. O'Hara plays the sympathetic gypsy girl Esmeralda to the tortured Quasimodo portrayed by Charles Laughton, her real-life discoverer and mentor.

HOW GREEN WAS MY VALLEY

(1941) 20th Century-Fox
Director John Ford's Oscar-winning film version of Richard Llewellyn's novel about a family of Welsh coal miners. O'Hara, in the first of her five films for Ford, is Angharad, the older sister of the young protagonist played by Roddy McDowall.

THE BLACK SWAN

(1942) 20th Century-Fox
One of several swashbucklers in which O'Hara is the damsel in distress—this time with pirate Tyrone Power dashing to the rescue.

MIRACLE ON 34TH STREET

(1947) 20th Century-Fox
A holiday classic about a Macy's Kris Kringle (Oscar-winner Edmund Gwenn) who attempts to prove he's the real thing. O'Hara is the realistic but warmhearted mother and Natalie Wood is her disbelieving child.

THE QUIET MAN

(1952) Republic
The second of O'Hara's five vehicles in which she costarred with her good friend John Wayne. John Ford directs the pair in this story of an American boxer who returns to his native Ireland and pursues a beautiful but hot-tempered lass.

THE BLACK SWAN, 1942

STYLENOTES

In 1959, the National Association of Hosiery Manufacturers named Maureen number one on their list of the ten women with the most beautiful legs in America.

When Hollywood wanted to give Maureen a nose job, she showed them how an Irish woman handles foolish requests: "My nose comes with me, I've got a big square face, and I need my big nose. If you don't like it, I'll go back where I came from."

Though Universal claimed that Maureen filmed *Lady Godiva*'s (1955) famous horseback ride in the nude, Maureen insists she wore a "full-length body leotard and underwear that was concealed by my long tresses."

Maureen loved the perks of filming *Miracle on 34th Street* in Macy's after hours—between takes, she admitted, she tried on everything in the store.

behindthescenes

MAUREEN O' HARA DESCRIBED HER IRISH CHILDHOOD AS SOMETHING NEARLY OUT OF *THE SOUND OF MUSIC*. THE SIX "BEAUTIFUL FITZSIMONS" CHILDREN DRESSED IN IDENTICAL OUTFITS MADE BY THEIR DESIGNER MOTHER, LINED UP IN THE EVENING FOR A MORAL INSPECTION, AND GATHERED AROUND THE FIREPLACE TO HEAR THEIR PARENTS SING BEFORE BEING TRUNDLED OFF TO BED.

MAUREEN AGREED TO WHISPER A PROVOCATIVE LINE AT THE END OF *THE QUIET MAN* ONLY IF SHE, DIRECTOR FORD, AND JOHN WAYNE WOULD SWEAR NEVER TO REVEAL IT. THAT PACT HAS HELD.

MARILYN MONROE ONCE TALKED MAUREEN INTO HIDING IN A BOX FOR JOE DIMAGGIO'S BIRTHDAY, SO THAT MARILYN COULD SAY, "NOW, JOE, AFTER I GIVE YOU THIS, I DON'T EVER WANT TO HEAR ABOUT MAUREEN O'HARA AGAIN." THE COUPLE SEPARATED SHORTLY BEFORE THE PLANNED STUNT.

MAUREEN MAY HAVE PLAYED A RETICENT EX-WIFE *IN THE PARENT TRAP* (1961), BUT SHE WASN'T SHY ABOUT FIGHTING DISNEY FOR HER STANDARD SALARY AND TOP BILLING. DISNEY MET HER SALARY REQUEST BUT BACKPEDALED ON THE BILLING, CREATING A RIFT THAT NEVER HEALED.

WHEN HER BELOVED HUSBAND CHARLIE DIED, MAUREEN STEPPED IN TO RUN ANTILLES AIR BOATS, BECOMING THE FIRST FEMALE PRESIDENT OF A SCHEDULED U.S. AIRLINE.

RIO GRANDE, 1950

Often known simply as "America's Sweetheart," she was a smart, tough negotiator who took charge of her career and almost single-handedly invented celebrity in Hollywood.

MARY
PICKFORD

Mary Pickford became a legend by taking on the budding motion picture industry, positioning herself from the very start to achieve fame and fortune. Many young girls were cowed by director D. W. Griffith, but Mary coolly talked him into paying her what she was worth. Her film debut in 1909 began her rapid rise in the industry, as audiences responded immediately to the Little Girl with the Golden Curls. Mary made dozens of movies in those first few years with Griffith, playing everything—comedies, dramas, romances, even Westerns—with a subtle, engaging style perfectly suited to the silent film. More loyal to her family and career than to Griffith, she jumped ship for a while to a company that paid more and then went back to Griffith for an even better salary. By 1912, she was known as "the Queen of the Movies," and the following year she signed with Famous Players Film Company, where her popularity continued to rise. In movie after movie, she played a girl or grown woman sweet enough to eat but fiery enough to right a wrong or settle a score. Mary's characters were often girlish, but it wasn't until *The Poor Little Rich Girl* (1917) that she actually played a little girl—and audiences ate it up, continuing to adore her in roles that featured "our Mary" in short skirts and long curls. The only male star who came close to Mary in popularity was the dashing action star Douglas Fairbanks Sr. When they fell in love and married, fans fell into a collective hysteria, showing up everywhere the couple went on their honeymoon, waiting hours for the merest glimpse of the stars. To guarantee a fair share of her films' profits, she joined with Fairbanks, Griffith, and Charles Chaplin in 1919 to form United Artists. The move made her a wealthy woman for the rest of her life. Despite her second Best Actress Oscar win for one of her first talking films, ultimately the advent of talkies and the fickleness of fame swept other women into Hollywood's white-hot spotlight. Yet Mary Pickford will always be the first: the first superstar, the first actress who negotiated her dominance every step of the way, the first little girl in America who dared to mess with the big boys and succeed beyond anyone's wildest dreams.

Born
Gladys Marie Smith
April 8, 1892
Toronto, Canada

Died
May 29, 1979
Santa Monica, California,
of a cerebral hemorrhage

Star Sign
Aries

Height
5'1"

Husbands and Children
Actor Owen Moore
(1911–20, divorced)

Actor Douglas Fairbanks Sr.
(1920–36, divorced)

Actor Charles "Buddy" Rogers
(1937–79, her death)
two adopted children,
Ronnie and Roxanne

Essential
MARYPICKFORDFilms

ACADEMY AWARDS

Won Best Actress
Coquette

Honorary Award in 1976 for "recognition of her unique contributions to the film industry and the development of film as an artistic medium"

STELLA MARIS

(1918) Artcraft
Showy double role for America's Sweetheart, with Pickford displaying her versatility as a pretty but crippled heiress (the title role) and as a homely and ill-treated maid. Both young women are in love with the same married man, and the maid takes shocking measures to ensure that at least one of them gets him.

POLLYANNA

(1920) United Artists
A hugely successful silent production for Pickford, who at age twenty-seven played novelist Eleanor Porter's always-optimistic twelve-year-old. When Pollyanna's father dies, she moves into her aunt's home in a New England village and teaches its residents to remain upbeat despite their troubles.

LITTLE LORD FAUNTLEROY

(1921) United Artists
Another daunting double role, this time with Pickford as both a young boy, Cedric Fauntleroy, and his mother, Dearest. In Frances Hodgson Burnett's story, Cedric and his mom manage to claim the boy's inheritance when another boy claims to be the rightful heir.

SPARROWS

(1926) United Artists
Again playing a character half her age, Pickford is the leader of a pack of orphans who rebel after being starved and overworked by an exploitative cruel farmer. This Pickford hit is highlighted by a scary escape through a swamp filled with real alligators.

COQUETTE

(1929) United Artists
Pickford's first talkie, and her Oscar-winning performance in a role performed onstage by Helen Hayes. Pickford plays a flirtatious Southern belle with a collection of three beaus and a violence-prone father.

COQUETTE, 1929

STYLENOTES

Mary's long curls were worshipped by her fans, but in 1928 she cut her hair in a dramatic display of independence attended by journalists and photographers. Fans were outraged, but Mary was determined to try the fashionable bob, calling her locks "shackles."

Before *Coquette* even finished filming, Mary had planned her outfit for the Academy Awards, a silk chiffon bias-cut gown with elaborate beading. As an Academy founder, she had secured her win, and she posed with the statue days before the official notification.

Mary was one of the first screen stars to fully understand the importance of makeup on screen. She complained repeatedly about her ghostly pallor on film; darker makeup finally solved the problem.

behindthe**scenes**

MARY PICKFORD IS BELIEVED TO HAVE BEEN THE SUBJECT OF THE SCREEN'S FIRST CLOSE-UP, IN *FRIENDS*, 1912.

DESPITE HER VIRTUOUS IMAGE, MARY OCCASIONALLY FOUND HERSELF THE FOCUS OF SCANDALS. IN 1920, SHE BECAME THE FIRST FILM STAR TO OBTAIN A NEVADA DIVORCE, MOVING THERE FOR SIX WEEKS TO ESTABLISH RESIDENCY BEFORE DIVORCING ACTOR OWEN MOORE SO SHE COULD MARRY DOUGLAS FAIRBANKS. THE SCANDAL MADE HEADLINES AROUND THE NATION, PARTICULARLY WHEN OUTRAGED MEMBERS OF THE NEVADA LEGISLATURE THREATENED TO REVERSE THE DIVORCE DECREE—WHICH WOULD HAVE MADE AMERICA'S SWEETHEART A BIGAMIST.

WHEN MARY NEGOTIATED WITH HER DISTRIBUTOR TO RETAIN RIGHTS TO HER FILMS AFTER FIVE YEARS, SHE THOUGHT SHE HAD A FOOLPROOF PLAN TO CONTROL HER CINEMATIC HISTORY. YET WHEN SHE HEARD THAT THE COMPANY, FIRST NATIONAL, MIGHT BE MERGING WITH FAMOUS PLAYERS-LASKY, MARY REALIZED HER DEAL WAS IN JEOPARDY. MARY, DOUGLAS FAIRBANKS, D. W. GRIFFITH, AND CHARLIE CHAPLIN FORMED UNITED ARTISTS ASSOCIATION, AND THE PRESS ANNOUNCED, "THE INMATES HAVE TAKEN OVER THE ASYLUM!"

IT WAS ONLY RIGHT THAT THE KING AND QUEEN OF THE MOVIES SHOULD LIVE IN A PALACE, AND MARY'S WAS A TWENTY-TWO-ROOM TUDOR ESTATE DUBBED "PICKFAIR" (COMBINING THE LAST NAMES OF MARY AND HUSBAND DOUGLAS FAIRBANKS SR.), WHERE A LARGE STAFF TENDED TO THE HOUSE, THE GROUNDS, THE BUSY COUPLE, AND THE MANY GUESTS WHO FREQUENTED THEIR LAVISH DINNER PARTIES.

She was fresh faced, bubbly, and utterly wholesome, but behind the sugar was plenty of spice: a determined and accomplished singer, dancer, actress, and stage artist with a survivor's spirit.

DEBBIE
REYNOLDS

Debbie Reynolds grew up with an inexhaustible list of passions: Girl Scouts, baton twirling, music, and sports, to name a few. She went after the title of Miss Burbank of 1948 to win the grand prize, a pretty shirt, little suspecting that talent scouts from MGM and Warner Bros. would be there. They flipped a coin over her, and Warner Bros. won, giving Debbie a contract for $65 a week. When they dropped her two years later, the MGM scout was still waiting. Debbie was determined to impress her new studio and pushed herself hard, taking lessons in singing, dancing, and acting. Within two films, she was generating an impressive amount of fan mail, most notably for chirping "Abba Dabba Honeymoon" in *Two Weeks with Love* (1950). Studio executives were so impressed that they awarded her the ingenue role opposite Gene Kelly in one of the most popular musicals of all time, *Singin' in the Rain* (1952). Debbie sang, danced, and beamed for MGM and other studios throughout the 1950s, becoming even more popular when she found love with singing sensation Eddie Fisher. Their whirlwind romance had fan magazines gushing and crowds cheering. Marriage, followed by the birth of two children, didn't detract from her perky image, but serious turns in *The Catered Affair* (1956) and *The Rat Race* (1960) showed her potential for deeper roles. The very public end of her marriage to Fisher in 1958 only made her more popular. Yet even as she scored in *The Unsinkable Molly Brown* (1964), she was struggling to survive a decade in which her bubbly, wholesome image was not much in demand. Always the trouper, Debbie resurrected an earlier nightclub act and became a popular performer both on the international stage and, for a few years, at her own club and casino in Las Vegas. She also hit Broadway for the first time, running for over a year in a revival of *Irene*. Debbie continues to act whenever a good part comes up, scoring laughs in movies such as *Mother* (1996) and *In and Out* (1997). In 2001 she costarred with Elizabeth Taylor and Shirley MacLaine in *These Old Broads*, a television movie written for her by her daughter, actress-writer Carrie Fisher.

Born
Mary Frances Reynolds
April 1, 1932
El Paso, Texas

Star Sign
Aries

Height
5'2"

Husbands and Children
Crooner Eddie Fisher
(1955–59, divorced)
two children, Carrie and Todd

Shoe manufacturer Harry Karl
(1960–73, divorced)

Real estate developer
Richard Hamlett
(1985–94, divorced)

Essential
DEBBIEREYNOLDSFilms

SINGIN' IN THE RAIN
(1952) MGM

A puddle-splashing musical and spoof of early talkies. Reynolds plays an aspiring actress who falls for an established star (Gene Kelly) and helps him deal with a banshee-voiced leading lady (Jean Hagen). Newcomer Reynolds holds her ground on the dance floor with super talents Gene Kelly and Donald O'Connor.

THE TENDER TRAP
(1955) MGM

A Broadway comedy success transferred to the screen, with Reynolds as a marriage-minded actress who snags a playboy agent (Frank Sinatra) by insisting that he stop seeing other women.

THE CATERED AFFAIR
(1956) MGM

A slice-of-life comedy-drama about a Bronx housewife (Bette Davis) who insists upon a lavish wedding for her daughter (Reynolds) even if it drives the family to bankruptcy. Ernest Borgnine is the beleaguered dad in this adaptation of a TV play by Paddy Chayefsky.

TAMMY AND THE BACHELOR
(1957) Universal

Reynolds as a backwoods Mississippi gal who nurses Southern gent Leslie Nielsen back to health after a plane crash and wins over the kinfolk at his plantation. The Ray Evans–Jay Livingston song "Tammy" was nominated for an Oscar and became a hit for Debbie.

THE UNSINKABLE MOLLY BROWN
(1964) MGM

The role for which Reynolds snagged her only Oscar nomination, a tour-de-force performance as a would-be socialite from Denver who became a real-life heroine during the sinking of the *Titanic*. As Molly Brown, Reynolds tears into a Meredith Willson score that includes "I Ain't Down Yet."

SINGIN' IN THE RAIN, 1952

STYLENOTES

Early in her career, Reynolds had to supply her own clothes for movie premieres and studio photo ops. Given her limited wardrobe, MGM designers Helen Rose, Edith Head, and Walter Plunkett would sketch out designs for the young actress, and her mother would make the gowns for her at home.

Athletic Debbie satisfied her early career dream of becoming a gym teacher by making an exercise video, *Do It Debbie's Way* (1983).

CIRCA 1951

behindthe**scenes**

GETTING THE FEMALE LEAD IN *SINGIN' IN THE RAIN* WAS THRILLING FOR DEBBIE, BUT DANCE REHEARSALS PROVED TO BE A NIGHTMARE. WITH JUST THREE MONTHS TO GET HER TO THE LEVEL OF COSTARS GENE KELLY AND DONALD O'CONNOR, MGM ASSIGNED HER THREE TEACHERS AND PRESCRIBED ALL-DAY DANCE SESSIONS. KELLY WAS SO BRUTALLY CRITICAL OF THE TERRIFIED NINETEEN-YEAR-OLD THAT DEBBIE WOULD LATER SAY, "*SINGIN' IN THE RAIN* AND CHILDBIRTH WERE THE HARDEST THINGS I EVER HAD TO DO IN MY LIFE." WHILE SHOOTING THE "GOOD MORNING" NUMBER, HE WORKED HER SO HARD THAT HER FEET BLED.

ONE OF THE BIGGEST HOLLYWOOD SCANDALS OF ALL TIME WAS EDDIE FISHER'S AFFAIR WITH THE VERY RECENTLY WIDOWED ELIZABETH TAYLOR. TAYLOR AND HER HUSBAND MICHAEL TODD HAD BEEN CLOSE FRIENDS WITH EDDIE AND DEBBIE FISHER. SHORTLY AFTER TODD DIED IN A PLANE CRASH, FISHER AND TAYLOR BEGAN A RELATIONSHIP THAT HORRIFIED THE PUBLIC. THE CLOUD OF SCANDAL EVENTUALLY LIFTED, ALTHOUGH FISHER'S CAREER NEVER FULLY RECOVERED. IN LATER YEARS, DEBBIE SPOKE OF THE SITUATION PHILOSOPHICALLY, ACKNOWLEDGING THAT LIFE WITH FISHER WAS NO PICNIC, EVEN SAYING, "LIZ DID ME A FAVOR." THE TWO WOMEN HAVE LONG SINCE BURIED THE HATCHET.

IN 1957, DEBBIE DEMONSTRATED HER POPULARITY BY LANDING A TOP TEN HIT WITH THE TITLE SONG "TAMMY" FROM HER UNIVERSAL ROMANCE *TAMMY AND THE BACHELOR*.

AMONG DEBBIE'S MOST PROMINENT RECENT ASSIGNMENTS IS A RECURRING ROLE AS GRACE'S LARGER-THAN-LIFE MOTHER ON THE HIT TELEVISION COMEDY *WILL & GRACE*. IN ONE EPISODE SHE ENTERED SINGING "GOOD MORNING," ONE OF HER NUMBERS FROM *SINGIN' IN THE RAIN*.

She may be best remembered dancing in the arms of longtime partner Fred Astaire—but she was also stellar in the romantic comedies and dramatic roles she embraced.

GINGER
ROGERS

Born
Virginia Katherine McMath
July 16, 1911
Independence, Missouri

Died
April 25, 1995
Rancho Mirage, California,
of congestive heart failure

Star Sign
Cancer

Height
5'4½"

Husbands
Singer Jack Culpepper
(1929–31, divorced)

Actor Lew Ayres
(1934–41, divorced)

Marine Jack Briggs
(1943–49, divorced)

Actor Jacques Bergerac
(1953–57, divorced)

Actor William Marshall
(1961–69, divorced)

Ginger Rogers was a young teen when her prize-winning rendition of the Charleston put her on the vaudeville circuit. In just a few years, nineteen-year-old Ginger found herself a Broadway star in *Girl Crazy*, earning $1,000 a week. Audiences loved her combination of all-American good looks and wisecracks delivered with a grin; she was the modern young woman you could still take home to mother. Ginger caught the eye of Paramount, whose executives offered her a seven-year contract. But making movies by day and lighting up Broadway by night was so exhausting that even with her indefatigable nature she couldn't keep it up forever. Her mother, Lela, adeptly got Ginger out of her Paramount contract, ostensibly for health reasons, but also to get her to a studio where the competition wasn't quite so overwhelming. Ginger made the most of her small part in the hit *42nd Street* (1933), yet it was her turn at RKO with Fred Astaire in *Flying Down to Rio* (1933) that put audiences in raptures, injecting an amusing musical with moments of sheer artistry. There were frequent rumors that their chemistry, so dynamic on screen, was not as positive off screen. Astaire is said to have disliked the constant presence of Rogers's mother, and Ginger bristled at the disparity between their salaries, at times striking and delaying production to get closer to Astaire's price. Yet Rogers always remained publicly supportive of her partner, saying in her biography, "We had fun, and it shows." Together Ginger and Fred made a total of ten movies highlighted by elegant, seemingly effortless dance numbers. Determined to prove that she could be a dramatic actress as well, she added impressive nuance to her role opposite Katharine Hepburn in *Stage Door* (1937). Finally, in 1940, Ginger delivered her ultimate dramatic performance in *Kitty Foyle* (1940), the tale of a working-class girl choosing between two men and two paths in life. She also proved to be skilled at screwball comedy in films like *Tom, Dick and Harry* (1941) and *The Major and the Minor* (1942). Ginger continued to star in films into the 1950s. Then she returned to Broadway to take over the lead in *Hello, Dolly!* which she also performed in Vietnam for the USO. Even in her seventies, she conquered new frontiers, making her directing debut with a revival of the musical *Babes in Arms*.

Essential
GINGERROGERSFilms

TOP HAT
(1935) RKO
Number four of the ten musicals Rogers made with Fred Astaire, directed by Mark Sandrich and featuring an Irving Berlin score that includes "Cheek to Cheek" and the title song. The plot is one of those mistaken-identity affairs, set in London and Venice, with Rogers mistaking Astaire for a married man.

SWING TIME
(1936) RKO
Number six in the Astaire-Rogers series, directed by versatile George Stevens and sporting a Jerome Kern–Dorothy Fields score that includes "A Fine Romance" and the Oscar-winning "The Way You Look Tonight."

STAGE DOOR
(1937) RKO
The Edna Ferber–George S. Kaufman comedy-drama, turned into a showcase for RKO's two top actresses, Rogers and Katharine Hepburn, plus Lucille Ball, Eve Arden, and Ann Miller. In this account of a boardinghouse filled with struggling New York actresses, Rogers is a streetwise performer who clashes with blue-blood Hepburn.

KITTY FOYLE
(1940) RKO
Rogers received a Best Actress Oscar for her role in Christopher Morley's story of a working-class Philadelphia woman torn between two loves—a millionaire (Dennis Morgan) and a poor but idealistic doctor (James Craig).

THE MAJOR AND THE MINOR
(1942) Paramount
Billy Wilder's Hollywood debut as a director, a comedy in which Rogers plays a New York woman who poses as an eleven-year-old to get a half-price train fare. When she meets up with Major Philip Kirby (Ray Milland), he becomes the protector of the "minor" (Rogers), finding his life in the process.

KITTY FOYLE, 1940

STYLENOTES

Ginger Rogers told *Look* magazine that she was happiest in a "shorts-and-bra outfit." She even designed her own angora bra, which she deemed "wonderful to wear while relaxing in the sun. It doesn't mark my skin."

Ginger adored her costumes. Putting on one of her dancing gowns made her instantly want to "turn and whirl in it. Dresses always affected me that way. I can never emphasize enough how important clothing was to me."

Fred Astaire hated Ginger's celebrated beaded and feathered on-screen dresses: the whirling beads were so heavy they left him black and blue when they hit him, and the feathers made him sneeze. He protested vehemently against the use of one of Ginger's all-time favorite costumes, the ice-blue ostrich-feather gown Bernard Newman created in 1935 for *Top Hat*'s "Cheek to Cheek" number. During film rehearsals, Rogers's dress shed feathers all over partner Astaire's suit, and he nicknamed her "Feathers" after the incident.

behindthescenes

GINGER ROGERS FIRST MET FRED ASTAIRE WHEN THEY WERE BOTH APPEARING ON BROADWAY, AND HE CAME IN TO HELP STAGE SOME OF THE DANCE NUMBERS IN *GIRL CRAZY*. THE STORY GOES THAT THEIR FIRST DATE CONCLUDED WITH A PASSIONATE KISS IN A TAXICAB BUT THAT THINGS DIDN'T PROGRESS FROM THERE.

UNLIKE MANY STARS WHO DECRIED THE ANTI-COMMUNIST WITCH HUNTS OR WERE BLACKLISTED THEMSELVES, CONSERVATIVE GINGER WAS A STAUNCH DEFENDER OF THE GOVERNMENT'S ATTEMPTS TO RID HOLLYWOOD OF SUBVERSIVE ELEMENTS. HER MOTHER, LELA, WAS ONE OF THE ORIGINAL FRIENDLY WITNESSES TESTIFYING TO CONGRESS ABOUT ALLEGED COMMUNIST INFILTRATION OF THE INDUSTRY. ONE "SUBVERSIVE" LINE GINGER REFUSED TO READ WAS FROM THE HOME-FRONT DRAMA *TENDER COMRADE* (1943): "SHARE AND SHARE ALIKE. THAT'S THE AMERICAN WAY."

GINGER INSPIRED A POPULAR FEMINIST MOTTO, SEEN IN RECENT YEARS ON EVERY-THING FROM BUMPER STICKERS TO T-SHIRTS: "GINGER ROGERS DID EVERYTHING FRED ASTAIRE DID—BUT BACKWARDS AND IN HIGH HEELS."

Smart and quick-witted, she set the standard for a new office archetype: the busy, never ruffled, and always-on-top-of-it modern working woman.

ROSALIND
RUSSELL

The clever schemes created by Rosalind Russell's characters were mirrored in her real-life professional savvy. From convincing her mother to let her attend the American Academy of Dramatic Arts (ostensibly to learn to teach acting) to finagling her way out of a Universal contract when MGM offered more money, Russell used her moxie to make up for her lack of drop-dead glamour (although some would argue that the young Rosalind—with her wide-set brown eyes, lustrous black hair, and milky complexion—hardly fell short in the looks department). Her years at MGM were spent in the shadow of Myrna Loy; studio executives used Russell as a threat whenever Loy wanted more money or turned down a role. Her early roles were more supporting than showstopping, but as cold, perfectionist housewife Harriet Craig in *Craig's Wife* (1936) she surprised critics and audiences with the depth of her performance. Although she was one of the last stars personally groomed by MGM production chief Irving Thalberg, it took Russell a while to hit her stride. Finally, in 1939, her true gifts shone forth in her comic performance as the oily, venomous Park Avenue snake Sylvia Fowler in *The Women*. Russell's comedic genius was at its peak a year later when she played Hildy Johnson, the wisecracking, sharp, and sexy reporter in *His Girl Friday*. The lightning-swift dialogue and carnival ride of a plot suited Russell to a tee and brought her a horde of fans. Her confidence rose with these twin successes, and she began to move into roles that put her on an equal footing with her male costars. Russell's sassy career gals were a movie staple, and she received her first of four Oscar nominations for her portrayal of the naive yet tough aspiring writer in *My Sister Eileen* (1942). When Hollywood production declined in the 1950s, Russell turned to Broadway for two of her biggest hits, *Wonderful Town* and *Auntie Mame*. She brought the latter to the screen in 1958. She finished her career in some of the best roles for older actresses available, including the ultimate stage mother in *Gypsy* (1962) and the mother superior in *The Trouble with Angels* (1966).

Born
Rosalind Russell
June 4, 1907
Waterbury, Connecticut

Died
November 28, 1976
Los Angeles, California,
of breast cancer

Star Sign
Gemini

Height
5'7"

Husband and Child
Stage and movie producer
Fred Brisson
(1941–76, her death)
son, Lance

Essential
ROSALINDRUSSELLFilms

ACADEMY AWARDS

Nominated for Best Actress
My Sister Eileen
Sister Kenny
Mourning Becomes Electra
Auntie Mame

**Jean Hersholt
Humanitarian Award in 1973**

NIGHT MUST FALL

(1937) MGM
In this film version of the Emlyn Williams stage shocker, a refined young Englishwoman (Rosalind Russell) remains attracted to a charming bellboy even after she realizes he's probably a murderer. Robert Montgomery plays the bellboy who employs a famous prop—a hatbox that may contain a severed head.

THE WOMEN

(1939) MGM
Director George Cukor's all-female comedy, based on the Clare Boothe Luce play, with Russell in a cast that includes Norma Shearer, Joan Crawford, Joan Fontaine, and Paulette Goddard. Russell is billed third, but as the gossipy Sylvia Fowler she steals all her scenes.

HIS GIRL FRIDAY

(1940) Columbia
The second film version of the Ben Hecht–Charles MacArthur play *The Front Page,* and the first adaptation to change the character of relentless reporter Hildy Johnson from male to female. A fast-talking Russell takes on the role under the direction of Howard Hawks, lending sexual spice to Hildy's confrontations with newspaper editor Cary Grant.

AUNTIE MAME

(1958) Warner Bros.
The film version of the Patrick Dennis novel, a tale of a larger-than-life socialite who takes on the responsibility of raising her orphaned nephew. Russell costarred with Forrest Tucker and Peggy Cass and received an Oscar nomination for her role.

GYPSY

(1962) Warner Bros.
Film version of the Jule Styne Stephen Sondheim stage musical based on the memoirs of stripper Gypsy Rose Lee. Russell, with some vocal help from Lisa Kirk, stepped into Ethel Merman's role as the ferocious stage mother of Gypsy (Natalie Wood).

HIS GIRL FRIDAY, 1940

STYLE NOTES

THE WOMEN, 1939

The daughter of a fashion editor, Rosalind Russell had innate style and was frequently acknowledged as one of America's best-dressed women. For a brief period, she marketed a clothing line of hats, sweaters, and jewelry.

Despite her careful devotion to appearance, Rosalind once said, "Taking joy in life is a woman's best cosmetic."

Rosalind played such a lengthy string of career gals that she could eventually predict exactly what she would get for her wardrobe. "I could order the clothes for my pictures in my sleep. I'd say . . . 'Make me a plaid suit, a striped suit, a grey flannel, and a negligee for the scene in the bedroom when I cry.'"

behind the scenes

ROSALIND RUSSELL HAD TROUBLE GETTING CAST IN HER BREAKTHROUGH ROLE IN *THE WOMEN*. SHE THOUGHT SHE'D BE PERFECT FOR THE GOSSIPY TROUBLEMAKER SYLVIA, AND SHE DEMANDED NOTICE FROM PRODUCER HUNT STROMBERG, SAYING, "WHY HAVEN'T YOU TESTED ME?" TO HER ASTONISHMENT, HE TOLD HER SHE WAS TOO BEAUTIFUL. "MY GOD," ROSALIND RECALLED RESPONDING, "BRING YOUR SECRETARY IN HERE. I'D LIKE YOU TO SAY THAT AGAIN IN FRONT OF A WITNESS."

WHEN ROSALIND COULDN'T GET ABOVE-THE-TITLE BILLING FOR *THE WOMEN* (POWERFUL STAR NORMA SHEARER HAD VETOED THE IDEA), SHE SUDDENLY "TOOK ILL." SHE GAMBLED ON BEING IRREPLACEABLE, AND SHE WON; SHEARER RELENTED SHORTLY AFTER ROSALIND STARTED HER SICK STRIKE. AT THE WRAP PARTY, A DIRECTOR SUGGESTED THAT IF SHE WANTED MORE CLOSE-UPS IN THE PICTURE, "YOU'D BETTER DANCE WITH NORMA SHEARER!" SO ROSALIND AND NORMA TOOK A SPIN AROUND THE FLOOR.

LIFE MAGAZINE HAD A HABIT OF SHOOTING PICTURES OF ROSALIND THAT THEY NEVER USED. THE THIRD TIME THEY SCHEDULED A PHOTO SHOOT, SHE SIMPLY STOOD IN HER DRIVEWAY IN A PAIR OF SLACKS, SAYING, "SNAP IT AND GO, BECAUSE YOU'RE NOT GOING TO USE IT ANYWAY." THAT WAS THE SHOT THEY RAN ON THE SEPTEMBER 3, 1939, COVER. IT WAS A DECISION THEY WOULD REGRET, BUT NOT BECAUSE OF ROSALIND'S CASUAL APPEARANCE. THAT WAS THE WEEK HITLER INVADED POLAND.

ONE OF THE BIGGEST OSCAR UPSETS EVER INVOLVED ROSALIND, HER GOOD FRIEND LORETTA YOUNG, AND THE 1947 BEST ACTRESS AWARD. ROSALIND WAS CONSIDERED SUCH A SHOO-IN FOR HER WORK IN *MOURNING BECOMES ELECTRA* THAT PRESENTER FREDRIC MARCH ACTUALLY STARTED TO SAY "ROZ," AND RUSSELL STOOD UP, BEFORE HE REALIZED HE HAD THE WRONG NAME. LORETTA YOUNG WAS SO ASTONISHED THAT SHE MADE MARCH SHOW HER THE CARD. IN CLASSIC GOOD-SPORT FASHION, ROSALIND CONGRATULATED THE WINNER AND POSED FOR PICTURES WITH YOUNG FOLLOWING THE CEREMONY. IRONICALLY, ROSALIND HAD TURNED DOWN THE ROLE IN *THE FARMER'S DAUGHTER* THAT WON YOUNG HER ONLY OSCAR.

A determined woman who willed herself to be beautiful, she honed her sense of style as seriously as she did her acting and took enormous chances to play modern, sexually charged women.

NORMA
SHEARER

Norma Shearer came to New York with her mother and sister determined to become an entertainer. She quickly got work as a film extra, but both director D. W. Griffith and Broadway producer Florenz Ziegfeld let her know that her looks fell short of starlet status. Undeterred, Norma worked hard until the parts grew bigger, and an audience was found for her luminous good looks and intelligent way of connecting with her roles. Norma's modern sensibility and upfront charm was perfect for the films Hollywood made before censorship. She was ambitious both professionally and personally and set her cap for MGM production head Irving Thalberg, waiting for his interest in her to grow, and then becoming the perfect, caring wife for the smart yet fragile executive. In *The Divorcée* (1931), Norma displayed a hitherto unsuspected sex appeal while playing an adulteress and loose woman with sympathy and depth; she took a calculated risk, and it made her a bigger star than ever. Thus began a series of roles that allowed Norma to display both sensuality and assertiveness. She was sexually charged without quite being promiscuous, walking a careful line that resonated with the increasingly liberated women of the era. When she let Clark Gable treat her like a tramp in *A Free Soul* (1931), it made him a star and raised her status even further. Because of her husband's health problems, Norma worked less in the late 1930s, yet she proved she was far more than the boss's wife when she continued to make successful films like *The Women* (1939) after Thalberg's death. The film career of this wealthy, still widely sought-after actress ended in 1942, when she left Hollywood for a ski instructor almost twenty years her junior.

Born
Edna Norma Shearer
August 10, 1900
Montreal, Canada

Died
June 10, 1983
Woodland Hills, California,
of pneumonia

Star Sign
Leo

Height
5'1"

Husbands and Children
Producer Irving Thalberg
(1927–36, his death)
two children,
Irving Jr. and Katherine

Ski instructor Martin Arouge
(1942–83, her death)

Essential
NORMASHEARERFilms

THEIR OWN DESIRE
(1929) MGM

Early talkie melodrama with Shearer as a young socialite who resents her father's (Lewis Stone) desertion of her mother (Belle Bennett) for another woman (Helene Millard). Shearer falls for handsome Robert Montgomery, only to discover that he is Millard's son.

THE DIVORCÉE
(1930) MGM

Shearer, in her Oscar-winning role, reunited with Robert Montgomery in another drama of marital entanglements. This time Shearer marries Chester Morris and, upon discovering him to be unfaithful, has her own adulterous affair with his best friend (Montgomery).

SMILIN' THROUGH
(1932) MGM

The much-filmed Jane Murfin–Jane Cowl play, with Shearer and Fredric March in the double roles of tragic lovers and their look-alike younger relatives who also fall in love. Leslie Howard figures in the story, as the man who was engaged to Shearer before her death at the hands of her jilted suitor (March).

MARIE ANTOINETTE
(1938) MGM

The turbulent career of the French queen as played by Shearer, with Robert Morley as her husband, King Louis XVI, and John Barrymore in the role of his father, Louis XV. Amid lavish sets, W. S. Van Dyke directed an impressive cast, including Tyrone Power as the handsome count with whom Marie has an affair.

THE WOMEN
(1939) MGM

Clare Boothe Luce comedy, with Shearer heading an all-female cast under the direction of George Cukor. She plays the wronged wife who learns to sharpen her claws (and paint them "jungle red") in order to compete with a husband-stealing shopgirl (Joan Crawford).

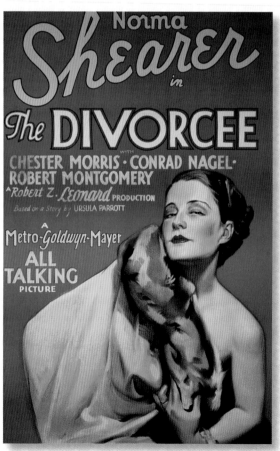

THE DIVORCÉE, 1930

TYLENOTES

Norma was meticulous about her appearance. Early in her career, she spent money she could barely afford on the services of an eye doctor, who trained her to strengthen a weak eye. She swam everyday, had massages to firm her figure, and dieted religiously. She experimented with makeup until she decided on a light tone that would illuminate her face on screen.

Although not cast as a sex symbol, Norma created a sensation when she wore a clinging bias-cut dress without undergarments in *Let Us Be Gay* (1930). The response was so huge that Norma instructed designer Adrian to make similar dresses for her next group of pictures. He dubbed the sexy dresses "Norma's nightgowns."

Norma used a variety of styles to convey her twin images of movie star and wife of a Hollywood mogul. She dazzled at premieres with gorgeous gowns, furs, and jewels. Yet for casual publicity shots with Thalberg, she dressed like an understated aristocrat, in sailor pants, sweaters, and scarves or berets.

behind the scenes

NORMA AND THALBERG WERE THE TOAST OF HOLLYWOOD, ENTERTAINING OFTEN AT THEIR BEACHSIDE HOME. DINNER PARTIES WERE LAVISH AFFAIRS. F. SCOTT FITZGERALD, A FREQUENT VISITOR TO THE THALBERG HOME, ADORED NORMA. HE BASED ONE OF HIS MOST FAMOUS STORIES, "CRAZY SUNDAY," ON A PARTY AT HER HOUSE.

NORMA WAS DYING TO STAR IN MGM'S RACY FILM *THE DIVORCÉE* (1930), BUT HUSBAND AND BOSS IRVING THALBERG DIDN'T THINK SHE WAS GLAMOROUS ENOUGH FOR THE PART. STILL DETERMINED, SHE COMMISSIONED PHOTOGRAPHER GEORGE HURRELL TO TAKE SOME SEXY SHOTS OF HER LOUNGING IN EXQUISITE GOWNS WITH A COME-HITHER GAZE. THALBERG WAS ASTOUNDED AT THE TRANSFORMATION, AND NORMA GOT THE ROLE.

EVEN AFTER HER RETIREMENT, NORMA MAINTAINED HER INTEREST IN THE FILM INDUSTRY. WHILE STAYING AT A SKI LODGE, SHE NOTICED A PHOTO OF THE RECEP-TIONIST'S DAUGHTER AND RECOMMENDED HER TO MGM—THAT GIRL BECAME THE STAR KNOWN AS JANET LEIGH. SHE ALSO DISCOVERED A HANDSOME YOUNG BUSINESSMAN BESIDE A SWIMMING POOL—NOW ACTOR-PRODUCER ROBERT EVANS.

CIRCA 1930

Thanks to her breezy sex appeal, pinup curves, and love of a good time, she was christened "the Oomph Girl," a playful name for an actress with a prolific career.

ANN SHERIDAN

Born
Clara Lou Sheridan
February 21, 1915
Denton, Texas

Died
January 21, 1967
Los Angeles, California,
of esophagus and
liver cancer

Star Sign
Pisces

Height
5'5"

Husbands
Actor Edward Norris
(1936–39, divorced)

Actor George Brent
(1942–43, divorced)

Actor Scott McKay
(1966–67, her death)

Born Clara Lou Sheridan of Denton, Texas, Ann Sheridan grew up on a ranch, and that tough, practical way of life shaped both her character and her straightforward acting style. Practically forced into the pictures when her sister sent her photo in to a beauty contest, Ann left college and her plans for teaching to sign a contract with Paramount. The stiff competition there disillusioned the young actress, but a change of agents led to a change of studios, and Ann found a solid home at Warner Bros., where she remained for over a decade. Starting in B movies, she worked her way to stardom using her ability to play both wisecracking dames and sophisticated ladies. Her big break came when she portrayed a girl drawn to the flashy life promised by ex-con James Cagney in *Angels with Dirty Faces* (1938). The studio started pushing her as "the Oomph Girl," capitalizing on her breezy sex appeal in the adventure comedy *Torrid Zone* (1940). They even rewrote James Cagney's final line to reflect her image: "You and your twenty-four-carat oomph!" Along with her on-screen "oomph," Sheridan was also respected off screen as a good sport and team player, even though the studio made her take a backseat to dramatic divas like Bette Davis. But she showed them all when, as a catty, glamorous stage star, she stole *The Man Who Came to Dinner* (1941) right out from under Davis's nose. She proved herself again when she fought for and won the role of Ronald Reagan's tough but sweet small-town love in *Kings Row* (1942). It would be her most acclaimed performance and could have led to better things had she not made the blunder of her career—turning down the title role in *Mildred Pierce* (1945) because she didn't want to play a woman with a grown daughter. Nevertheless, Ann's popularity held through the 1940s, largely thanks to her tireless work for the war effort and her popularity as a pinup girl. She left Warner Bros. in the late 1940s, a tough time for many Hollywood players. Despite a hit opposite Cary Grant in *I Was a Male War Bride* (1949), she found good roles hard to come by, and so she turned to stage work and even daytime soaps (*Another World* in 1965). She had bounced back with the lead role in the Western sitcom *Pistols and Petticoats* (1966) when she learned she had terminal cancer.

Essential
ANN SHERIDAN Films

THE MAN WHO CAME TO DINNER
(1941) Warner Bros.
The screen version of the George S. Kaufman–Moss Hart stage comedy about an irascible radio commentator (Monty Woolley) who overstays his welcome in a Midwestern home. In a cast that includes everyone from Bette Davis to Jimmy Durante, Sheridan shines as a chic Broadway star based on Gertrude Lawrence.

KINGS ROW
(1942) Warner Bros.
Sheridan plays Randy, the good-hearted girl devoted to a young man whose legs are amputated (Ronald Reagan, in his most celebrated role) in this drama of life in a Midwestern town full of shocking secrets.

SHINE ON, HARVEST MOON
(1944) Warner Bros.
This biographical musical stars Dennis Morgan and a radiant Sheridan as turn-of-the-century entertainers Jack Norworth and Nora Bayes. Featured in the film are several Norworth songs, including his famous title track.

NORA PRENTISS
(1947) Warner Bros.
Sheridan was never sexier than when she played a sultry nightclub singer whose love drives a doctor to fake his own death in this intriguing film noir.

I WAS A MALE WAR BRIDE
(1949) 20th Century-Fox
A comedy of errors featuring Sheridan as the WAC wife of French Army officer Cary Grant—who dresses in drag in order to accompany her back to the States. Hilarious complications ensue, with Sheridan's dry comedy style providing perfect counterpoint to Grant's antics.

NORA PRENTISS, 1947

STYLENOTES

Ann's earliest movie parts were literally parts—the studio used parts of her body to double for those of other actresses: "I used to go to Grauman's Chinese or Pantages and sit there waiting to see my faceless body on the screen."

Ann had a large gap between her front teeth. She always wore a porcelain cap when having her picture taken.

Ann credits her weight loss at Paramount to constricting corsets; she laced them so tight she could barely breathe, let alone eat.

Ann was known to tell her makeup artist to "come over and put some oomph on me."

ANGELS WITH DIRTY FACES, 1938

behindthescenes

A MODELING CONTEST BROUGHT ANN TO HOLLYWOOD, AFTER THE PHOTOS OF FINALISTS WERE TOSSED IN THE AIR AND HERS REPEATEDLY LANDED RIGHT-SIDE UP. UPON LEARNING THE REASON FOR HER BIG BREAK, ANN RESPONDED, "YES, YOU S.O.B., AND I'VE BEEN ON MY BACK EVER SINCE."

WARNER BROS. WAS EAGER TO PORTRAY ANN AS A "GIRL ABOUT TOWN," SO HER CONTRACT DEMANDED THAT SHE HIT THE NIGHTCLUBS AT LEAST THREE TIMES A WEEK.

ACCORDING TO AN ARTICLE IN THE NEWARK EVENING NEWS, ANN KEPT BUSY DURING HER 1941 STRIKE FROM WARNER BROS. BY REBUILDING ABANDONED CARS AT A FRIEND'S GARAGE.

IN 1939, A FRATERNITY BET INSPIRED A UCLA STUDENT TO HANDCUFF HIMSELF TO ANN DURING A MOVIE PREVIEW AND THEN SWALLOW THE KEY. A LOCKSMITH HAD TO BE SUMMONED TO THE THEATER.

EDGE OF DARKNESS, 1943

She talked tough, worked hard, and was a little rough around the edges, but her ability to imbue a part with unflinching emotional commitment made her a star.

BARBARA
STANWYCK

Charles Dickens might have written the story of Barbara Stanwyck's childhood, which was, by her own admission, "completely awful." Born into poverty, she lost her mother at age two and was orphaned at four when her father abandoned his children to go off to sea. She went on the stage, first as a dancer, and then as an actress, to support herself and her siblings. Marriage at twenty to vaudeville star Frank Fay brought Barbara to a Hollywood that was slow to warm up to her. The turning point came after a screen test was brought to the attention of director Frank Capra. His *Ladies of Leisure* (1930) revealed to the world a new star, an actress who, as Capra himself said "doesn't act a scene—she lives it." After a brief stint at Warner Bros., Barbara never signed another long-term studio contract, preferring to work as a free agent. Barbara's star rose even higher when she played the ultimate in self-sacrificing motherhood, the title character in *Stella Dallas* (1937). Next she proved herself adept at comedy in a pair of 1941 films, director Preston Sturges's *The Lady Eve*, which also showed her in her first really glamorous on-screen wardrobe, and director Howard Hawks's *Ball of Fire* (1941). On a dare from writer-director Billy Wilder, she created one of the most memorable femmes fatales in film history, the seductive murderess in *Double Indemnity* (1944). Adding to her display of versatility were several Westerns, starting with Cecil B. DeMille's *Union Pacific* (1939), in which she often did her own stunts. Reeling from a painful divorce from second husband Robert Taylor, Stanwyck buried herself in work, including low-budget Westerns and television programs. It was on television that she scored one of her most memorable roles, tough matriarch Victoria Barkley in the Western series *The Big Valley* (1965–69). When she lost out on the chance to costar with Henry Fonda in *On Golden Pond* (1980), Barbara threw herself into another television part, the sex-starved land baron in *The Thorn Birds* (1983), a role that brought her an Emmy

Born
Ruby Stevens
July 16, 1907
Brooklyn, New York

Died
January 20, 1990
Santa Monica, California,
of congestive heart failure

Star Sign
Cancer

Height
5'5"

Husbands and Child
Entertainer Frank Fay
(1928–36, divorced)
adopted son, Dion

Robert Taylor
(1939–51, divorced)

Essential
BARBARASTANWYCKFilms

STELLA DALLAS

(1937) United Artists
The archetypal tearjerker, with Stanwyck as the self-sacrificing mother Stella Dallas, a performance that earned her the first of four Oscar nominations. King Vidor directs, and Anne Shirley plays the daughter Stella gives up because her own vulgarity stands in the way of the girl's social acceptance.

THE LADY EVE

(1941) Paramount
The sparkling Preston Sturges sexual satire, with Stanwyck as a glamorous cardshard who falls for wealthy Henry Fonda and then extracts an amusing revenge when he learns of her profession and dumps her. Posing as the British Lady Eve, she convinces the gullible millionaire that she's a different dame altogether.

BALL OF FIRE

(1941) RKO
Stanwyck and Gary Cooper in the second of three teamings, in director Howard Hawks's comedy about a nightclub performer who assists a group of encyclopedia-writing professors in learning about slang. Drawing on her showgirl roots, Stanwyck plays Sugarpuss O'Shea to Cooper's bedazzled Professor Potts.

DOUBLE INDEMNITY

(1944) Paramount
Stanwyck set the standard for the femme fatale in director Billy Wilder's film noir version of the James M. Cain story. Slinky in blonde wig and ankle bracelet, Oscar-nominated Stanwyck seduces insurance agent Fred MacMurray into murdering her husband.

SORRY, WRONG NUMBER

(1948) Paramount
The suspenseful Lucille Fletcher radio play, expanded into a film vehicle for Stanwyck as the neurotic wife who overhears her own murder being plotted on the telephone. Stanwyck, once more nominated for an Oscar, realizes too late that she has driven her weak-willed husband (Burt Lancaster) over the brink.

DOUBLE INDEMNITY, 1944

STYLENOTES

Baby Face (1933) was a rare early opportunity for Barbara to reveal the glamour girl within, and Warner Bros. pulled out all the stops: an eye-catching wardrobe by Orry-Kelly featuring furs, jewels, and ruffles, set off by a collection of blonde wigs in all the latest styles.

Barbara was known for her powerful, confident stride. Rumor has it that she acquired "the Stanwyck walk" by going to the zoo and observing the panthers.

Barbara's marriage to gorgeous actor Robert Taylor didn't change her unadorned style. Yet when they attended a premiere and she was accidentally hustled away with the casually dressed, screaming fans, she decided it was time to spruce up her look.

behindthescenes

BARBARA'S NO-NONSENSE ATTITUDE TOWARD HER PROFESSION IS REFLECTED IN THIS CLASSIC QUOTE: "CAREER IS TOO POMPOUS A WORD. IT WAS A JOB, AND I HAVE ALWAYS FELT PRIVILEGED TO BE PAID FOR WHAT I LOVE DOING."

DURING THE FILMING OF *FORTY GUNS*, A STUNTMAN REFUSED TO BE DRAGGED BY A HORSE, CLAIMING THAT IT WAS TOO DANGEROUS. DESPITE THE FACT THAT SHE WAS NEARING FIFTY, TOUGH-AS-NAILS BARBARA AGREED TO DO THE STUNT. THREE TAKES AND SOME PRETTY SERIOUS BRUISES LATER, THEY HAD THE SHOT.

FRANK CAPRA LOVED HOW EMOTIVE BARBARA WAS, BUT HE FOUND THAT SHE GAVE EVERYTHING SHE HAD ON THE FIRST TAKE. FOR THIS REASON, HE TOOK TO REHEARSING THE OTHER ACTORS WITHOUT HER, NOT BRINGING BARBARA IN UNTIL THE CAMERAS WERE READY TO ROLL. ACCORDING TO CAPRA, ONE TAKE WAS ENOUGH—SHE NEVER MISSED A LINE.

A glamorous and iconic silent star, forever remembered for her legendary, gutsy comeback in a film made thirty years after her heyday, *Sunset Blvd.*

GLORIA
SWANSON

Born
Gloria Josephine May Swenson
March 27, 1898
Chicago, Illinois

Died
April 4, 1983
New York, New York,
of natural causes

Star Sign
Aries

Height
4'11 ½"

Husbands and Children
Actor Wallace Beery
(1916–19, divorced)

President of
Equity Pictures
Herbert K. Somborn
(1919–22, divorced)
daughter, Gloria
adopted son, Joseph

Marquis Henri de la
Falaise de la Coudraye
(1925–31, divorced)

Actor and sportsman
Michael Farmer
(1931–34, divorced)
daughter, Michelle

Retired businessman
George W. Davey
(1945–46, divorced)

Author William Dufty
(1976–83, her death)

Gloria Swanson didn't start out intending to be an actress. She dreamed of singing, but when an aunt took her to visit the Essanay Studios in 1913, she was captivated, particularly when she was offered a job as an extra. She did extra work until she caught the eye of comedy legend Mack Sennett, who starred her in a series of short films. But the young Gloria felt stifled in comedy and left Sennett in 1917 to work at Triangle Studios. Her serious dramas there garnered enough attention for director Cecil B. DeMille to sign her. Their first picture together, *Don't Change Your Husband* (1919), typed Gloria as a society woman bravely negotiating the new immoral order of the Jazz Age. With her DeMille films, Gloria became a fashion icon in movies that equated high fashion with superior living. By 1920, she was a household name and a huge box office draw. The studio, Famous Players–Lasky (which later became Paramount Pictures), separated Swanson and DeMille in an attempt to double their box office returns, and it worked. By 1926, she was making $6,500 a week (over $3.5 million a year by today's standards). Then she turned down the studio's offer of $1 million a year and left to form her own production company with Joseph Kennedy. Gloria continued to score hits, most notably with the daring *Sadie Thompson* (1928), but when she and Kennedy pulled the plug on director Erich Von Stroheim's lavish and decidedly kinky *Queen Kelly* (1928), they lost a bundle. After she made a successful transition to talking films in *The Trespasser* (1929), her lavish vehicles began to fall out of favor with Depression-era audiences. With the failure of the musical *Music in the Air* (1934), she left the screen. In 1949, writer-director Billy Wilder offered her the comeback role of all time, Norma Desmond in *Sunset Blvd.* (1950). Gloria received an Oscar nomination and almost universal praise, but her performance as the insane former actress typed her all over again. Producers expected her to be as tempestuous and disturbed as her character, and future film offers didn't materialize. Instead, Gloria did more stage work, including a popular run in the comedy *Butterflies Are Free*. She also created her own fashion line and traveled the world promoting health foods. Through it all, she remained the epitome of movie-star glamour.

Essential
GLORIA**SWANSON**Films

SADIE THOMPSON
(1928) United Artists
W. Somerset Maugham's famous heroine, brought to life by Oscar-nominated Swanson in a silent version of the play *Rain*. Thompson is the shady lady who prowls the South Seas happily seducing U.S. marines—until she runs afoul of a religious hypocrite (Lionel Barrymore) who claims he wants to save her soul but can't resist her body.

QUEEN KELLY
(1928) United Artists
Director Erich von Stroheim's final silent film, taken over by producer and star Swanson a third of the way through shooting because she disapproved of his extravagant methods and strange story ideas. Swanson plays a convent girl who is seduced by a German nobleman and then banished to East Africa, where she marries a manager of brothels (Tully Marshall).

THE TRESPASSER
(1929) United Artists
Swanson's first talking picture, a melodrama in which she plays a self-sacrificing secretary who marries into a wealthy family, only to have her marriage annulled after one night. Pregnant but too proud to say so, she turns to her former boss for help, leading people to gossip that she is his mistress.

FATHER TAKES A WIFE
(1941) RKO
A comedy marking Swanson's return to films after her "retirement" seven years earlier, In her only movie of the 1940s, she plays a famous actress who marries a shipping magnate (Adolphe Menjou), but both newlyweds soon become jealous of their spouse's younger companions.

SUNSET BLVD.
(1950) Paramount
Swanson's iconic depiction of silent-screen diva Norma Desmond, in director Billy Wilder's corrosive study of Hollywood morals. William Holden plays the young screenwriter who becomes her kept man, and Erich von Stroheim is her very odd butler.

SUNSET BLVD., 1950

STYLENOTES

SADIE THOMPSON, 1928

Gloria is said to be Hollywood's first serious fashion influence—no one before her had ever dressed in the same glamorous clothes both on screen and off. She was the first movie star required by contract to be fashionably dressed when out in public. At the height of her extravagance, Gloria's professional and personal clothing bill topped $100,000 a year, with $10,000 spent just for her elegant stockings.

When Gloria returned to Hollywood from France after shooting *Madame Sans-Gene* (1925), she brought with her the film's costumer, Rene Hubert—and thus she became one of the first Hollywood stars to hire a French couturier to do her films.

In 1950, Gloria signed with the Puritan Dress Company to create her own clothing line, Gowns by Gloria, producing high fashion at a lower cost. When Neiman Marcus honored her with a fashion award that same year, she personally designed three gowns for the affair.

behindthescenes

IN 1917, GLORIA WENT ON STRIKE TO GET MACK SENNETT TO RAISE HER SALARY. HE GOT HER TO RETURN TO WORK BY BUYING HER A $100 GREEN SUIT TRIMMED WITH SQUIRREL FUR.

IN THE DEMILLE FILM *MALE AND FEMALE* (1919), SWANSON LIES DOWN WITH A LION, WHICH PLACES A PAW ON HER BACK. WHEN A SHAKEN GLORIA DEMANDED THE NEXT DAY OFF TO RECOVER, DEMILLE PLACATED HER BY ALLOWING HER TO PICK ANYTHING SHE WANTED FROM A LARGE CACHE OF JEWELS. SHE SELECTED A GOLD MESH BAG AND IMMEDIATELY SAID SHE FELT MUCH BETTER.

IN THE SILENT ERA, STUDIOS USUALLY HAD MUSICIANS PLAY DURING FILMING TO PUT THE STARS IN THE RIGHT MOOD. THE SIZE OF THE MUSICAL ENSEMBLE USUALLY REFLECTED THE STAR'S STATURE. FOR SWANSON IN HER PRIME, PARAMOUNT HIRED A SEVENTY-PIECE ORCHESTRA.

THE *SUNSET BLVD.* SCENE IN WHICH NORMA WATCHES ONE OF HER OLD MOVIES HAS AN ADDED BENEFIT FOR HER FANS—IT FEATURES A SCENE FROM HER UNFINISHED EPIC, *QUEEN KELLY.*

Beginning with her screen debut at age ten, she has riveted audiences with her stunning beauty, violet eyes, and emotional depth; she is a legend for the ages—the quintessential movie star.

ELIZABETH
TAYLOR

Born
Elizabeth Rosemond Taylor
February 27, 1932
London, England

Height
5'4"

Star Sign
Pisces

Husbands and Children
Hotel heir
Conrad "Nicky" Hilton Jr.
(1950–51, divorced)

British actor Michael Wilding
(1952–57, divorced)
two sons,
Christopher and Michael Jr.

Entrepreneur Michael Todd
(1957–58, his death)
daughter, Liza

Crooner Eddie Fisher
(1959–64, divorced)

Richard Burton
(1964–74 and 1975–76,
divorced both times)
daughter, Maria

Senator John W. Warner
(1976–82, divorced)

Construction worker and
fellow rehab patient
Larry Fortensky
(1991–96, divorced)

Elizabeth Taylor was born with such otherworldly beauty that it seemed she was never truly a child. Right from the start she was an icon in the making. According to legend, when she was just a little girl, agents approached her parents about testing her to play Scarlett and Rhett's daughter in *Gone with the Wind* (1939). True or not, she made her screen debut at age ten opposite Carl "Alfalfa" Switzer in *There's One Born Every Minute* (1942). A contract player with MGM at eleven, Elizabeth fought hard for the lead role in film *National Velvet* (1944), and her performance as the young rider led her to stardom. By the time she was sixteen, her grown-up beauty was bringing her adult roles opposite heartthrobs like Robert Taylor and Montgomery Clift. Her first marriage, which began just as the comedy *Father of the Bride* (1950) was hitting film screens, proved a publicity bonanza, while her performance as the society beauty who falls for Clift in *A Place in the Sun* (1951) made critics aware of her mature acting abilities. Life has both enriched and scarred Elizabeth, and she learned to use her life experience to project her complex personality onto the screen in huge hits like *Cat on a Hot Tin Roof* (1958) and *Butterfield 8* (1960). Her lavish star turn in *Cleopatra* (1963) changed her life when she took up with her costar, dashing Welsh actor Richard Burton. "Liz and Dick," as they were called, made several movies together (most notably *Who's Afraid of Virginia Woolf?* in 1966) while living large in the public eye. But some of the films they made to support that lifestyle, and her personal decision to take a backseat to his career, ended her reign as a box office star. Elizabeth's battles with alcohol and drugs have greatly increased attention given to rehabilitation programs. Her support of one-time costar Rock Hudson during his last days turned her into an outspoken AIDS activist, bringing her worldwide acclaim. Despite a series of significant health issues and public scandals, her strong sense of self and ever-present sense of humor have kept her afloat.

Essential
ELIZABETH**TAYLOR**Films

FATHER OF THE BRIDE
(1950) MGM
A family comedy developed from Edward Streeter's book about a middle-class man whose life is turned upside down when his wife decides that their daughter should have an elaborate wedding. Spencer Tracy is the uptight lawyer father, Taylor the radiant bride, Joan Bennett the suffering mom.

A PLACE IN THE SUN
(1951) Paramount
A film marking Taylor's emergence as an adult actress, playing the rich beauty who makes Montgomery Clift wish he'd never become involved with factory worker Shelley Winters. George Stevens directed this moving version of Theodore Dreiser's *An American Tragedy.*

CAT ON A HOT TIN ROOF
(1958) MGM
The sultry Tennessee Williams drama about a Southern family's squabbles over the fortune of dying patriarch Big Daddy Pollitt (Burl Ives). Paul Newman and Taylor, both Oscar nominated, play alcoholic son Brick and Maggie the Cat, the wife driven to desperation by her husband's indifference.

SUDDENLY, LAST SUMMER
(1959) Columbia
Another Tennessee Williams drama that brought more Oscar nominations, this time for Taylor and Katharine Hepburn. Hepburn plays the mother of a poet named Sebastian who died under horrible circumstances, with Taylor as the niece who is threatened with a lobotomy if she continues to "babble" the truth.

WHO'S AFRAID OF VIRGINIA WOOLF?
(1966) Warner Bros.
Director Mike Nichols's taboo-breaking film of the searing Edward Albee play, in which Taylor and then-husband Richard Burton are the middle-aged married couple who tear each other apart in front of their younger guests (George Segal and fellow Oscar-winner Sandy Dennis).

CAT ON A HOT TIN ROOF, **1958**

STYLENOTES

Costumer Edith Head's simple, pretty designs for Elizabeth Taylor in *A Place in the Sun* influenced "young miss" collections nationwide. Her white party dress with a daisy-covered bust was the country's most popular prom dress that season.

In both *Butterfield 8* and *Cat on a Hot Tin Roof*, Elizabeth appears on screen wearing nothing but a little white slip. Designer Michael Kors admired the way Elizabeth wore it "with real bravado."

Elizabeth loves jewelry and has many fabulous pieces, often gifts from the men in her life. Recently she wrote a book entitled *Elizabeth Taylor: My Love Affair with Jewelry* in which she shows off her collection, including snippets about the origin of each piece.

behindthescenes

BY THE EARLY 1960S, ELIZABETH WAS THE HIGHEST-PAID ACTRESS AROUND, THE FIRST TO COMMAND A $1 MILLION SALARY (FOR *CLEOPATRA*).

WHEN HER FILM CAREER STARTED TO WANE IN THE 1980S, ELIZABETH TOOK TO THE STAGE IN AN ACCLAIMED BROADWAY PRODUCTION OF LILLIAN HELLMAN'S *THE LITTLE FOXES* AND A POPULAR TOUR OF NOEL COWARD'S *PRIVATE LIVES*, THE LATTER PAIRING HER AGAIN WITH EX-HUSBAND RICHARD BURTON.

ELIZABETH MOVED INTO THE FASHION WORLD BY CREATING HER OWN PERFUME COMPANY. SCENTS RELEASED UNDER HER NAME INCLUDE PASSION, WHITE DIAMONDS, DIAMONDS AND RUBIES, DIAMONDS AND EMERALDS, DIAMONDS AND SAPPHIRES, AND BLACK PEARLS.

MANY WERE DISMAYED TO HEAR THAT ELIZABETH HAD BEEN CHOSEN OVER BETTE DAVIS TO STAR IN *WHO'S AFRAID OF VIRGINIA WOOLF?* FANS OF EDWARD ALBEE'S POWERFUL PLAY FEARED SHE WOULD TURN IT INTO A GLAMOROUS ROLE. THE FINISHED PRODUCT, HOWEVER, REVEALS THAT THEY NEEDN'T HAVE WORRIED; SHE GAINED WEIGHT, ESCHEWED GLAMOROUS MAKEUP, AND EVEN PUT GRAY IN HER HAIR TO CAPTURE HER ROLE AS A FROWSY, FOUL-MOUTHED UNIVERSITY WIFE.

One of the great beauties of the 1940s and 1950s, she lit up the screen with her stunning green eyes and beautifully sculpted face—but it was her performance in the haunting noir classic *Laura* that proved unforgettable.

GENE TIERNEY

Born into affluence, the spectacularly beautiful Gene Tierney set out to put her life of privilege to good use, dreaming more of saving the world than of gracing the movies she enjoyed so thoroughly. She changed her mind when she turned the head of noted director Anatole Litvak, who spotted her while she toured Warner Bros. on a family vacation. A screen test led to a $150-a-week contract offer, yet Tierney's father refused to let her enter what he considered a disreputable business. A deal was struck between father and daughter: if Tierney made her society debut, he would help her pursue an acting career—but on Broadway, not in Hollywood. Gene was quickly cast in bit parts on stage, but the movie industry again took notice. A brief, disastrous contract with Columbia sent her back to Broadway, where she scored her first real break in a critically acclaimed performance as a college cheerleader in *The Male Animal*. Magazines like *Vogue* and *LIFE* ran photos of the luscious young actress, and 20th Century-Fox became eager to sign her. Their arrangement was unusual: she could return to Broadway yearly and have some creative control over her appearance. Tierney impressed film critics with her beauty, scoring her greatest hits with two films noir, *Laura* (1944) and *Leave Her to Heaven* (1945). Her Oscar nomination for the latter, in which she plays a relentlessly immoral woman, rid many of the notion that her assets were merely visual. Tierney herself was thrilled to get the part, acknowledging that "few actresses can resist playing bitchy women." Tierney also showed she could charm audiences in touching romances like *Heaven Can Wait* (1943) and *The Ghost and Mrs. Muir* (1947), and she intrigued famously picky directors like Otto Preminger, who cast her in four of his films. Her career in the 1950s was overshadowed by personal problems, including a disastrous affair with Aly Khan and a bout with mental illness. In the 1960s, however, she received solid reviews for *Toys in the Attic* (1963) and found marital happiness and satisfying work for a number of charities, returning to the passion for helping others that had originally fueled her fantasies.

Born
GENE ELIZA TIERNEY
November 19, 1920
Brooklyn, New York

Died
November 6, 1991
Houston, Texas,
of emphysema

Star Sign
Scorpio

Height
5'7"

Husbands and Children
Couturier Oleg Cassini
(1941–52, divorced)
two daughters,
Daria and Christina

Oil man Howard Lee
(1960–81, his death)

Essential
GENETIERNEYFilms

ACADEMY AWARDS

Nominated for Best Actress
Leave Her to Heaven

HEAVEN CAN WAIT

(1943) 20th Century-Fox
Ernst Lubitsch's fantasy-comedy
about a recently deceased man
(Don Ameche) who recounts his
"sinful" past as he attempts to gain
entry into Hades. Tierney appears
in flashbacks as Ameche's lovely,
understanding wife.

LAURA

(1944) 20th Century-Fox
The twisted murder mystery
based on Vera Caspary's novel. A
detective, played by Dana Andrews,
falls in love with a painting of a
woman (Gene Tierney) who is
believed to have been murdered. Of
all her roles, this is Tierney's most
well known and highly praised.

LEAVE HER TO HEAVEN

(1945) 20th Century-Fox
Screen version of the Ben Ames
Williams novel, with Tierney as
the woman who brings death and
disaster to those who threaten her
closeness to her husband (Cornel
Wilde). Tierney, coolly ravishing
in Leon Shamroy's Oscar-winning
Technicolor cinematography, won
her only Oscar nomination as the
monstrous Ellen.

THE RAZOR'S EDGE

(1946) 20th Century-Fox
W. Somerset Maugham's story of a
man (Tyrone Power) searching for
the deeper meaning of existence,
with Tierney and Oscar-winner
Anne Baxter as the women in his
life. Tierney, dressed by husband
Oleg Cassini, is the chic socialite
who dallies with Power before
marrying another man.

THE GHOST AND MRS. MUIR

(1947) 20th Century-Fox
A fantasy providing Tierney
with one of her most appealing
characters, a widow who discovers
that her English cottage is haunted
by the ghost of a charming sea
captain (Rex Harrison). Joseph L.
Mankiewicz directed a cast that
includes a very young Natalie
Wood as Tierney's daughter.

LEAVE HER TO HEAVEN, 1945

STYLENOTES

When Gene Tierney saw herself on screen for the first time, she was horrified by her voice ("I sounded like an angry Minnie Mouse"). She started smoking to lower her voice, but it came at a great price—she died of emphysema.

The portrait of Gene that figures so heavily in the plot of *Laura* was actually an enlarged photograph. Dissatisfied with the painting of Gene created by a popular artist, director Otto Preminger had her pose for a studio photographer and then had the results enlarged and brushed over with paint.

LAURA, 1944

THE SHANGHAI GESTURE, 1941

behindthescenes

GENE TIERNEY'S ELOPEMENT WITH DESIGNER OLEG CASSINI SO ANGERED STUDIO EXECUTIVES (WHO WARNED HER AGAINST THE UNION) THAT THEY BLACKLISTED HIM FROM FILM WORK AND OSTRACIZED THE COUPLE FROM THE HOLLYWOOD SOCIAL SCENE FOR MONTHS.

WHILE SEPARATED FROM CASSINI, GENE FELL FOR JOHN F. KENNEDY WHEN HE VISITED THE SET OF *DRAGONWYCK* (1946). THEIR ROMANCE RUFFLED HER FAMILY'S FEATHERS. "THEY WERE EPISCOPALIAN REPUBLICANS, WHO DIDN'T TAKE KINDLY TO THE CATHOLIC DEMOCRAT WITH LOFTY IDEAS ABOUT HELPING THE POOR," SHE WOULD LATER SAY.

UNTIL GENE WAS MARRIED, 25 PERCENT OF HER SALARY WENT DIRECTLY TO HER FATHER'S INSURANCE COMPANY, BELLE-TIER CORPORATION. WHEN SHE EVENTUALLY BROKE FROM HER FATHER'S MANAGEMENT, HE SUED HER. THE TRIAL REVEALED THAT HE HAD BEEN STEALING FROM HER FOR YEARS.

GENE CONTRACTED GERMAN MEASLES DURING A USO APPEARANCE, ALLEGEDLY BECAUSE A FEMALE MARINE WITH THE ILLNESS BROKE QUARANTINE TO MEET HER FAVORITE STAR. AS A RESULT, GENE'S FIRST CHILD WAS BORN BLIND AND WITH SEVERE DEVELOPMENTAL DISABILITIES. THE PAINFUL INCIDENT WAS THE INSPIRATION FOR THE AGATHA CHRISTIE MYSTERY *THE MIRROR CRACK'D* (1980), IN WHICH ELIZABETH TAYLOR PLAYS A ROLE MODELED ON GENE'S HISTORY.

WHILE FILMING *PLYMOUTH ADVENTURE* (1952) AT MGM, GENE HAD A BRIEF FLING WITH SPENCER TRACY. GREATLY IMPRESSED WITH HER INNER BEAUTY, HE WOULD LATER SAY, "ALTHOUGH SHE WAS BEAUTIFUL IN HER FILMS, THEY COULDN'T QUITE CAPTURE ALL OF HER. FORTUNATELY I DID, EVEN IF IT WAS LATE IN MY LIFE."

Early in her career, she was known as "the Sweater Girl," a teasing, fun-loving blonde bombshell who grew up to become the benchmark for Hollywood glamour.

LANA TURNER

Born
Julia Jean Mildred Frances Turner
February 8, 1921
Wallace, Idaho

Died
June 29, 1995
Century City, California,
of throat cancer

Star Sign
Aquarius

Height
5'3"

Husbands and Child
Musician Artie Shaw
(1940, divorced)

Restaurateur Stephen Crane
(1942–43, annulled;
1943–44, divorced)
daughter, Cheryl

Millionaire Henry J.
"Bob" Topping Jr.
(1948–52, divorced)

Former Tarzan Lex Barker
(1953–57, divorced)

Rancher Fred May
(1960–62, divorced)

Businessman Robert Eaton
(1965–69, divorced)

Nightclub hypnotist
Ronald Dante
(1969–72, divorced)

It was impossible to tell Lana Turner the person from Lana Turner the Hollywood icon. She was one star who never let her glamour drop even off screen, and her life was marked with enough scandal and heartache for any of her films. When she was eight, her father was murdered, triggering a family move to California in search of work. She really wasn't discovered at the soda counter at Schwab's Drug Store; it was Currie's Drug Store, across the street from her high school. The talent agent who spied Lana took her to see director Mervyn LeRoy, who was looking for a provocative young actress for a small role as a murder victim in *They Won't Forget* (1937). Publicists dubbed her "the Sweater Girl" in honor of her form-fitting costume, and when LeRoy moved to MGM, he brought her with him. She scored as a small-town siren in *Love Finds Andy Hardy* (1938), and the studio started building her up as both a star and a glamour girl. Lana didn't stay long in juvenile roles; she was only twenty when she played torrid love scenes with gangster Robert Taylor in *Johnny Eager* (1941) and not much older when she seduced John Garfield on screen in the classic film noir *The Postman Always Rings Twice* (1946). Critics often derided her acting, but her screen presence was electric. And the scandals that might have destroyed other careers—seven failed marriages and additional disastrous affairs—only made her more popular. They also made her the perfect choice for the hard-drinking, lovelorn movie star in director Vincente Minnelli's Hollywood tell-all *The Bad and the Beautiful* (1952). Lana felt a bit lost after leaving MGM in the 1950s, but she reinvented herself as a melodrama queen in *Peyton Place* (1957). As that hit was going into national release, Lana's abusive relationship with gangster Johnny Stompanato climaxed when her daughter, Cheryl Crane, killed the thug to protect her mother. The scandal drove ticket sales, and Turner launched a series of popular on-screen melodramas, including *Imitation of Life* (1959). She later turned to television, most notably as a woman who turns out to be the head of an international crime syndicate on the prime-time soap *Falcon Crest*. Even in her sixties, she was glamorous, explosive, and compellingly watchable.

Essential
LANATURNERFilms

ACADEMY AWARDS

Nominated for Best Actress
Peyton Place

ZIEGFELD GIRL

(1941) MGM
Turner's star-making role in MGM's
tale of three ambitious showgirls,
Judy Garland, Hedy Lamarr, and
Turner, vying for prominence on a
Ziegfeld stage. Fourth-billed Turner,
teamed romantically with James
Stewart, steals the spotlight with
a memorable walk down those
Ziegfeld stairs.

THE POSTMAN ALWAYS RINGS TWICE

(1946) MGM
The James M. Cain story of adultery
and murder, transformed into
MGM's most accomplished film noir.
Turner, platinum blonde, dressed
all in white, creates heat with John
Garfield, who plays the drifter who
helps her knock off her husband
(Cecil Kellaway).

THE BAD AND THE BEAUTIFUL

(1952) MGM
Vincente Minnelli's dramatic study
of a ruthless Hollywood producer
(Kirk Douglas) and his destructive
impact on the lives of those around
him, including Turner as an actress
seduced by the producer and
then discarded in favor of another
woman. The cast also includes Dick
Powell, Barry Sullivan, and Oscar-
winner Gloria Grahame.

PEYTON PLACE

(1957) 20th Century-Fox
The film version of then-scandalous
novel by Grace Metalious about
sexual escapades in an outwardly
straight-laced New England town.
Turner is the mother who worries
that her illegitimate daughter (Diane
Varsi) may repeat her own mistakes.

IMITATION OF LIFE

(1959) Universal
Turner steps into Claudette Colbert's
role as the career woman who
befriends her black housekeeper
and her daughter (Susan Kohner)
who passes for white.

THE POSTMAN ALWAYS RINGS TWICE, 1946

STYLENOTES

After Turner bounced across the screen in her tight sweater, in a brief but explosive performance in *They Won't Forget* (1937), actresses around Hollywood began padding their bras—the birth of bosom mania.

When Lana's personal makeup artist was drafted right before *The Postman Always Rings Twice* (1946), she made him teach her his techniques so she could do the job herself.

Lana favored tight clothes in simple, strong colors. Diamonds were a staple, and a fur, preferably white, was often draped over one shoulder. Glamour was the key. Lana Turner was a movie star and dressed for the part nearly every day of her life.

When Lana's apartment building caught fire, she had only minutes to grab a few of her most precious items. She took her lipstick, eyebrow pencil, and hair dryer.

behind the scenes

WHEN LANA RECEIVED HER FIRST PAYCHECK, SHE TOLD HER MOTHER, "QUIT YOUR HAIRDRESSING JOB, MOM. YOU'LL NEVER HAVE TO WORK ANOTHER DAY IN YOUR LIFE." THIS TURNED OUT TO BE TRUE.

THE STOMPANATO CASE WAS FICTIONALIZED IN HAROLD ROBBINS'S BEST-SELLER *WHERE LOVE HAS GONE.* WHEN PARAMOUNT ANNOUNCED PLANS TO FILM THE BOOK IN 1964, LANA AGREED TO STAR UNTIL FRIENDS POINTED OUT THE SIMILARITIES TO HER OWN LIFE. SHE PULLED OUT OF THE FILM, LEAVING THE ROLE TO SUSAN HAYWARD. YEARS LATER ELAINE STRITCH WOULD PLAY ANOTHER CHARACTER INSPIRED BY LANA'S ROLE IN THE SCANDAL IN DIRECTOR WOODY'S ALLEN'S *SEPTEMBER* (1987).

WHEN TURNER FIRST AGREED TO STAR IN *PEYTON PLACE,* HER FANS WERE UPSET THAT HOLLYWOOD'S SEXY SWEATER GIRL WAS GOING TO PLAY A MIDDLE-AGED MOTHER. YET LANA WAS INSPIRED BY THE WAY JOAN CRAWFORD HAD REINVENTED HER CAREER PLAYING MOTHERS AND WON AN OSCAR FOR IT IN *MILDRED PIERCE* (1945), AND SO SHE WENT AHEAD WITH HER PLANS.

With a swish of the hips, a roll of the eyes, and a saucy "Come up sometime, see me," she earned the title "the Empress of Sex," and she did it all through suggestion, often in period gowns that covered her from head to toe.

MAE
WEST

Mae West spent most of her career at war with the censors, a battle she was born for as the daughter of a boxer and a former corset model. Performing in vaudeville from an early age, West developed a sexually charged act modeled on the moves of female impersonators and African American entertainers. She scored some hits on Broadway, too, but when she couldn't find a suitable script, she wrote her own, *SEX*. The 1926 show was a hit, even though the police closed it and sent her to jail for ten days. Her later plays, especially *Diamond Lil* (1928), were even bigger. When old friend George Raft got Paramount Pictures to offer her a small part in his next film, *Night After Night* (1932), she rewrote her dialogue and, according to Raft, "stole everything but the cameras." Still, Paramount offered her a lucrative contract to write and star. At the age of forty, when most actresses would have begun easing into maternal roles, she launched a series of vehicles in which she played women pursuing romantic conquests as avidly and independently as any man. Her first—*She Done Him Wrong* (1933), an adaptation of *Diamond Lil*—saved the studio from bankruptcy, and by 1935 Mae was the highest paid woman in America. But by then Hollywood had entered a new era of tougher film censorship, partly prompted by Mae's bawdy films. When she performed as Eve on a 1937 radio broadcast, it triggered a national uproar that led to her being banned from the medium. With declining box office returns, she returned to the stage with sellout revivals of *Diamond Lil*. In 1952 she launched a hit Vegas act surrounded by a chorus of muscle men. And in 1958 she made her TV debut vamping Rock Hudson while singing "Baby, It's Cold Outside" at the Academy Awards. Mae remained in the public eye with carefully chosen television and stage appearances and the publication of her memoir, *Goodness Had Nothing to Do with It*, in 1959. She returned to the screen with a showy role as a Hollywood agent in *Myra Breckinridge* (1970). In one of her best one-liners, she sizes up a group of handsome aspiring actors and quips, "OK, boys, take out your resumes." In her last film, *Sextette* (1978), she was romanced by Timothy Dalton and George Hamilton. She was still the Empress of Sex—at eighty-five.

Born
Mary Jane West
August 17, 1893
Brooklyn, New York

Died
November 22, 1980
Hollywood, California,
of heart failure
following multiple strokes

Star Sign
Leo

Height
5'

Husband
Vaudeville partner Frank Wallace
(1911–42, divorced)

Essential
MAE WEST Films

SHE DONE HIM WRONG

(1933) Paramount
West's first starring vehicle in films—
the one that saved Paramount
Pictures from bankruptcy and the
one in which she tells Cary Grant,
"Why don't you come up sometime
and see me?" Repeating her stage
role of "Diamond Lil," West plays a
Gay Nineties entertainer, and Grant
is a detective posing as a Salvation
Army worker.

I'M NO ANGEL

(1933) Paramount
West and Grant in a follow-up
even more successful than their
first film, with Mae as a circus
performer who wriggles her way
out of a robbery charge and
insinuates herself into high society.
She dallies with Grant in between
songs and such suggestive nuggets
as "It's not the men in my life,
but the life in my men."

BELLE OF THE NINETIES

(1934) Paramount
West's first film under the Hays
Production Code that was
established partly in reaction to
her naughty movies. She plays a
cabaret entertainer who has no lack
of suitors but, in keeping with the
Code's guidelines, goes on to wed
her true love.

KLONDIKE ANNIE

(1936) Paramount
Another West adventure about a
kept woman in San Francisco who
is accused of killing her abusive
benefactor. She runs away to
Alaska and poses as a missionary
seeking to save souls, all the while
beguiling a Mountie (Philip Reed)
who doesn't realize she's the
fugitive he's tracking.

EVERY DAY'S A HOLIDAY

(1937) Paramount
A tale of a turn-of-the-century con
woman who poses as a famous
French singer. This was the West
vehicle that ended her relationship
with Paramount, even though it was
lavishly produced and featured an
unusually strong supporting cast.

I'M NO ANGEL, 1933

STYLENOTES

Mae appeared at her first meeting with costumer Walter Plunkett wearing ten-inch wedge heels, two-inch eyelashes, a foot-long blonde wig, and absolutely nothing else. "Honey," she said, "I thought you'd like to see the beautiful body you're gonna have the opportunity of dressin'."

After insisting that Paris-based Elsa Schiaparelli design her costumes for *Every Day's a Holiday* (1937), Mae had a dress form sent to France in lieu of traveling there for a fitting. When the designer first laid eyes on the form, she reportedly exclaimed, "Shocking!" That moment inspired Schiaparelli's first fragrance, aptly named "Shocking," and the bottle is still a miniature of West's dress form.

Mae's dresses for *She Done Him Wrong* started a trend in Paris called *La Vogue Mae West*. Like the actress, fashionable women wore velvet and satin hourglass gowns, feathers on their hats, and boas around their necks.

behindthescenes

IN AN APPARENT CONTRADICTION TO HER HEDONISTIC PERSONA, MAE NEITHER SMOKED NOR DRANK AND WAS A HEAVY CONTRIBUTOR TO CATHOLIC CHARITIES. WHEN SHE BECAME SPIRITUAL TOWARD THE END OF HER LIFE, ESP WAS LIKE A RELIGION TO HER. IN 1975 SHE WROTE A BOOK, *MAE WEST ON SEX, HEALTH AND ESP.*

THE IDEA FOR *DIAMOND LIL* CAME FROM A MANHATTAN HOTEL PORTER WHO DELIGHTED MAE WITH STORIES OF HIS BOWERY SWEETHEART, A GREAT BEAUTY WHO COLLECTED DIAMONDS FROM HER MANY ADMIRERS.

WHEN MAE TOURED *DIAMOND LIL* TO LOS ANGELES IN 1930, UNIVERSAL PICTURES EXECUTIVES WANTED TO FILM IT BUT WERE BLOCKED BY THE CENSORS. PARAMOUNT ONLY GOT TO MAKE A FILM VERSION THREE YEARS LATER BY AGREEING TO CHANGE THE TITLE AND THE CHARACTER NAMES (DIAMOND LIL BECAME LADY LOU).

IN 1942, ENGLAND'S ROYAL AIR FORCE NAMED THEIR INFLATABLE LIFE JACKETS "MAE WESTS" BECAUSE OF THE WAY THEY MADE THE WEARER'S CHEST STICK OUT. MAE WAS DELIGHTED, QUIPPING, "I'VE BEEN IN *WHO'S WHO,* AND I KNOW WHAT'S WHAT, BUT IT'S THE FIRST TIME I EVER MADE THE DICTIONARY."

AFTER HER PARAMOUNT CONTRACT ENDED, MAE TURNED DOWN THE CHANCE TO COSTAR WITH CLARK GABLE AT MGM. THE FILM WOULD HAVE CAST HER AS THE OWNER OF A HOCKEY TEAM WHO DATED THE PLAYERS, BUT MAE REFUSED TO PLAY A WOMAN WHO HAD TO PAY MEN TO DATE HER.

MAE FORGED A LIFELONG FRIENDSHIP WITH COSTUME DESIGNER EDITH HEAD WHEN THEY WORKED TOGETHER ON *SHE DONE HIM WRONG* (1933). ALTHOUGH THEY WOULDN'T WORK TOGETHER ON FILM AGAIN UNTIL *MYRA BRECKINRIDGE* IN 1970, HEAD WOULD DESIGN MUCH OF MAE'S PERSONAL WARDROBE. OFF SCREEN, WEST PREFERRED PALE PASTELS—PINK, POWDER BLUE, AND LAVENDER—TO SET OFF HER CREAMY COMPLEXION. THE ONLY FILM TO REFLECT THIS WAS *SEXTETTE* (1978), WHICH FEATURED CLOTHES FROM HER PRIVATE WARDROBE.

MGM's Million Dollar Mermaid, she created the aquatic musical and made history with astounding athletic stunts and a glamorous approach to swimwear that made her an all-American dream girl.

ESTHER
WILLIAMS

Like many young people, Esther Williams dreamt of fame and awards—but she was pining for Olympic gold, not Oscar. An accomplished swimmer, Esther had to put Olympic fantasies to rest when Hitler's march on Europe caused the 1940 games to be cancelled. She settled for joining showman Billy Rose's San Francisco Aquacade, where her combination of looks and water ballet caught the eye of MGM talent scouts. Despite a lack of acting, singing, or dancing experience, Esther was put under contract. After scoring in small roles, she was cast as a swimming gym teacher in the Red Skelton comedy *Mr. Coed*. MGM executives were so impressed with her performance that they built up the role and changed the title to *Bathing Beauty* (1944). For eleven years, Esther swam through eighteen films shot on Stage 30, which consisted of a large, specially equipped swimming pool built just for her. She was game for almost anything, yet the elaborate tricks her directors put her through were not without peril, and she nearly died more than once while filming. A fifty-foot dive at the climax of *Million Dollar Mermaid* (1952) resulted in a nearly broken neck and half a year in a body cast. Esther's physical toughness was matched by her professional calm, and neither Louis B. Mayer's famous tantrums nor the constant advances from directors and costars could daunt her. When the studio system fell apart in the 1950s, Esther tried moving into dramatic roles, but with little success. Instead, she became a successful businesswoman, marketing her own lines of swimsuits and swimming pools. Even after a long retirement from the public eye, Esther reemerged to launch a successful swimsuit line for the mature woman, write a best-selling biography, *The Million Dollar Mermaid*, and use her influence to promote both synchronized swimming and the benefits of swimming for everyone.

Born
August 8, 1922
Los Angeles, California

Star Sign
Leo

Height
5'8½"

Husbands and Children
Medical student Leonard Kovner
(1940–44, divorced)

Personal manager Ben Gage
(1945–59, divorced)
three children,
Benjamin, Kimball,
and Susan

Fernando Lamas
(1962–82, his death)

Businessman Edward Bell
(1994–present)

Essential
ESTHERWILLIAMSFilms

BATHING BEAUTY

(1944) MGM

Williams's first big splash as a swimming star, and the creation of a new genre: the MGM swim musical. Originally, the film was planned strictly as a comedy vehicle for costar Red Skelton, but the focus changed once everyone got a load of Esther's aquatic performance as the pretty swimming instructor he marries.

NEPTUNE'S DAUGHTER

(1949) MGM

A typical Williams entertainment, with spectacular swim sequences, musical interludes, and Skelton's ample doses of comedy. Williams, playing a swimsuit designer, pairs with love interest Ricardo Montalban to sing the Oscar-winning ditty "Baby, It's Cold Outside."

MILLION DOLLAR MERMAID

(1952) MGM

Williams's favorite among her films, the screen bio of earlier aquatic star Annette Kellerman. Victor Mature costars as the flashy promoter who wins Kellerman's heart, and choreographer Busby Berkeley stages the truly spectacular water ballets.

DANGEROUS WHEN WET

(1953) MGM

Lighthearted romp with music and a touch of drama, Williams plays a farm girl who plans to swim the English Channel with her entire family. Along the way, she takes a dip with future husband Fernando Lamas and the cartoon characters Tom and Jerry.

EASY TO LOVE

(1953) MGM

Williams on water skis, as the star performer of an aquacade in Cypress Gardens, Florida. Busby Berkeley again stages the aquatic production numbers, with costar Van Johnson and Tony Martin providing the love interest.

BATHING BEAUTY, 1944

206

STYLENOTES

All the top swimsuit designers watched Esther's movies and copied her swimwear. Irene, Esther's favorite designer on and off screen, made many of her swimsuits, as did costumer Helen Rose. After a time, Esther participated in the swimsuit design process and made decisions about the fabric herself.

In order to keep Esther looking glamorous under water, MGM covered the star in a thick cream makeup and lathered her hair in baby oil and petroleum jelly. She recalled, "By the time I came out of hair and makeup, I was waterproof as a mallard."

THIS TIME FOR KEEPS, 1947

behindthescenes

A MARRIED WOMAN AT EIGHTEEN AND NO STRANGER TO SHOW-BIZ LECHERY (JOHNNY WEISSMULLER WOULD SLIP OFF HIS TRUNKS AND CHASE HER AROUND BACKSTAGE AT THE AQUACADE), ESTHER WILLIAMS WAS USED TO DEALING WITH THE MALE LIBIDO. YET NOTHING COULD PREPARE HER FOR THE MOMENT WHEN HER IDOL, CLARK GABLE, SPENT A SCREEN TEST GIVING HER SMOOCHES WHILE JOKING WITH WIFE, CAROLE LOMBARD, "WELL, BABY, I TOLD YOU I WAS GOING TO KISS ME A MERMAID TODAY."

ACCORDING TO ESTHER'S AUTOBIOGRAPHY, SHE ALMOST MARRIED MOVIE STAR JEFF CHANDLER, WHOM SHE MET WHILE WORKING ON A RARE DRAMATIC FILM, *RAW WIND IN EDEN* (1958). SHE BROKE OFF THE RELATIONSHIP WHEN SHE DISCOVERED HE WAS A CROSS-DRESSER.

ESTHER'S THIRD MARRIAGE, TO DASHING ACTOR FERNANDO LAMAS, WAS LONG LASTING YET IMBUED WITH A UNIQUE COMPROMISE: HER THREE CHILDREN WERE FORBIDDEN TO ENTER THE HOUSE, SO EVERY DAY ESTHER SURREPTITIOUSLY DROVE TO THEIR FATHER'S HOUSE TO SPEND TIME WITH THEM. TOLERANT ESTHER SAW FERNANDO'S JEALOUSY AS THE RESULT OF HIS LATIN BACKGROUND, BUT SHE DEFIED HIS STRICTURES TO ATTEND HER DAUGHTER'S WEDDING.

She morphed effortlessly from the sweetest of child stars to a captivating and vulnerable young woman in performances that epitomized the complex generation coming of age in the 1950s.

NATALIE
WOOD

Born
Natalia Nikolaevna Zakharenko
July 20, 1938
San Francisco, California

Died
November 29, 1981
Santa Catalina Island, California,
in an accidental drowning

Star Sign
Cancer

Height
5'

Husbands and Children
Robert Wagner
(1957–62, divorced;
1972–81, her death)
daughter, Courtney

Richard Gregson
(1969–71, divorced)
daughter, Natasha

Natalie Wood was the child of Russian immigrant parents. Her mother felt her child's beauty should be seen in the movies, and so Natalie was in her first picture at age five, quickly becoming a very busy child star. Although she rarely carried her films, she was such a scene stealer that she was once dubbed "the most talented juvenile in America." Even the difficult-to-impress Orson Welles, star of 1946's *Tomorrow Is Forever,* said, "She was so good, she frightened me." She even stole scenes from Santa Claus in the Christmas classic *Miracle on 34th Street* (1947). Some speculate that it was Natalie's "second banana" child star status that allowed her to develop a career as a young adult. It certainly didn't hurt that she blossomed physically, going from a pretty little girl to an exquisite older teen. At age sixteen, after working steadily in the business for more than a decade, Natalie joined a group of young Method actors, including James Dean, in a classic of adolescent angst, *Rebel Without a Cause* (1955). Her stock continued to rise in Hollywood, particularly in 1961, when she gave well-received performances as young women driven to desperate measures for love in both *West Side Story* and *Splendor in the Grass.* Natalie's stunning looks and emotionally riveting performances made her one of the most popular stars of the 1950s and 1960s. In the 1960s, she also expanded into comedy, capped by the successful satire of sexual liberation, 1969's *Bob and Carol and Ted and Alice.* The following decade Natalie worked more in television, and although her career had clearly peaked she always had her fans. In 1981, she was in the midst of her second marriage to actor Robert Wagner and filming *Brainstorm* with actor Christopher Walken. The three were out on the couple's yacht that Thanksgiving weekend when Natalie disappeared late at night, tragically drowning in the frigid waters off Catalina Island. Natalie's untimely death was devastating not just for her family and friends but for legions of fans around the world who had never tired of her beauty, vivacity, and passion.

Essential
NATALIE**WOOD**Films

REBEL WITHOUT A CAUSE

(1955) Warner Bros.
Nicholas Ray's influential study of teen delinquency in the 1950s, marking Wood's Oscar-nominated breakthrough as young adult star. James Dean, in an iconic role, stars as a high-schooler who serves as protector for two other trouble-prone youngsters: Wood, the girl he loves, and misfit Sal Mineo.

WEST SIDE STORY, 1961

WEST SIDE STORY

(1961) United Artists
Robert Wise's screen version of the Leonard Bernstein–Stephen Sondheim Broadway musical inspired by *Romeo and Juliet,* with Wood and Richard Beymer as the star-crossed lovers in a New York City ghetto. Wood's songs were dubbed over with Marni Nixon's voice, but she acquitted herself well in the Jerome Robbins choreography.

SPLENDOR IN THE GRASS

(1961) Warner Bros.
Wood's only film with director Elia Kazan, the William Inge screenplay set in 1920s Kansas. Wood is the repressed schoolgirl whose passion for a handsome young man (Warren Beatty) leads to a mental breakdown.

LOVE WITH THE PROPER STRANGER

(1963) Paramount
A comedy-drama from director Robert Mulligan, with Wood playing a young Italian American who considers an abortion after becoming pregnant by an irresponsible jazz musician (Steve McQueen). Supporting cast included Tom Bosley and Edie Adams.

BOB & CAROL & TED & ALICE

(1969) Columbia
A satirical comedy in which Bob, Carol, Ted, and Alice (Robert Culp, Natalie Wood, Elliott Gould, and Dyan Cannon) explore the difference between free love and loving relationships during the sexual revolution.

STYLENOTES

Natalie always wore a heavy gold bracelet on her left arm in order to cover a large knot left by an unhealed broken wrist. Friends claim that she was never seen without the bump covered.

Costumer Edith Head's designs for *Love with the Proper Stranger* so delighted Natalie that from then on she usually requested Edith to design her costumes and other clothes. The two worked together to design Natalie's dress when she wed Richard Gregson.

With no time to fuss over hair after a long day of shooting, Natalie surprised those at the 1956 Academy Awards with a cropped hairstyle that was popular in Europe at the time. Natalie's appeal made its popularity among American women soar.

behindthescenes

WHEN SIXTEEN-YEAR-OLD NATALIE WOOD READ FOR A PART IN *REBEL WITHOUT A CAUSE*, SOME AT WARNER BROS. WERE NOT CONVINCED SHE COULD MAKE THE ROLE BELIEVABLE. DENNIS HOPPER WAS ALREADY SET TO STAR IN THE FILM WHEN ONE NIGHT HE TOOK NATALIE AND A FRIEND OF HERS FOR A DRIVE. ALL THREE WOUND UP LITERALLY THROWN FROM HOPPER'S CONVERTIBLE, AND AT THE HOSPITAL NATALIE INSISTED THAT THE STAFF CALL DIRECTOR NICHOLAS RAY, NOT HER PARENTS. WHEN HE ARRIVED AT THE SCENE, SHE SAID, "NICK, THEY CALLED ME A GODDAMN JUVENILE DELINQUENT. NOW DO I GET THE PART?"

NATALIE'S BEAUTY AND SPUNKY SPIRIT BROUGHT HER A WIDE ARRAY OF ADMIRERS. ELVIS PRESLEY ONCE BROUGHT HER DOWN TO HIS PARENT'S HOUSE, PLANNING A WEEK-LONG VISIT THAT NATALIE ENDED AFTER ONE DAY—SHE GOT THE FEELING HIS MOTHER DIDN'T LIKE HER. SHE HAD A TORRID AFFAIR WITH WARREN BEATTY THAT ALSO CAME TO AN ABRUPT END. ONE NIGHT THEY WERE DINING OUT WHEN HE LEFT THE TABLE, SUPPOSEDLY TO MAKE A PHONE CALL. HE THEN TALKED THE HATCHECK GIRL INTO QUITTING HER JOB, AND THEY LEFT THE RESTAURANT TOGETHER, NEVER TO RETURN.

NATALIE REALLY PROVED SHE HAD A SENSE OF HUMOR ABOUT HERSELF WHEN, DESPITE SOME OSCAR-WORTHY PERFORMANCES, *THE HARVARD LAMPOON* AWARDED HER A PRIZE FOR "THE WORST ACTRESS OF THIS YEAR, NEXT YEAR, AND THE FOLLOWING YEAR." MUCH TO THEIR SURPRISE, NATALIE OFFERED TO COME TO HARVARD AND ACCEPT THE AWARD IN PERSON, WHICH SHE DID.

NATALIE'S DEATH BY DROWNING WAS PARTICULARLY IRONIC: SHE HAD DEVELOPED A STRONG FEAR OF THE WATER AFTER A SWIMMING ACCIDENT ON THE SET OF THE *GREEN PROMISE* (1949). WHEN SHE WAS SUPPOSED TO SWIM IN THE OCEAN FOR A SCENE IN *THE STAR* (1952), SHE WENT INTO A PANIC. BETTE DAVIS, STARRING AS HER MOTHER, ORDERED THE DIRECTOR TO CHANGE THE SCENE. YEARS LATER, DIRECTOR ELIA KAZAN LIED WHEN HE PROMISED HER A DOUBLE FOR SWIMMING SCENES IN *SPLENDOR IN THE GRASS*. HER HYSTERIA IN THE SCENES WAS NOT ACTING.

From the twilight of silent films to the dawn of television's Golden Age, she graced the screen with her ladylike charm, her liquid, luminous eyes peering out from more than one hundred films.

LORETTA
YOUNG

Born
Gretchen Michaela Young
January 6, 1913
Salt Lake City, Utah

Died
August 12, 2000
Los Angeles, California,
of ovarian cancer

Star Sign
Capricorn

Height
5'6"

Husbands and Children
Actor Grant Withers
(1930–31, divorced)

Daughter Judy
fathered by Clark Gable
out of wedlock in 1936

Advertising executive
Tom Lewis (1940–69, divorced)
two sons, Christopher Paul
and Peter Charles

Costume designer Jean Louis
(1993–97, his death)

Loretta Young's show business resume began with extra work in silent films as a child. Barely a teenager, she got a showy supporting role in the film *Naughty but Nice* (1927), a part she snagged when someone called for her older sister, who wasn't available at the time. Her large blue eyes, striking cheekbones, and graceful presence made the crew sit up and take notice, and more parts followed. Loretta was fortunate as the talkies took hold: "My voice matched my face," she said years later. Clark Gable appeared with her in the adventure *Call of the Wild* (1935), and a host of other on-screen romances followed. She worked with such costars as Don Ameche, who invented the telephone for her in *The Story of Alexander Graham Bell* (1939), and *Tyrone Power*. Loretta's romantic comedies with Power were big hits, and by the late 1930s she was a major studio star. With new, younger actresses appearing in the 1940s, she kept her star value by changing with the times. Her knack for playing pretty innocents made her a fresh choice for film noir, most notably in her first foray into the genre, *The Stranger* (1946). The next year, Loretta won critical acclaim and a long-overdue Oscar for *The Farmer's Daughter* (1947). She was smart enough to move to television in the 1950s, but she always cited "absurdly lucky" timing as the reason for her enormous success with *The Loretta Young Show,* which lasted eight seasons. This half-hour anthology opened each week with her sweeping entrance in a lovely evening gown. Each episode might have her appearing as any of a number of characters, from a glamorous stage star to a Japanese housemaid, for which she won three Emmys. From there, Loretta continued to act in television when she was intrigued by a role, yet she also spent time writing, pursuing business interests, and continuing a nearly lifelong devotion to Catholic charities.

Essential
LORETTAYOUNGFilms

ACADEMY AWARDS

Won Best Actress
The Farmer's Daughter

Nominated for Best Actress
Come to the Stable

KENTUCKY
(1938) 20th Century-Fox
A melodrama with Young in early Technicolor as a Kentuckian who falls in love with a handsome horse trainer (Richard Greene) despised by her uncle (Walter Brennan) because of a family feud dating to the Civil War. After Greene secretly trains Brennan's thoroughbred, the family conflict reaches a climax at the Kentucky Derby.

THE STRANGER
(1946) RKO
Postwar thriller cowritten by, directed by, and starring Orson Welles, who plays a college professor living quietly in New England with his wife (Young). What she doesn't know is that he is actually a notorious Nazi war criminal, and that a war-crimes commissioner (Edward G. Robinson) is closing in.

THE FARMER'S DAUGHTER
(1947) RKO
A charming comedy featuring Young as a Swedish woman who leaves her Minnesota farm, heads to the big city, and becomes a housekeeper for a congressman (Joseph Cotten), who falls in love with her.

THE BISHOP'S WIFE
(1947) RKO
The ultracharming Cary Grant, David Niven, and Young star in this comedy about a guardian angel (Grant) who descends at Christmastime to aid an Episcopalian bishop (Niven) working to raise funds for a new cathedral. Young is the bishop's wife, who also benefits from Grant's heavenly influence.

COME TO THE STABLE
(1949) 20th Century-Fox
Another Christmas classic, this one with Young and Celeste Holm as French nuns who come to the New England town of Bethlehem to raise money for a children's hospital. Among those helping them realize their dream are a struggling painter (Elsa Lanchester) and a songwriter (Hugh Marlowe).

THE STRANGER, 1946

STYLENOTES

At fourteen, Loretta Young hadn't yet acquired the womanly curves needed to play her star-making role in *Laugh, Clown, Laugh* (1928), so the wardrobe department fitted her with some selectively placed padding. "I had the most divine figure that ever walked in front of a camera, courtesy of the studio," she once said. "It was all pads—false hips, false front, false behind."

Loretta demanded that her appearances at the beginning of each episode of *The Loretta Young Show* be removed from syndicated reruns, insisting that the once-high-style gowns, hairstyles, and makeup she donned in those segments would make her look dated. When NBC didn't comply, she successfully sued the network.

LAUGH, CLOWN, LAUGH, 1928

behindthescenes

WHEN LORETTA YOUNG STARRED WITH THE CLARK GABLE IN *CALL OF THE WILD* (1935), SPARKS FLEW. AFTER FILMING, YOUNG TOOK TO HER BED WITH AN "INTERNAL CONDITION." IN ACTUALITY SHE GAVE BIRTH TO GABLE'S DAUGHTER, JUDY, AND PLACED HER IN AN ORPHANAGE IN ORDER TO ADOPT HER PUBLICLY A YEAR LATER. DENYING FOR DECADES THAT JUDY WAS THE BIOLOGICAL CHILD OF THE MARRIED GABLE, LORETTA FINALLY CONFIRMED THE LONG-HELD RUMOR IN AN AUTHORIZED BIOGRAPHY PUBLISHED AFTER HER DEATH.

LORETTA WASN'T A SAINT, BUT SHE HAD STRONG FEELINGS ABOUT PROPER BEHAVIOR ON THE SET. WHILE FILMING *RACHEL AND THE STRANGER* (1948), SHE ESTABLISHED THE FIRST OF HER SWEAR BOXES, FINING ANYONE WHO USED PROFANITY WITHIN HER HEARING. ONE STORY HAS IT THAT COSTAR ROBERT MITCHUM WOULD THRUST A FEW BILLS INTO THE BOX EACH MORNING, TELLING YOUNG, "THIS SHOULD COVER ME FOR THE DAY." SEVERAL INDUSTRY PEOPLE, FROM ACTRESS BARBARA STANWYCK TO WRITER-DIRECTOR JOSEPH L. MANKIEWICZ, HAVE CLAIMED THAT THEY STUFFED A FIVE-DOLLAR BILL IN THE BOX AND THEN TOLD LORETTA WHERE TO GET OFF, IN NO UNCERTAIN TERMS.

LORETTA'S SON PETER LEWIS WAS A MEMBER OF THE 1960S ROCK GROUP MOBY GRAPE.

THE FARMER'S DAUGHTER, 1947

FILMOGRAPHIES

JEAN ARTHUR

Cameo Kirby, 1923
Biff Bang Buddy, 1924
Fast and Fearless, 1924
Bringin' Home the Bacon, 1924
Thundering Romance, 1924
Travelin' Fast, 1924
Seven Chances, 1925
Drug Store Cowboy, 1925
The Fighting Smile, 1925
Tearin' Loose, 1925
A Man of Nerve, 1925
Hurricane Horseman, 1925
Thundering Through, 1925
Under Fire, 1926
Born to Battle, 1926
The Fighting Cheat, 1926
Double Daring, 1926
Lighting Bill, 1926
Twisted Triggers, 1926
The Cowboy Cop, 1926
The College Boob, 1926
The Block Signal, 1926
Husband Hunters, 1927
The Broken Gate, 1927
Horse Shoes, 1927
The Poor Nut, 1927
Flying Luck, 1927
Wallflowers, 1928
Warming Up, 1928
Brotherly Love, 1928
Sins of the Fathers, 1928
The Canary Murder Case, 1929
Stairs of Sand, 1929
*The Mysterious
    Dr. Fu Manchu*, 1929
The Greene Murder Case, 1929
The Saturday Night Kid, 1929
Halfway to Heaven, 1929
Street of Chance, 1930
Young Eagles, 1930
*The Return of
    Dr. Fu Manchu*, 1930
Danger Lights, 1930
The Silver Horde, 1930
The Gang Buster, 1931
The Virtuous Husband, 1931
The Lawyer's Secret, 1931
Ex-Bad Boy, 1931
The Past of Mary Holmes, 1933
Get That Venus, 1933
Whirlpool, 1934
*The Most Precious Thing
    in Life*, 1934
The Defense Rests, 1934
*The Whole Town's
    Talking*, 1935
Party Wire, 1935
Public Hero No. 1, 1935
Diamond Jim, 1935
The Public Menace, 1935

If You Could Only Cook, 1935
Mr. Deeds Goes to Town, 1936
The Ex-Mrs. Bradford, 1936
Adventure in Manhattan, 1936
More Than a Secretary, 1936
The Plainsman, 1936
History Is Made at Night, 1937
Easy Living, 1937
You Can't Take It With You, 1938
Only Angels Have Wings, 1939
*Mr. Smith Goes to
    Washington*, 1939
Too Many Husbands, 1940
Arizona, 1940
The Devil and Miss Jones, 1941
The Talk of the Town, 1942
The More the Merrier, 1943
A Lady Takes a Chance, 1943
The Impatient Years, 1944
A Foreign Affair, 1948
Shane, 1953

LAUREN BACALL

To Have and Have Not, 1944
Confidential Agent, 1945
The Big Sleep, 1946
Two Guys From Milwakee, 1946
Dark Passage, 1947
Key Largo, 1948
Young Man with a Horn, 1950
Bright Leaf, 1950
*How to Marry
    a Millionaire*, 1953
Woman's World, 1954
The Cobweb, 1955
Blood Alley, 1955
Written on the Wind, 1956
Designing Woman, 1957
The Gift of Love, 1958
North West Frontier, 1959
Shock Treatment, 1964
Sex and the Single Girl, 1964
Harper, 1966
*Murder on the
    Orient Express*, 1974
The Shootist, 1976
The Fan, 1981
H.E.A.L.T.H., 1979
Appointment with Death, 1988
Mr. North, 1988
Tree of Hands, 1989
Misery, 1990
All I Want for Christmas, 1991
A Star for Two, 1991
Prêt-à-Porter, 1994
The Mirror Has Two Faces, 1996
Le Jour et la Nuit, 1997
Diamonds, 1999
The Venice Project, 1999
Presence of Mind, 1999
The Limit, 2003
Dogville, 2003
Birth, 2004
Manderlay, 2005

INGRID BERGMAN

*Munkbrogreven/The Count of the Old
    Monk's Bridge*, 1934
Bränningar/The Surf, 1935
Swedenhielms, 1935
*Valborgsmässoafton/
    Walpurgis Night*, 1935
*På Solisidan/
    On the Sunny Side*, 1936
Intermezzo, 1937
Dollar, 1938
*Die Vier Gesellen/
    The Four Companions*, 1938
*En Kvinnas Ansikte/
    A Woman's Face*, 1938
En Enda Natt/One Single Night, 1938
Intermezzo: A Love Story, 1939
Juninatten/A Night in June, 1940
Rage in Heaven, 1941
Adam Had Four Sons, 1941
Dr. Jekyll and Mr. Hyde, 1941
Casablanca, 1942
For Whom the Bell Tolls, 1943
Gaslight, 1944
Spellbound, 1945
Saratoga Trunk, 1945
The Bells of St. Mary's, 1945
Notorious, 1946
Arch of Triumph, 1948
Joan of Arc, 1948
Under Capricorn, 1949
Stromboli, 1950
Europa '51, 1951
*Viaggio in Italia/
    Journey to Italy*, 1953
La Paura/Fear, 1954
*Giovanna D'Arco al Rogo/
    Joan at the Stake*, 1954
*Elena et les Hommes/
    Paris Does Strange Things*, 1956
Anastasia, 1956
Indiscreet, 1958
*The Inn of the Sixth
    Happiness*, 1958
Goodbye Again, 1961
The Visit, 1964
The Yellow Rolls-Royce, 1965
Stimulantia, 1967
Cactus Flower, 1969
A Walk in the Spring Rain, 1970
*From the Mixed-Up Files
    of Mrs. Basil E. Frankweiler*, 1973
Murder on the Orient Express, 1974
A Matter of Time, 1976
*Höstsonaten/
    Autumn Sonata*, 1978

CLARA BOW

Beyond the Rainbow, 1922
Down to the Sea in Ships, 1922
The Enemies of Women, 1923
The Daring Years, 1923
Maytime, 1923
Black Oxen, 1924
Grit, 1924
Poisoned Paradise, 1924
Daughters of Pleasure, 1924
Wine, 1924
Empty Hearts, 1924
Helen's Babies, 1924
This Woman, 1924
Black Lightning, 1924
Capital Punishment, 1925
The Adventurous Sex, 1925
Eve's Lover, 1925
Lawful Cheaters, 1925
The Scarlet West, 1925
My Lady's Lips, 1925
Parisian Love, 1925
Kiss Me Again, 1925
The Keeper of the Bees, 1925
The Primrose Path, 1925
Free to Love, 1925
The Best Bad Man, 1925
The Plastic Age, 1925
The Ancient Mariner, 1925
My Lady of Whims, 1926
The Shadow of the Law, 1926
Two Can Play, 1926
Dancing Mothers, 1926
Fascinating Youth, 1926
The Runaway, 1926
Mantrap, 1926
Kid Boots, 1926
It, 1927
Children of Divorce, 1927
Rough House Rosie, 1927
Wings, 1927
Hula, 1927
Get Your Man, 1927
Red Hair, 1928
Ladies of the Mob, 1928
The Fleet's In, 1928
Three Week-Ends, 1928
The Wild Party, 1929
Dangerous Curves, 1929
The Saturday Night Kid, 1929
True to the Navy, 1930
Love Among the Millionaires, 1930
Her Wedding Night, 1930
No Limit, 1931
Kick In, 1931
Call Her Savage, 1932
Hoopla, 1933

LOUISE BROOKS

The American Venus, 1926
Love 'Em and Leave 'Em, 1926
A Social Celebrity, 1926
It's the Old Army Game, 1926
The Show-Off, 1926
Just Another Blonde, 1926
Evening Clothes, 1927
Rolled Stockings, 1927
Now We're in the Air, 1927
The City Gone Wild, 1927
A Girl in Every Port, 1928
Beggars of Life, 1928
Die Büchse der Pandora/
    Pandora's Box, 1929
The Canary Murder Case, 1929
Das Tagebuch einer Verlorenen/
    Diary of a Lost Girl, 1929
Prix de Beauté/
    Miss Europe, 1930
It Pays to Advertise, 1931
God's Gift to Women, 1931
Empty Saddles, 1936
Overland Stage Raiders, 1938

CLAUDETTE COLBERT

For the Love of Mike, 1927
The Hole in the Wall, 1929
The Lady Lies, 1929
Young Man of Manhattan, 1929
La Grande Mare/
    The Big Pond, 1930
Manslaughter, 1930
L'Énigmatique M. Parkes, 1930
Honor Among Lovers, 1931
The Smiling Lieutenant, 1931
Secrets of a Secretary, 1931
His Woman, 1931
The Wise Sex, 1932
The Misleading Lady, 1932
The Man from Yesterday, 1932
The Phantom President, 1932
The Sign of the Cross, 1932
Tonight Is Ours, 1933
I Cover the Waterfront, 1933
Three-Cornered Moon, 1933
Torch Singer, 1933
Four Frightened People, 1934
It Happened One Night, 1934
Cleopatra, 1934
Imitation of Life, 1934
The Gilded Lily, 1935
Private Worlds, 1935
She Married Her Boss, 1935
The Bride Comes Home, 1935
Under Two Flags, 1936
Maid of Salem, 1937
I Met Him in Paris, 1937
Tovarich, 1937
Bluebeard's Eighth Wife, 1938
Zaza, 1939
Midnight, 1939
It's a Wonderful World, 1939
Drums Along the Mohawk, 1939

Boom Town, 1940
Arise, My Love, 1940
Skylark, 1941
Remember the Day, 1941
The Palm Beach Story, 1942
No Time for Love, 1943
So Proudly We Hail! 1943
Since You Went Away, 1944
Practically Yours, 1944
Guest Wife, 1945
Tomorrow Is Forever, 1946
Without Reservations,
    1946
The Secret Heart, 1946
The Egg and I, 1947
Sleep, My Love, 1948
Family Honeymoon, 1949
Bride for Sale, 1949
Three Came Home, 1950
The Secret Fury, 1950
Thunder on the Hill, 1951
Let's Make It Legal, 1951
The Planter's Wife, 1951
Destinées, 1954
Si Versailles M'était Conté/
    Royal Affairs in Versailles, 1954
Texas Lady, 1955
Parrish, 1961

JOAN CRAWFORD

Pretty Ladies, 1925
Old Clothes, 1925
Sally, Irene and Mary, 1925
Tramp, Tramp, Tramp, 1926
The Boob, 1926
Paris, 1926
Winners of the Wilderness, 1927
The Taxi Dancer, 1927
The Understanding Heart, 1927
The Unknown, 1927
Twelve Miles Out, 1927
Spring Fever, 1927
West Point, 1928
The Law of the Range, 1928
Rose-Marie, 1928
Across to Singapore, 1928
Four Walls, 1928
Our Dancing Daughters, 1928
Dream of Love, 1928
The Duke Steps Out, 1929
Our Modern Maidens, 1929
Untamed, 1929
Montana Moon, 1930
Our Blushing Brides, 1930
Paid, 1931
Dance, Fools, Dance, 1931
Laughing Sinners, 1931
This Modern Age, 1931
Possessed, 1931
Grand Hotel, 1932
Letty Lynton, 1932
Rain, 1932
Today We Live, 1933

JOAN CRAWFORD (con't)

Dancing Lady, 1933
Sadie McKee, 1934
Chained, 1934
Forsaking All Others, 1934
No More Ladies, 1935
I Live My Life, 1935
The Gorgeous Hussy, 1936
Love on the Run, 1936
The Last of Mrs. Cheyney, 1937
The Bride Wore Red, 1937
Mannequin, 1937
The Shining Hour, 1938
Ice Follies of 1939, 1939
The Women, 1939
Strange Cargo, 1940
Susan and God, 1940
A Woman's Face, 1941
When Ladies Meet, 1941
They All Kissed the Bride, 1942
Reunion in France, 1942
Above Suspicion, 1943
Mildred Pierce, 1945
Humoresque, 1946
Possessed, 1947
Daisy Kenyon, 1947
Flamingo Road, 1949
The Damned Don't Cry, 1950
Harriet Craig, 1950
Goodbye, My Fancy, 1951
The Woman Is Dangerous, 1952
Sudden Fear, 1952
Torch Song, 1953
Johnny Guitar, 1954
Female on the Beach, 1955
Queen Bee, 1955
Autumn Leaves, 1956
Good-by, My Lady, 1956
*The Story of
    Esther Costello*, 1957
The Best of Everything, 1959
*What Ever Happened
    to Baby Jane?* 1962
The Caretakers, 1963
Strait-Jacket, 1964
I Saw What You Did, 1965
The Karate Killers, 1967
Berserk! 1967
Trog, 1970

MARION DAVIES

Runaway Romany, 1917
Cecilia of the Pink Roses, 1918
The Burden of Proof, 1918
The Belle of New York, 1919
Getting Mary Married, 1919
The Dark Star, 1919
The Cinema Murder, 1919
April Folly, 1920
The Restless Sex, 1920
Buried Treasure, 1921
Enchantment, 1921
The Bride's Play, 1921
Beauty's Worth, 1922
The Young Diana, 1922
*When Knighthood
    Was in Flower*, 1922

Adam and Eva, 1923
Little Old New York, 1923
Yolanda, 1924
Janice Meredith, 1924
Zander the Great, 1925
Lights of Old Broadway, 1925
Beverly of Graustark, 1926
The Red Mill, 1926
Tillie the Toiler, 1927
The Fair Co-ed, 1927
Quality Street, 1927
The Patsy, 1927
The Cardboard Lover, 1928
Show People, 1928
Marianne, 1929
Not So Dumb, 1930
The Florodora Girl, 1931
The Bachelor Father, 1931
It's a Wise Child, 1931
Polly of the Circus, 1931
Blondie of the Follies, 1932
Peg o' My Heart, 1933
Going Hollywood, 1933
Operator 13, 1934
Page Miss Glory, 1935
Hearts Divided, 1936
Cain and Mabel, 1936
Ever Since Eve, 1937

BETTE DAVIS

The Bad Sister, 1931
Seed, 1931
Waterloo Bridge, 1931
Way Back Home, 1931
The Menace, 1932
Hell's House, 1932
The Man Who Played God, 1932
So Big, 1932
*The Rich Are
    Always with Us*, 1932
The Dark Horse, 1932
The Cabin in the Cotton, 1932
Three on a Match, 1932
*20,000 Years
    in Sing Sing*, 1932
Parachute Jumper, 1933
The Working Man, 1933
Ex-Lady, 1933
*Bureau of
    Missing Persons*, 1933
The Big Shakedown, 1934
Fashions of 1934, 1934
Jimmy the Gent, 1934
Fog Over Frisco, 1934
Of Human Bondage, 1934
Housewife, 1934
Bordertown, 1935
*The Girl from
    10th Avenue*, 1935
Front Page Woman, 1935
Special Agent, 1935
Dangerous, 1935
The Petrified Forest, 1936

The Golden Arrow, 1936
Satan Met a Lady, 1936
Marked Woman, 1937
Kid Galahad, 1937
That Certain Woman, 1937
It's Love I'm After, 1937
Jezebel, 1938
The Sisters, 1938
Dark Victory, 1939
Juarez, 1939
The Old Maid, 1939
*The Private Lives of
    Elizabeth and Essex*, 1939
All This, and Heaven Too, 1940
The Letter, 1940
The Great Lie, 1941
The Bride Came C.O.D., 1941
The Little Foxes, 1941
*The Man Who
    Came to Dinner*, 1942
In This Our Life, 1942
Now, Voyager, 1942
Watch on the Rhine, 1943
Old Acquaintance, 1943
Mr. Skeffington, 1944
The Corn Is Green, 1945
A Stolen Life, 1946
Deception, 1946
Winter Meeting, 1948
June Bride, 1948
Beyond the Forest, 1949
All About Eve, 1950
Payment on Demand, 1951
Another Man's Poison, 1952
*Phone Call
    from a Stranger*, 1952
The Star, 1952
The Virgin Queen, 1955
The Catered Affair, 1956
Storm Center, 1956
John Paul Jones, 1959
The Scapegoat, 1959
Pocketful of Miracles, 1961
*What Ever Happened
    to Baby Jane?* 1962
*La Noia/
    The Empty Canvas*, 1963
Dead Ringer, 1964
Where Love Has Gone, 1964
*Hush . . . Hush,
    Sweet Charlotte*, 1964
The Nanny, 1965
The Anniversary, 1968
Connecting Rooms, 1970
Bunny O'Hare, 1971
Madame Sin, 1972
*Lo Scopone Scientifico/The Scientific
    Cardplayer*, 1972
Burnt Offerings, 1976
*Return from
    Witch Mountain*, 1978
Death on the Nile, 1978
*The Watcher
    in the Woods*, 1980
The Whales of August, 1987
Wicked Stepmother, 1989

DORIS DAY

Romance on the High Seas, 1948
My Dream Is Yours, 1949
It's a Great Feeling, 1949
Young Man with a Horn, 1950
Tea for Two, 1950
West Point Story, 1950
Storm Warning, 1951
Lullaby of Broadway, 1951
On Moonlight Bay, 1951
I'll See You in My Dreams, 1951
Starlift, 1951
The Winning Team, 1952
April in Paris, 1952
By the Light
* of the Silvery Moon*, 1953
Calamity Jane, 1953
Lucky Me, 1954
Young at Heart, 1954
Love Me or Leave Me, 1955
The Man Who
* Knew Too Much*, 1956
Julie, 1956
The Pajama Game, 1957
Teacher's Pet, 1958
The Tunnel of Love, 1958
It Happened to Jane, 1959
Pillow Talk, 1959
Please Don't
* Eat the Daisies*, 1960
Midnight Lace, 1960
Lover Come Back, 1961
That Touch of Mink, 1962
Billy Rose's Jumbo, 1962
The Thrill of It All, 1963
Move Over, Darling, 1963
Send Me No Flowers, 1964
Do Not Disturb, 1965
The Glass Bottom Boat, 1966
The Ballad of Josie, 1967
Caprice, 1967
Where Were You When the
* Lights Went Out ?* 1968
With Six You Get Eggroll, 1968

OLIVIA DE HAVILLAND

Alibi Ike, 1935
The Irish in Us, 1935
A Midsummer
* Night's Dream*, 1935
Captain Blood, 1935
Anthony Adverse, 1936
The Charge
* of the Light Brigade*, 1936
Call It a Day, 1937
It's Love I'm After, 1937
The Great Garrick, 1937
Gold Is Where You Find It, 1938
The Adventures
* of Robin Hood*, 1938
Four's a Crowd, 1938
Hard to Get, 1938
Wings of the Navy, 1939
Dodge City, 1939
The Private Lives of
* Elizabeth and Essex*, 1939
Gone with the Wind, 1939
Raffles, 1940
My Love Came Back, 1940
Santa Fe Trail, 1940

The Strawberry Blonde, 1941
Hold Back the Dawn, 1941
They Died with
* Their Boots On*, 1941
The Male Animal, 1942
In This Our Life, 1942
Princess O'Rourke, 1943
Government Girl, 1943
To Each His Own, 1946
Devotion, 1946
The Well-Groomed Bride, 1946
The Dark Mirror, 1946
The Snake Pit, 1948
The Heiress, 1949
My Cousin Rachel, 1953
That Lady, 1955
Not as a Stranger, 1955
The Ambassador's
* Daughter*, 1956
The Proud Rebel, 1958
Libel, 1959
Light in the Piazza, 1962
Lady in a Cage, 1964
Hush . . . Hush, Sweet
* Charlotte*, 1965
The Adventurers, 1970
Pope Joan, 1972
Airport '77, 1977
The Swarm, 1978
The Fifth Musketeer, 1979

MARLENE DIETRICH

So Sind die Männer/
* The Little Napoleon*, 1922
Der Mensch am Wege/
* Man by the Roadside*, 1923
Tragödie der Liebe/
* Love Tragedy*, 1923
Der Sprung ins Leben/
* Leap into Life*, 1923
Der Mönch von Santarem/
* The Monk from Santarem*, 1924
Manon Lescaut, 1926
Kopf hoch, Charly!/
* Heads Up, Charley*, 1926
Der Juxbaron/
* The Imaginary Baron*, 1926
Dubarry von Heute, Eine/
* A Modern Dubarry*, 1927
Café Elektric/
* Cafe Electric*, 1927
Sein Größter Bluff/
* His Greatest Bluff*, 1927
Prinzessin Olala/
* Art of Love*, 1928
Ich Küsse Ihre Hand,
* Madame/I Kiss Your*
* Hand, Madame*, 1929
Das Schiff der
* Verlorenen Menschen/*
* Grischa the Cook*, 1929
Gefahren der Brautzeit/
* Dangers of the*
* Engagement*, 1929
Die Frau Nach der Man Sich Sehnt/
* The Woman One Longs For*, 1929
Der Blaue Engel/
* The Blue Angel*, 1930

Morocco, 1930
Dishonored, 1931
Shanghai Express, 1932
Blonde Venus, 1932
The Song of Songs, 1933
The Scarlet Empress, 1934
The Devil Is a Woman, 1935
Desire, 1936
The Garden of Allah, 1936
I Loved a Soldier, 1936
Knight Without Armor, 1937
Angel, 1937
Destry Rides Again, 1939
Seven Sinners, 1940
The Flame
* of New Orleans*, 1941
Manpower, 1941
The Lady Is Willing, 1942
The Spoilers, 1942
Pittsburgh, 1942
Kismet, 1944
Martin Roumagnac/
* The Room Upstairs*, 1946
Golden Earrings, 1947
A Foreign Affair, 1948
Stage Fright, 1950
No Highway in the Sky, 1951
Rancho Notorious, 1952
Around the World
* in 80 Days*, 1956
Monte Carlo, 1956
Witness for
* the Prosecution*, 1957
Touch of Evil, 1958
Judgment at Nuremberg, 1961
Schöner Gigolo, Armer Gigolo/
* Just a Gigolo*, 1979

IRENE DUNNE

Leathernecking, 1930
Cimarron, 1931
Bachelor Apartment, 1931
The Great Lover, 1931
Consolation Marriage, 1931
Symphony of Six Million, 1932
Back Street, 1932
Thirteen Women, 1932
No Other Woman, 1933
The Secret of
* Madame Blanche*, 1933
The Silver Cord, 1933
Ann Vickers, 1933
If I Were Free, 1933
This Man Is Mine, 1934
Stingaree, 1934
The Age of Innocence, 1934
Sweet Adeline, 1934
Roberta, 1935
Magnificent Obsession, 1935
Show Boat, 1936
Theodora Goes Wild, 1936
High, Wide,
* and Handsome*, 1937
The Awful Truth, 1937
Joy of Living, 1938
Love Affair, 1939
Invitation to Happiness, 1939
When Tomorrow Comes, 1939
My Favorite Wife, 1940
Penny Serenade, 1941

IRENE DUNNE (con't)

Unfinished Business, 1941
Lady in a Jam, 1942
A Guy Named Joe, 1943
The White Cliffs of Dover, 1944
Together Again, 1944
Over 21, 1945
*Anna and
    the King of Siam*, 1946
Life with Father, 1947
I Remember Mama, 1948
Never a Dull Moment, 1950
The Mudlark, 1950
It Grows on Trees, 1952

GRETA GARBO

*Luffarpetter/
    Peter the Tramp*, 1922
*Gösta Berlings saga/
    The Saga of Gösta Berling*, 1924
*Die Freudlose Gasse/
    The Joyless Street*, 1925
Torrent, 1926
The Temptress, 1926
Flesh and the Devil, 1926
Love, 1927
The Divine Woman, 1928
The Mysterious Lady, 1928
A Woman of Affairs, 1928
Wild Orchids, 1929
The Single Standard, 1929
The Kiss, 1929
Anna Christie, 1930
Romance, 1930
Inspiration, 1931
*Susan Lenox
    (Her Fall and Rise)*, 1931
Mata Hari, 1931
Grand Hotel, 1932
As You Desire Me, 1932
Queen Christina, 1933
The Painted Veil, 1934
Anna Karenina, 1935
Camille, 1936
Conquest, 1937
Ninotchka, 1939
Two-Faced Woman, 1941

AVA GARDNER

Ghosts on the Loose, 1943
Maisie Goes to Reno, 1944
Three Men in White, 1944
She Went to the Races, 1945
Whistle Stop, 1946
The Killers, 1946
Singapore, 1947
The Hucksters, 1947
One Touch of Venus, 1948
The Bribe, 1949
The Great Sinner, 1949
East Side, West Side, 1949
*Pandora and
    the Flying Dutchman*, 1951
My Forbidden Past, 1951
Show Boat, 1951
Lone Star, 1952
The Snows of Kilimanjaro, 1952
Ride, Vaquero! 1953
Mogambo, 1953

Knights of the Round Table, 1953
The Barefoot Contessa, 1954
Bhowani Junction, 1956
The Little Hut, 1957
The Sun Also Rises, 1957
The Naked Maja, 1959
On the Beach, 1959
The Angel Wore Red, 1960
55 Days at Peking, 1963
Seven Days in May, 1964
The Night of the Iguana, 1964
La Bibbia, 1966
Mayerling, 1968
Tam Lin, 1970
*The Life and Times
    of Judge Roy Bean*, 1972
Earthquake, 1974
Permission to Kill, 1975
The Blue Bird, 1976
The Cassandra Crossing, 1976
The Sentinel, 1977
City on Fire, 1979
*The Kidnapping
    of the President*, 1980
Priest of Love, 1981
Regina Roma, 1982

JUDY GARLAND

Pigskin Parade, 1936
Every Sunday, 1936
Broadway Melody of 1938, 1937
Thoroughbreds Don't Cry, 1937
Everybody Sing, 1938
Love Finds Andy Hardy, 1938
Listen, Darling, 1938
The Wizard of Oz, 1939
Babes in Arms, 1939
*Andy Hardy
    Meets Debutante*, 1940
Strike Up the Band, 1940
Little Nellie Kelly, 1940
Ziegfeld Girl, 1941
*Life Begins
    for Andy Hardy*, 1941
Babes on Broadway, 1941
For Me and My Gal, 1942
Presenting Lily Mars, 1943
Girl Crazy, 1943
Meet Me in St. Louis, 1944
The Clock, 1945
The Harvey Girls, 1946
Ziegfeld Follies, 1946
Till the Clouds Roll By, 1947
Words and Music, 1948
The Pirate, 1948
Easter Parade, 1948
*In the Good
    Old Summertime*, 1949
Summer Stock, 1950
A Star Is Born, 1954
Judgment at Nuremberg, 1961
A Child Is Waiting, 1963
I Could Go On Singing, 1963

GREER GARSON

Goodbye, Mr. Chips, 1939
Remember? 1939
Pride and Prejudice, 1940
Blossoms in the Dust, 1941
When Ladies Meet, 1941
Mrs. Miniver, 1942
Random Harvest, 1942
The Youngest Profession, 1943
Madame Curie, 1943
Mrs. Parkington, 1944
The Valley of Decision, 1945
Adventure, 1945
Desire Me, 1947
Julia Misbehaves, 1948
That Forsyte Woman, 1949
The Miniver Story, 1950
The Law and the Lady, 1951
Scandal at Scourie, 1953
Julius Caesar, 1953
Her Twelve Men, 1954
Strange Lady in Town, 1955
Sunrise at Campobello, 1960
The Singing Nun, 1966
The Happiest Millionaire, 1967

LILLIAN GISH

The New York Hat, 1912
The One She Loved, 1912
My Baby, 1912
Two Daughters of Eve, 1912
An Unseen Enemy, 1912
Gold and Glitter, 1912
The Informer, 1912
In the Aisles of the Wild, 1912
A Cry for Help, 1912
*The Musketeers
    of Pig Alley*, 1912
The Burglar's Dilemma, 1912
The Painted Lady, 1912
A Timely Interception, 1913
The Unwelcome Guest, 1913
So Runs the Way, 1913
During the Round-Up, 1913
*The Battle at
    Elderbush Gulch*, 1913
A Woman in the Ultimate, 1913
Oil and Water, 1913
A Misunderstood Boy, 1913
A Modest Hero, 1913
Madonna of the Storm, 1913
The Mothering Heart, 1913
The House of Darkness, 1913
An Indian's Loyalty, 1913
Just Gold, 1913
The Left-Handed Man, 1913
The Lady and the Mouse, 1913
Judith of Bethulia, 1914
The Hunchback, 1914
The Battle of the Sexes, 1914
The Quicksands, 1914
Home, Sweet Home, 1914
Lord Chumley, 1914
The Sisters, 1914
The Tear That Burned, 1914
*The Rebellion
    of Kitty Belle*, 1914
Man's Enemy, 1914

Silent Sandy, 1914
The Escape, 1914
The Angel of Contention, 1914
The Folly of Anne, 1914
His Lesson, 1914
The Birth of a Nation, 1915
The Lost House, 1915
Enoch Arden, 1915
Captain Macklin, 1915
The Lily and the Rose, 1915
Souls Triumphant, 1915
Daphne and the Pirate, 1916
Sold for Marriage, 1916
An Innocent Magdalene, 1916
Intolerance, 1916
Diane of the Follies, 1916
The Children Pay, 1916
Pathways of Life, 1916
Flirting with Fate, 1916
*The House
    Built Upon Sand*, 1917
Hearts of the World, 1918
The Great Love, 1918
The Greatest Thing in Life, 1918
*A Romance
    of Happy Valley*, 1919
Broken Blossoms, 1919
True Heart Susie, 19119199
The Greatest Question, 1919
Way Down East, 1920
Orphans of the Storm, 1922
The White Sister, 1923
Romola, 1924
La Bohème, 1926
The Scarlet Letter, 1926
Annie Laurie, 1927
The Enemy, 1928
The Wind, 1928
One Romantic Night, 1930
His Double Life, 1933
*The Commandos
    Strike at Dawn*, 1942
Top Man, 1943
Miss Susie Slagle's, 1945
Duel in the Sun, 1946
Portrait of Jennie, 1948
The Cobweb, 1955
The Night of the Hunter, 1955
Orders to Kill, 1958
The Unforgiven, 1960
Follow Me, Boys! 1966
Warning Shot, 1967
The Comedians, 1967
Twin Detectives, 1976
A Wedding, 1978
Hambone and Hillie, 1984
Sweet Liberty, 1986
The Whales of August, 1987

JEAN HARLOW

The Saturday Night Kid, 1929
Hell's Angels, 1930
The Secret Six, 1931
Public Enemy, 1931
Iron Man, 1931
Goldie, 1931
Platinum Blonde, 1931
Three Wise Girls, 1932
Beast of the City, 1932
Red-Headed Woman, 1932
Red Dust, 1932
Hold Your Man, 1933
Dinner at Eight, 1933
Bombshell, 1933
The Girl from Missouri, 1934
Reckless, 1935
China Seas, 1935
Riffraff, 1935
Wife vs. Secretary, 1936
Suzy, 1936
Libeled Lady, 1936
Personal Property, 1937
Saratoga, 1937

SUSAN HAYWARD

Girls on Probation, 1938
Beau Geste, 1939
Our Leading Citizen, 1939
$1,000 a Touchdown, 1939
Adam Had Four Sons, 1941
Sis Hopkins, 1941
Among the Living, 1941
Reap the Wild Wind, 1942
The Forest Rangers, 1942
I Married a Witch, 1942
Young and Willing, 1943
Hit Parade of 1943, 1943
Jack London, 1943
The Fighting Seabees, 1944
The Hairy Ape, 1944
And Now Tomorrow, 1944
Deadline at Dawn, 1946
Canyon Passage, 1946
*Smash-up:
    The Story of a Woman*, 1947
They Won't Believe Me, 1947
The Lost Moment, 1947
The Saxon Charm, 1948
Tulsa, 1949
Tap Roots, 1948
House of Strangers, 1949
My Foolish Heart, 1949
*I'd Climb the
    Highest Mountain*, 1951
Rawhide, 1951
*I Can Get It
    for You Wholesale*, 1951
David and Bathsheba, 1951
With a Song in My Heart, 1952
The Snows of Kilimanjaro, 1952
The Lusty Men, 1952
The President's Lady, 1953
White Witch Doctor, 1953

*Demetrius and
    the Gladiators*, 1954
Garden of Evil, 1954
Untamed, 1955
Soldier of Fortune, 1955
I'll Cry Tomorrow, 1955
The Conqueror, 1956
Top Secret Affair, 1957
I Want to Live! 1958
Thunder in the Sun, 1959
Woman Obsessed, 1959
The Marriage-Go-Round, 1960
Ada, 1961
Back Street, 1961
I Thank a Fool, 1962
Stolen Hours, 1963
Where Love Has Gone, 1964
The Honey Pot, 1967
Valley of the Dolls, 1967
The Revengers, 1972

RITA HAYWORTH

Under the Pampas Moon, 1935
Charlie Chan in Egypt, 1935
Dante's Inferno, 1935
Paddy O'Day, 1935
Dancing Pirate, 1936
Human Cargo, 1936
Meet Nero Wolfe, 1936
Rebellion, 1936
Old Louisiana, 1937
Hit the Saddle, 1937
Trouble in Texas, 1937
Criminals of the Air, 1937
Girls Can Play, 1937
The Game That Kills, 1937
Paid to Dance, 1937
The Shadow, 1937
Who Killed Gail Preston? 1938
Special Inspector, 1938
There's Always a Woman, 1938
Convicted, 1938
Juvenile Court, 1938
The Renegade Ranger, 1939
Homicide Bureau, 1939
The Lone Wolf Spy Hunt, 1939
Only Angels Have Wings, 1939
Music in My Heart, 1940
Blondie on a Budget, 1940
Susan and God, 1940
The Lady in Question, 1940
Angels Over Broadway, 1940
The Strawberry Blonde, 1941
Affectionately Yours, 1941
Blood and Sand, 1941
You'll Never Get Rich, 1941
My Gal Sal, 1942
Tales of Manhattan, 1942
You Were Never Lovelier, 1942
Cover Girl, 1944
Tonight and Every Night, 1945

RITA HAYWORTH (con't)

Gilda, 1946
Down to Earth, 1947
The Lady from Shanghai, 1948
The Loves of Carmen, 1948
Affair in Trinidad, 1952
Salome, 1952
Miss Sadie Thompson, 1953
Fire Down Below, 1957
Pal Joey, 1957
Separate Tables, 1958
They Came to Cordura, 1959
The Story on Page One, 1959
The Happy Thieves, 1962
Circus World, 1964
The Money Trap, 1966
The Poppy Is Also a Flower, 1966
L'Avventuriero/The Rover, 1967
I Bastardi, 1969
The Naked Zoo, 1970
La Route de Salina/
    Road to Salina, 1971
The Wrath of God, 1972

AUDREY HEPBURN

Laughter in Paradise, 1951
One Wild Oat, 1951
The Lavender Hill Mob, 1951
Young Wives' Tale, 1951
Monte Carlo Baby, 1951
The Secret People, 1952
Nous Irons à Monte Carlo/
    We Will All Go to Monte Carlo, 1952
Roman Holiday, 1953
Sabrina, 1954
War and Peace, 1956
Funny Face, 1957
Love in the Afternoon, 1957
Green Mansions, 1959
The Nun's Story, 1959
The Unforgiven, 1960
Breakfast at Tiffany's, 1961
The Children's Hour, 1961
Charade, 1963
Paris—When It Sizzles, 1964
My Fair Lady, 1964
How to Steal a Million, 1966
Two for the Road, 1967
Wait Until Dark, 1967
Robin and Marian, 1976
Bloodline, 1979
They All Laughed, 1981
Love Among Thieves, 1987
Always, 1989

KATHARINE HEPBURN

A Bill of Divorcement, 1932
Christopher Strong, 1933
Morning Glory, 1933
Little Women, 1933
Spitfire, 1934
The Little Minister, 1934
Break of Hearts, 1935
Alice Adams, 1935
Sylvia Scarlett, 1935
Mary of Scotland, 1936
A Woman Rebels, 1936
Quality Street, 1937
Stage Door, 1937
Bringing Up Baby, 1938
Holiday, 1938
The Philadelphia Story, 1940
Woman of the Year, 1942
Keeper of the Flame, 1942
Dragon Seed, 1944
Without Love, 1945
Undercurrent, 1946
The Sea of Grass, 1947
Song of Love, 1947
State of the Union, 1948
Adam's Rib, 1949
The African Queen, 1951
Pat and Mike, 1952
Summertime, 1955
The Rainmaker, 1956
The Iron Petticoat, 1956
Desk Set, 1957
Suddenly, Last Summer, 1959
Long Day's Journey
    Into Night, 1962
Guess Who's
    Coming to Dinner? 1967
The Lion in Winter, 1968
The Madwoman
    of Chaillot, 1969
The Trojan Women, 1971
A Delicate Balance, 1973
Rooster Cogburn, 1975
Olly, Olly, Oxen Free, 1978
On Golden Pond, 1981
Grace Quigley, 1984
Love Affair, 1994

LENA HORNE

The Duke Is Tops, 1938
Panama Hattie, 1942
Cabin in the Sky, 1943
Stormy Weather, 1943
Thousands Cheer, 1943
I Dood It, 1943
Swing Fever, 1944
Broadway Rhythm, 1944
Two Girls and a Sailor, 1944
Ziegfeld Follies, 1946
Till the Clouds Roll By, 1947
Words and Music, 1948
Duchess of Idaho, 1950
Meet Me in Las Vegas, 1956
Death of a Gunfighter, 1969
The Wiz, 1978

GRACE KELLY

Fourteen Hours, 1951
High Noon, 1952
Mogambo, 1953
Dial M for Murder, 1954
Rear Window, 1954
The Country Girl, 1954
Green Fire, 1954
The Bridges at Toko-Ri, 1955
To Catch a Thief, 1955
The Swan, 1956
High Society, 1956

DEBORAH KERR

Major Barbara, 1941
Love on the Dole, 1941
Penn of Pennsylvania, 1941
Hatter's Castle, 1941
The Day Will Dawn, 1942
The Life and Death
    of Colonel Blimp, 1943
Perfect Strangers, 1945
I See a Dark Stranger, 1946
Black Narcissus, 1947
The Hucksters, 1947
If Winter Comes, 1947
Edward, My Son, 1949
King Solomon's Mines, 1950
Please Believe Me, 1950
Quo Vadis, 1951
The Prisoner of Zenda, 1952
Thunder in the East, 1952
Young Bess, 1953
Julius Caesar, 1953
Dream Wife, 1953
From Here to Eternity, 1953
The End of the Affair, 1955
The Proud
    and the Profane, 1956
The King and I, 1956
Tea and Sympathy, 1956
Heaven Knows,
    Mr. Allison, 1957
An Affair to Remember, 1957
Bonjour Tristesse, 1958
Separate Tables, 1958
The Journey, 1959
Count Your Blessings, 1959
Beloved Infidel, 1959
The Sundowners, 1960
The Grass Is Greener, 1960
The Naked Edge, 1961
The Innocents, 1961
The Chalk Garden, 1964
The Night of the Iguana, 1964
Marriage on the Rocks, 1965
Casino Royale, 1967
Eye of the Devil, 1967
Prudence and the Pill, 1968
The Gypsy Moths, 1969
The Arrangement, 1969
The Assam Garden, 1985

HEDY LAMARR

Die Koffer des Herrn O.F./
   The Trunks of Mr. O.F., 1931
Mein Braucht Kein Geld/
   We Need No Money, 1931
Extase/Ecstasy, 1933
Algiers, 1938
Lady of the Tropics, 1939
I Take This Woman, 1940
Boom Town, 1940
Comrade X, 1940
Come Live with Me, 1941
Ziegfeld Girl, 1941
H. M. Pulham, Esq., 1941
Tortilla Flat, 1942
Crossroads, 1942
White Cargo, 1942
The Heavenly Body, 1943
The Conspirators, 1944
Experiment Perilous, 1944
Her Highness
   and the Bellboy, 1945
The Strange Woman, 1946
Dishonored Lady, 1947
Let's Live a Little, 1948
Samson and Delilah, 1949
A Lady Without
   a Passport, 1950
Copper Canyon, 1951
My Favorite Spy, 1951
L'Amante di Paride/Loves
   of Three Queens, 1954
The Story of Mankind, 1957
The Female Animal, 1958
Instant Karma, 1990

VIVIEN LEIGH

Things Are Looking Up, 1935
The Village Squire, 1935
Gentlemen's Agreement, 1935
Look Up and Laugh, 1935
Fire Over England, 1937
Dark Journey, 1937
Storm in a Teacup, 1937
A Yank at Oxford, 1938
Sidewalks of London, 1938
Gone with the Wind, 1939
Twenty-One Days, 1940
Waterloo Bridge, 1940
That Hamilton Woman, 1941
Caesar and Cleopatra, 1946
Anna Karenina, 1948
A Streetcar Named Desire, 1951
The Deep Blue Sea, 1955
Ship of Fools, 1965

CAROLE LOMBARD

A Perfect Crime, 1921
Marriage in Transit, 1925
Hearts and Spurs, 1925
Durand of the Badlands, 1925
The Divine Sinner, 1928
Me, Gangster, 1928
Show Folks, 1928
Ned McCobb's Daughter, 1928

High Voltage, 1929
Big News, 1929
The Racketeer, 1929
The Arizona Kid, 1930
Safety in Numbers, 1930
Fast and Loose, 1930
It Pays to Advertise, 1931
Man of the World, 1931
Ladies' Man, 1931
Up Pops the Devil, 1931
I Take This Woman, 1931
No One Man, 1932
Sinners in the Sun, 1932
Virtue, 1932
No More Orchids, 1932
No Man of Her Own, 1932
From Hell to Heaven, 1933
Supernatural, 1933
The Eagle and the Hawk, 1933
Brief Moment, 1933
White Woman, 1933
Bolero, 1934
We're Not Dressing, 1934
Twentieth Century, 1934
Now and Forever, 1934
Lady by Choice, 1934
The Gay Bride, 1934
Rumba, 1935
Hands Across the Table, 1935
Love Before Breakfast, 1936
The Princess
   Comes Across, 1936
My Man Godfrey, 1936
Nothing Sacred, 1937
Swing High, Swing Low, 1937
True Confession, 1937
Fools for Scandal, 1938
Made for Each Other, 1939
In Name Only, 1939
Vigil in the Night, 1940
They Knew
   What They Wanted, 1940
Mr. and Mrs. Smith, 1941
To Be or Not to Be, 1942

SOPHIA LOREN

La Favorita, 1952
E' Arrivato l'Accordatore/
   The Piano Tuner Has Arrived, 1952
Aida, 1953
Africa Sotto I Mari/
   Africa Under the Seas, 1953
*La Tratta Delle Bianche/*Girls Marked for
   Danger, 1953
Pellegrini d'Amore, 1953
Il Paese Dei Campanelli, 1953
Due Notti Con Cleopatra/
   Two Nights with Cleopatra, 1953
La Domenica della
   Buona Gente, 1953
Ci Troviamo in Galleria, 1953
Tempi Nostri/
   The Anatomy of Love, 1954
Miseria E Nobilta, 1954
L'oro di Napoli/
   The Gold of Naples, 1954
Un Giorno in Pretura/
   A Day in Court, 1954

Carosello Napoletano/
   Neapolitan Carousel, 1954
Attila, 1954
Il Segno di Venere/
   The Sign of Venus, 1955
*La Bella Mugnaia/*The
   Miller's Beautiful Wife, 1955
A Donna del Fiume/
   The River Girl, 1955
Peccato Che
   Sia di Essere Donna/
   Too Bad She's Bad, 1955
Pane, amore e . . ./
   Scandal in Sorrento, 1955
La Fortuna di Essere Donna/
   Lucky to Be a Woman, 1956
Boy on a Dolphin, 1957
The Pride and the Passion, 1957
Timbuctù/
   Legend of the Lost, 1957
Desire Under the Elms, 1958
The Key, 1958
The Black Orchid, 1959
Houseboat, 1959
That Kind of Woman, 1959
Heller in Pink Tights, 1960
It Started in Naples, 1960
A Breath of Scandal, 1960
La Ciociara/Two Women, 1961
The Millionairess, 1961
El Cid, 1961
Boccaccio '70, 1962
Madame Sans-Géne, 1962
I Sequestrata di Altona/
   The Condemned of Altona, 1962
Le Couteau Dans la Plaie/
   Five Miles to Midnight, 1962
Ieri, Oggi, Domaini/
   Yesterday, Today and
   Tomorrow, 1963
The Fall of
   the Roman Empire, 1964
Matrimonio all'Italiana/
   Marriage, Italian Style, 1964
Operation Crossbow, 1965
Lady L., 1965
Judith, 1966
Arabesque, 1966
A Countess
   from Hong Kong, 1967
C'Era una Volta/
   More than a Miracle, 1967
Questi Fantasmi/
   Ghosts—Italian Style, 1968
I Girasoli/Sunflower, 1970
La Moglie del Preta/
   The Priest's Wife, 1971
Bianco, Rosso e . . ., 1972
Man of La Mancha, 1972
Il Viaggio/The Voyage, 1974
Verdict, 1974
La Pupa del Gangster, 1975
The Cassandra Crossing, 1976
Una Giornata Particulare/
   A Special Day, 1977

SOPHIA LOREN (con't)

Angela, 1978
*Fatto di Sangue fra Due Uomini
    per Causa di una Vedova—
    Si Sospettano Moventi Politici/*
    Blood Feud, 1978
Brass Target, 1979
Firepower, 1979
Qualcosa di Biondo, 1984
Prêt-à-Porter, 1994
Grumpier Old Men, 1995
Soleil, 1997
Between Strangers, 2002

MYRNA LOY

What Price Beauty? 1925
The Caveman, 1926
Why Girls Go Back Home, 1926
The Gilded Highway, 1926
Exquisite Sinner, 1926
So This Is Paris, 1926
Don Juan, 1926
Across the Pacific, 1926
Finger Prints, 1927
Bitter Apples, 1927
The Climbers, 1927
Simple Sis, 1927
The Heart of Maryland, 1927
A Sailor's Sweetheart, 1927
The Jazz Singer, 1927
The Girl from Chicago, 1927
If I Were Single, 1927
*Ham and Eggs
    at the Front*, 1927
Beware of Married Men, 1928
Turn Back the Hours, 1928
The Crimson City, 1928
Pay as You Enter, 1928
State Street Sadie, 1928
The Midnight Taxi, 1928
Fancy Baggage, 1929
Hardboiled Rose, 1929
The Desert Song, 1929
The Black Watch, 1929
The Squall, 1929
Noah's Ark, 1929
The Great Divide, 1929
Evidence, 1929
The Show of Shows, 1929
Cameo Kirby, 1930
Isle of Escape, 1930
Under a Texas Moon, 1930
Cock o' the Walk, 1930
Bride of the Regiment, 1930
The Last of the Duanes, 1930
The Jazz Cinderella, 1930
The Bad Man, 1930
Renegades, 1930
Rogue of the Rio Grande, 1930
The Truth about Youth, 1930
The Devil to Pay! 1930
The Naughty Flirt, 1931
Body and Soul, 1931
A Connecticut Yankee, 1931
Hush Money, 1931
Transatlantic, 1931
Rebound, 1931
Skyline, 1931
Consolation Marriage, 1931
Arrowsmith, 1931

Emma, 1931
Vanity Fair, 1932
The Wet Parade, 1932
The Woman in Room 13, 1932
New Morals for Old, 1932
Love Me Tonight, 1932
Thirteen Women, 1932
The Mask of Fu Manchu, 1932
The Animal Kingdom, 1932
Topaze, 1933
The Barbarian, 1933
The Prizefighter and the Lady, 1933
When Ladies Meet, 1933
Penthouse, 1933
Night Flight, 1933
Men in White, 1934
Manhattan Melodrama, 1934
The Thin Man, 1934
Stamboul Quest, 1934
Evelyn Prentice, 1934
Broadway Bill, 1934
Wings in the Dark, 1935
Whipsaw, 1935
Wife vs. Secretary, 1936
Petticoat Fever, 1936
The Great Ziegfeld, 1936
To Mary—with Love, 1936
Libeled Lady, 1936
After the Thin Man, 1936
Parnell, 1937
Double Wedding, 1937
Test Pilot, 1938
Man-Proof, 1938
Too Hot to Handle, 1938
Lucky Night, 1939
The Rains Came, 1939
Another Thin Man, 1939
I Love You Again, 1940
Third Finger, Left Hand, 1940
Love Crazy, 1941
Shadow of the Thin Man, 1941
The Thin Man Goes Home, 1945
So Goes My Love, 1946
*The Best Years
    of Our Lives*, 1946
*The Bachelor
    and the Bobby-Soxer*, 1947
Song of the Thin Man, 1947
*The Senator
    Was Indiscreet*, 1947
*Mr. Blandings Builds
    His Dream House*, 1948
The Red Pony, 1949
That Dangerous Age, 1949
Cheaper by the Dozen, 1950
Belles on Their Toes, 1952
*The Ambassador's
    Daughter*, 1956
Lonelyhearts, 1958
From the Terrace, 1960
Midnight Lace, 1960
The April Fools, 1969
Airport 1975, 1974
The End, 1978
*Just Tell Me
    What You Want*, 1980

SHIRLEY MACLAINE

The Trouble with Harry, 1955
Artists and Models, 1955
*Around the World
    in 80 Days*, 1956
The Sheepman, 1958
The Matchmaker, 1958
Hot Spell, 1958
Some Came Running, 1958
Ask Any Girl, 1959
Career, 1959
Can-Can, 1960
The Apartment, 1960
Ocean's Eleven, 1960
All in a Night's Work, 1961
Two Loves, 1961
The Children's Hour, 1961
My Geisha, 1962
Two for the Seesaw, 1962
Irma la Douce, 1963
What a Way to Go! 1964
The Yellow Rolls-Royce, 1964
*John Goldfarb,
    Please Come Home*, 1965
Gambit, 1966
Woman Times Seven, 1967
The Bliss of Mrs. Blossom, 1968
Sweet Charity, 1969
Two Mules for Sister Sara, 1970
Desperate Characters, 1971
*The Possession
    of Joel Delaney*, 1972
The Turning Point, 1977
Being There, 1979
Loving Couples, 1980
A Change of Seasons, 1980
Terms of Endearment, 1983
Cannonball Run II, 1984
Madame Sousatzka, 1988
Steel Magnolias, 1989
Waiting for the Light, 1990
Postcards from the Edge, 1990
Used People, 1992
Wrestling Ernest Hemingway, 1993
Guarding Tess, 1994
Ms. Winterbourne, 1996
The Evening Star, 1996
Bruno, 2000
Carolina, 2003
In Her Shoes, 2005

MARILYN MONROE

Dangerous Years, 1947
Scudda Hoo! Scudda Hay! 1948
Ladies of the Chorus, 1949
Love Happy, 1949
A Ticket to Tomahawk, 1950
The Asphalt Jungle, 1950
The Fireball, 1950
All About Eve, 1950
Right Cross, 1950
Hometown Story, 1951
As Young as You Feel, 1951
Love Next, 1951
Let's Make It Legal, 1951
Clash by Night, 1952
We're Not Married! 1952
Don't Bother to Knock, 1952

Monkey Business, 1952
O. Henry's Full House, 1952
Niagara, 1953
Gentlemen Prefer Blondes, 1953
*How to Marry
    a Millionaire*, 1953
River of No Return, 1954
*There's No Business
    Like Show Business*, 1954
The Seven Year Itch, 1955
Bus Stop, 1956
*The Prince and
    the Showgirl*, 1957
Some Like it Hot, 1959
Let's Make Love, 1960
The Misfits, 1961

KIM NOVAK

Pushover, 1954
Phffft! 1954
Five Against the House, 1955
Picnic, 1955
*The Man with
    the Golden Arm*, 1955
The Eddy Duchin Story, 1956
Jeanne Eagels, 1957
Pal Joey, 1957
Vertigo, 1958
Bell, Book and Candle, 1958
Middle of the Night, 1959
*Strangers
    When We Meet*, 1960
The Notorious Landlady, 1962
Boys' Night Out, 1962
Of Human Bondage, 1964
Kiss Me, Stupid, 1964
*The Amorous Adventures
    of Moll Flanders*, 1965
*The Legend
    of Lylah Clare*, 1968
The Great Bank Robbery, 1969
*Tales That
    Witness Madness*, 1973
The White Buffalo, 1977
*Schöner Gigolo, Armer Gigolo/
    Just a Gigolo*, 1979
The Mirror Crack'd, 1980
The Children, 1990
Liebestraum, 1991

MAUREEN O'HARA

My Irish Molly, 1938
Jamaica Inn, 1939
*The Hunchback
    of Notre Dame*, 1939
A Bill of Divorcement, 1940
Dance, Girl, Dance, 1940
They Met in Argentina, 1941
How Green Was My Valley, 1941
To the Shores of Tripoli, 1941
*Ten Gentlemen
    from West Point*, 1942
The Black Swan, 1942
Immortal Sergeant, 1943
This Land Is Mine, 1943
The Fallen Sparrow, 1943
Buffalo Bill, 1944
The Spanish Main, 1945
Sentimental Journey, 1946

Do You Love Me? 1946
Sinbad the Sailor, 1947
The Homestretch, 1947
Miracle on 34th Street, 1947
The Foxes of Harrow, 1947
Sitting Pretty, 1948
A Woman's Secret, 1949
Britannia Mews, 1949
Father Was a Fullback, 1949
Bagdad, 1949
Comanche Territory, 1950
Tripoli, 1950
Rio Grande, 1950
Flame of Araby, 1951
At Sword's Point, 1951
Kangaroo, 1952
The Quiet Man, 1952
Against all Flags, 1952
*The Redhead
    from Wyoming*, 1953
War Arrow, 1953
Malaga, 1954
The Long Gray Line, 1955
The Magnificent Matador, 1955
Lady Godiva, 1955
Lisbon, 1956
Everything but the Truth, 1956
The Wings of Eagles, 1957
Our Man in Havana, 1959
The Deadly Companions, 1961
The Parent Trap, 1961
*Mr. Hobbs
    Takes a Vacation*, 1962
McLintock! 1963
Spencer's Mountain, 1963
*The Battle of
    the Villa Fiorita*, 1965
The Rare Breed, 1966
How Do I Love Thee? 1970
Big Jake, 1971
Only the Lonely, 1991

MARY PICKFORD

Mrs. Jones Entertains; 1908
Oh, Uncle! 1909
The Necklace, 1909
The Peachbasket Hat, 1909
The Mexican Sweethearts, 1909
The Mountaineer's Honor, 1909
The Lonely Villa, 1909
The Seventh Day, 1909
The Sealed Room, 1909
The Renunciation, 1909
The Restoration, 1909
Slave, 1909
His Wife's Visitor, 1909
His Lost Love, 1909
*In the Watches
    of the Night*, 1909
His Duty, 1909
The Little Teacher, 1909
The Little Darling, 1909
*Lines of White
    on a Sullen Sea*, 1909

*The Indian
    Runner's Romance*, 1909
The Light That Came, 1909
Her First Biscuits, 1909
The Country Doctor, 1909
The Deception, 1909
The Children's Friend, 1909
*The Fascinating
    Mrs. Francis*, 1909
The Faded Lilies, 1909
The Gibson Goddess, 1909
Sweet and Twenty, 1909
The Broken Locket, 1909
*The Cardinal's
    Conspiracy*, 1909
Test, 1909
The Son's Return, 1909
Tender Hearts, 1909
A Sweet Revenge, 1909
They Would Elope, 1909
A Strange Meeting, 1909
A Midnight Adventure, 1909
In Old Kentucky, 1909
The Awakening, 1909
To Save Her Soul, 1909
Getting Even, 1909
Serious Sixteen, 1910
Smoker, 1910
*The Song of
    the Wildwood Flute*, 1910
*The Sorrows
    of the Unfaithful*, 1910
Simple Charity, 1910
The Twisted Trail, 1910
The Thread of Destiny, 1910
*That Chink at
    Golden Gulch*, 1910
A Summer Tragedy, 1910
Sunshine Sue, 1910
*A Romance
    of the Western Hills*, 1910
*When We
    Were in Our Teens*, 1910
White Roses, 1910
What the Daisy Said, 1910
The Woman from Mellon's, 1910
Wilful Peggy, 1910
The Two Brothers, 1910
The Unchanging Sea, 1910
Usurer, 1910
Waiter No. 5, 1910
A Victim of Jealousy, 1910
An Arcadian Maid, 1910
The Face at the Window, 1910
A Flash of Light, 1910
*Examination
    Day at School*, 1910
The Iconoclast, 1910
A Gold Necklace, 1910
In the Border States, 1910
Call, 1910
A Child's Impulse, 1910
The Englishman and the Girl, 1910
A Child's Stratagem, 1910
A Rich Revenge, 1910
Never Again, 1910
The Newlyweds, 1910

Mary Pickford (con't)

Muggsy's First Sweetheart, 1910
A Plain Song, 1910
In the Season of Buds, 1910
Little Angels of Luck, 1910
Love Among the Roses, 1910
Muggsy Becomes a Hero, 1910
May and December, 1910
As It is in Life, 1910
The Call to Arms, 1910
An Affair of Hearts, 1910
Ramona, 1910
Their First Misunderstanding, 1911
Three Sisters, 1911
The Message in the Bottle, 1911
The Rose's Story, 1911
Mirror, 1911
A Manly Man, 1911
Conscience, 1911
Little Red Riding Hood, 1911
When a Man Loves, 1911
The Better Way, 1911
The Italian Barber, 1911
Her Awakening, 1911
Little Nell's Tobacco, 1911
For Her Brother's Sake, 1911
Dream, 1911
In the Sultan's Garden, 1911
The House That Jack Built, 1911
In Old Madrid, 1911
Madame Rex, 1911
A Decree of Destiny, 1911
A Dog's Tale, 1911
Artful Kate, 1911
The Aggressor, 1911
Fate's Interception, 1912
A Child's Remorse, 1912
A Siren of Impulse, 1912
With the Enemy's Help, 1912
So Near, Yet So Far, 1912
The Schoolteacher
   and the Waif, 1912
Just Like a Woman, 1912
Friends, 1912
A Beast at Bay, 1912
The Female
   of the Species, 1912
A Feud in the
   Kentucky Hills, 1912
Iola's Promise, 1912
The Inner Circle, 1912
Lena and the Geese, 1912
A Lodging for the Night, 1912
Home Folks, 1912
The Informer, 1912
An Indian Summer, 1912
A Pueblo Legend, 1912
The Old Actor, 1912
The New York Hat, 1912
The One She Loved, 1912
The Mender of Nets, 1912
My Baby, 1912
The Narrow Road, 1912
Fate, 1913
The Unwelcome Guest, 1913
The Bishop's Carriage, 1913
Caprice, 1913

Hearts Adrift, 1914
A Good Little Devil, 1914
Tess of the Storm Country, 1914
The Eagle's Mate, 1914
Such a Little Queen, 1914
Behind the Scenes, 1914
Cinderella, 1914
Mistress Nell, 1915
Fanchon the Cricket, 1915
The Dawn of Tomorrow, 1915
Little Pal, 1915
Rags, 1915
Esmerelda, 1915
A Girl of Yesterday, 1915
Madame Butterfly, 1915
The Foundling, 1916
Poor Little Peppina, 1916
The Eternal Grind, 1916
Hulda from Holland, 1916
Less than the Dust, 1916
The Pride of the Clan, 1917
The Poor Little Rich Girl, 1917
A Romance of
   the Redwoods, 1917
The Little American, 1917
Rebecca of
   Sunnybrook Farm, 1917
A Little Princess, 1917
Stella Maris, 1918
Amarilly of
   Clothes-Line Alley, 1918
M'Liss, 1918
How Could You, Jean? 1918
Johanna Enlists, 1918
Captain Kidd, Jr., 1919
Daddy-Long-Legs, 1919
The Hoodlum, 1919
The Heart o' the Hills, 1919
Pollyanna, 1920
Suds, 1920
The Love Light, 1921
Through the Back Door, 1921
Little Lord Fauntleroy, 1921
Tess of the
   Storm Country, 1922
Rosita, 1923
Dorothy Vernon
   of Haddon Hall, 1924
Little Annie Rooney, 1925
Sparrows, 1926
My Best Girl, 1927
Coquette, 1929
The Taming of the Shrew, 1929
Kiki, 1931
Secrets, 1933

DEBBIE REYNOLDS

June Bride, 1948
The Daughter
   of Rosie O'Grady, 1950
Three Little Words, 1950
Two Weeks with Love, 1950
Mr. Imperium, 1951
Singin' in the Rain, 1952
Skirts Ahoy, 1952
I Love Melvin, 1953
The Affairs of Dobie Gillis, 1953
Give a Girl a Break, 1953
Susan Slept Here, 1954
Athena, 1954
Hit the Deck, 1955
The Tender Trap, 1955
The Catered Affair, 1956
Bundle of Joy, 1956
Meet Me in Las Vegas, 1956
Tammy and the Bachelor, 1957
This Happy Feeling, 1958
Say One for Me, 1959
The Gazebo, 1959
The Mating Game, 1959
It Started with a Kiss, 1959
The Rat Race, 1960
The Second Time Around, 1961
The Pleasure
   of His Company, 1961
How the West Was Won, 1962
My Six Loves, 1963
Mary, Mary, 1963
The Unsinkable
   Molly Brown, 1964
Goodbye Charlie, 1964
The Singing Nun, 1965
Divorce American Style, 1967
How Sweet It Is! 1968
What's the
   Matter with Helen? 1971
The Bodyguard, 1992
Heaven & Earth, 1993
Mother, 1996
In and Out, 1997
Zack and Reba, 1998

GINGER ROGERS

Young Man of Manhattan, 1930
The Sap from Syracuse, 1930
Queen High, 1930
Office Blues, 1930
Follow the Leader, 1930
Honor Among Lovers, 1931
The Tip-Off, 1931
Suicide Fleet, 1931
Carnival Boat, 1932
The Tenderfoot, 1932
The Thirteenth Guest, 1932
Hat Check Girl, 1932
You Said a Mouthful, 1932
42nd Street, 1933
Broadway Bad, 1933
Gold Diggers of 1933, 1933
Professional Sweetheart, 1933

Don't Bet on Love, 1933
A Shriek in the Night, 1933
Rafter Romance, 1933
Chance at Heaven, 1933
Sitting Pretty, 1933
Flying Down to Rio, 1933
*Twenty Million
    Sweethearts*, 1934
Upperworld, 1934
Finishing School, 1934
Change of Heart, 1934
The Gay Divorcee, 1934
Romance in Manhattan, 1935
Roberta, 1935
Star of Midnight, 1935
Top Hat, 1935
In Person, 1935
Follow the Fleet, 1936
Swing Time, 1936
Shall We Dance, 1937
Stage Door, 1937
Vivacious Lady, 1938
Having Wonderful Time, 1938
Carefree, 1938
*The Story of Vernon
    and Irene Castle*, 1939
Bachelor Mother, 1939
Fifth Ave Girl, 1939
Primrose Path, 1940
Lucky Partners, 1940
Kitty Foyle, 1940
Tom, Dick and Harry, 1941
Roxie Hart, 1942
Tales of Manhattan, 1942
The Major and the Minor, 1942
Once Upon a Honeymoon, 1942
Tender Comrade, 1943
Lady in the Dark, 1944
I'll Be Seeing You, 1945
Week-End at the Waldorf, 1945
Heartbeat, 1946
Magnificent Doll, 1946
It Had to Be You, 1947
*The Barkleys
    of Broadway*, 1949
Perfect Strangers, 1950
Storm Warning, 1951
The Groom Wore Spurs, 1951
We're Not Married! 1952
Dreamboat, 1952
Monkey Business, 1952
Forever Female, 1953
Black Widow, 1954
Beautiful Stranger, 1954
Tight Spot, 1955
*The First
    Traveling Saleslady*, 1956
Teenage Rebel, 1956
Oh, Men! Oh, Women! 1957
The Confession, 1964
Harlow, 1964

ROSALIND RUSSELL

Evelyn Prentice, 1934
The President Vanishes, 1934
Forsaking All Others, 1934
The Night Is Young, 1935
The Casino Murder Case, 1935
West Point of the Air, 1935
Reckless, 1935
China Seas, 1935
Rendezvous, 1935
It Had to Happen, 1936
Under Two Flags, 1936
Craig's Wife, 1936
Trouble for Two, 1936
Night Must Fall, 1937
Live, Love and Learn, 1937
Man-Proof, 1938
Four's a Crowd, 1938
The Citadel, 1938
Fast and Loose, 1939
The Women, 1939
His Girl Friday, 1940
No Time for Comedy, 1940
Hired Wife, 1940
This Thing Called Love, 1941
They Met in Bombay, 1941
The Feminine Touch, 1941
Design for Scandal, 1941
Take a Letter, Darling, 1942
My Sister Eileen, 1942
Flight for Freedom, 1943
What a Woman, 1943
Roughly Speaking, 1945
She Wouldn't Say Yes, 1945
Sister Kenny, 1946
The Guilt of Janet Ames, 1946
*Mourning
    Becomes Electra*, 1947
The Velvet Touch, 1948
Tell It to the Judge, 1949
A Woman of Distinction, 1950
Never Wave at a WAC, 1952
The Girl Rush, 1955
Picnic, 1955
Auntie Mame, 1958
A Majority of One, 1961
Five Finger Exercise, 1961
Gypsy, 1962
The Trouble with Angels, 1966
*Oh, Dad, Poor Dad, Mama's
    Hung You in the Closet and
    I'm Feeling So Sad*, 1967
Rosie! 1967
*Where Angels Go . . .
    Trouble Follows*, 1968
Mrs. Pollifax—Spy, 1971

NORMA SHEARER

The Stealers, 1920
The Man Who Paid, 1922
*Channing of
    the Northwest*, 1922
The Bootleggers, 1922
A Clouded Name, 1923
Man and Wife, 1923
The Devil's Partner, 1923
Pleasure Mad, 1923
The Wanters, 1923
Lucretia Lombard, 1923
The Trail of the Law, 1924
The Wolf Man, 1924
Blue Water, 1924
Broadway After Dark, 1924
Empty Hands, 1924
Broken Barriers, 1924
He Who Gets Slapped, 1924
The Snob, 1924
Excuse Me, 1925
Lady of the Night, 1925
Waking Up the Town, 1925
Pretty Ladies, 1925
A Slave of Fashion, 1925
The Tower of Lies, 1925
His Secretary, 1925
The Devil's Circus, 1926
The Waning Sex, 1926
Upstage, 1926
The Demi-Bride, 1927
After Midnight, 1927
*The Student Prince
    in Old Heidelberg*, 1927
The Latest from Paris, 1928
The Actress, 1928
A Lady of Chance, 1928
The Trial of Mary Dugan, 1929
The Last of Mrs. Cheyney, 1929
Their Own Desire, 1929
The Divorcée, 1930
Let Us Be Gay, 1930
Strangers May Kiss, 1931
A Free Soul, 1931
Private Lives, 1931
Smilin' Through, 1932
Strange Interlude, 1932
Riptide, 1934
*The Barretts of
    Wimpole Street*, 1934
Romeo and Juliet, 1936
Marie Antoinette, 1938
Idiot's Delight, 1939
The Women, 1939
Escape, 1940
We Were Dancing, 1942
Her Cardboard Lover, 1942

ANN SHERIDAN

Search for Beauty, 1934
Come on Marines! 1934
Shoot the Works, 1934
Kiss and Make Up, 1934
Ladies Should Listen, 1934
Behold My Wife, 1934
Home on the Range, 1935
Car 99, 1935
Rocky Mountain Mystery, 1935
Red Blood of Courage, 1935
The Glass Key, 1935
Fighting Youth, 1935
Black Legion, 1937
The Great O'Malley, 1937
San Quentin, 1937
Wine, Women and Horses, 1937
The Footloose Heiress, 1937
Alcatraz Island, 1937
She Loved a Fireman, 1937
The Patient in Room 18, 1938
Mystery House, 1938
Little Miss Thoroughbred, 1938
Cowboy from Brooklyn, 1938
Letter of Introduction, 1938
Broadway Musketeers, 1938
Angels with Dirty Faces, 1938
They Made Me a Criminal, 1939
Dodge City, 1939
Naughty but Nice, 1939
Winter Carnival, 1939
Indianapolis Speedway, 1939
*The Angels Wash
    Their Faces*, 1939
Castle on the Hudson, 1940
It All Came True, 1940
Torrid Zone, 1940
They Drive by Night, 1940
City for Conquest, 1940
Honeymoon for Three, 1941
Navy Blues, 1941
*The Man Who
    Came to Dinner*, 1942
Kings Row, 1942
Juke Girl, 1942
Wings for the Eagle, 1942
*George Washington
    Slept Here*, 1942
Edge of Darkness, 1943
Shine On, Harvest Moon, 1944
The Doughgirls, 1944
One More Tomorrow, 1946
Nora Prentiss, 1947
The Unfaithful, 1947
Silver River, 1948
Good Sam, 1948
I Was a Male War Bride, 1949
Stella, 1950
Woman on the Run, 1950
Steel Town, 1952
Just Across the Street, 1952
Take Me to Town, 1953
*Appointment
    in Honduras*, 1953
Come Next Spring, 1956
The Opposite Sex, 1956
Woman and the Hunter, 1957

BARBARA STANWYCK

Broadway Nights, 1927
The Locked Door, 1929
Mexicali Rose, 1929
Ladies of Leisure, 1930
Illicit, 1931
Ten Cents a Dance, 1931
Night Nurse, 1931
The Miracle Woman, 1931
Forbidden, 1932
Shopworn, 1932
So Big, 1932
The Purchase Price, 1932
*The Bitter Tea
    of General Yen*, 1933
Ladies They Talk About, 1933
Baby Face, 1933
Ever in My Heart, 1933
Gambling Lady, 1934
A Lost Lady, 1934
The Secret Bride, 1935
The Woman in Red, 1935
Red Salute, 1935
Annie Oakley, 1935
A Message to Garcia, 1936
The Bride Walks Out, 1936
His Brother's Wife, 1936
Banjo on my Knee, 1936
The Plough and the Stars, 1936
*Internes Can't
    Take Money*, 1937
This Is My Affair, 1937
Stella Dallas, 1937
Breakfast for Two, 1937
Always Goodbye, 1938
The Mad Miss Manton, 1938
Union Pacific, 1939
Golden Boy, 1939
Remember the Night, 1940
The Lady Eve, 1941
Meet John Doe, 1941
You Belong to Me, 1941
Ball of Fire, 1941
The Great Man's Lady, 1942
The Gay Sisters, 1942
Lady of Burlesque, 1943
Flesh and Fantasy, 1943
Double Indemnity, 1944
Christmas in Connecticut, 1945
My Reputation, 1946
The Bride Wore Boots, 1946
*The Strange Love
    of Martha Ivers*, 1946
California, 1946
The Two Mrs. Carrolls, 1947
Cry Wolf, 1947
The Other Love, 1947
B.F.'s Daughter, 1948
Sorry, Wrong Number, 1948
The Lady Gambles, 1949
East Side, West Side, 1949

*The File on
    Thelma Jordan*, 1949
No Man of Her Own, 1950
The Furies, 1950
To Please a Lady, 1950
The Man with a Cloak, 1951
Clash by Night, 1952
Jeopardy, 1953
Titanic, 1953
All I Desire, 1953
The Moonlighter, 1953
Blowing Wild, 1953
Witness to Murder, 1954
Executive Suite, 1954
Cattle Queen of Montana, 1954
The Violent Men, 1955
Escape to Burma, 1955
There's Always Tomorrow, 1956
The Maverick Queen, 1956
These Wilder Years, 1956
Crime of Passion, 1957
Trooper Hook, 1957
Forty Guns, 1957
Walk on the Wild Side, 1962
Roustabout, 1964
The Night Walker, 1964

GLORIA SWANSON

The Broken Pledge, 1915
*The Fable of Elvira and
    Farina and the Meal Ticket*, 1915
His New Job, 1915
The Sultan's Wife, 1915
*The Ambition
    of the Baron*, 1915
Teddy at the Throttle, 1916
The Nick of Time Baby, 1916
A Pullman Bride, 1917
Society for Sale, 1918
Every Woman's Husband, 1918
The Secret Code, 1918
Wife or Country, 1918
*You Can't
    Believe Everything*, 1918
Station Content, 1918
Shifting Sands, 1918
Her Decision, 1918
*Don't Change
    Your Husband*, 1919
For Better, For Worse, 1919
Male and Female, 1919
Why Change Your Wife? 1920
*Something to
    Think About*, 1920
The Great Moment, 1921
The Affairs of Anatol, 1921
Under the Lash, 1921
Don't Tell Everything, 1921
*Her Husband's
    Trademark*, 1922
Her Gilded Cage, 1922
Beyond the Rocks, 1922
*The Impossible
    Mrs. Bellew*, 1922
My American Wife, 1922
Prodigal Daughters, 1923
Bluebeard's Eighth Wife, 1923

Zaza, 1923
The Humming Bird, 1924
A Society Scandal, 1924
Manhandled, 1924
Her Love Story, 1924
Wages of Virtue, 1924
Madame Sans-Gêne, 1924
The Coast of Folly, 1925
Stage Struck, 1925
The Untamed Lady, 1926
Fine Manners, 1926
The Love of Sunya, 1927
Sadie Thompson, 1928
The Trespasser, 1929
Queen Kelly, 1929
    (released in 1950)
What a Widow! 1930
Indiscreet, 1931
Tonight or Never, 1931
Perfect Understanding, 1933
Music in the Air, 1934
Father Takes a Wife, 1941
Sunset Blvd., 1950
Three for Bedroom C, 1952
Mio Figlio Nerone/
    Nero's Mistress, 1956
Killer Bees, 1974
Airport 1975, 1974

ELIZABETH TAYLOR
There's One
    Born Every Minute, 1942
Lassie Come Home, 1943
Jane Eyre, 1944
The White Cliffs of Dover, 1944
National Velvet, 1944
Courage of Lassie, 1946
Life with Father, 1947
Cynthia, 1947
A Date with Judy, 1948
Julia Misbehaves, 1948
Little Women, 1949
Conspirator, 1949
The Big Hangover, 1950
Father of the Bride, 1950
Father's Little Dividend, 1951
A Place in the Sun, 1951
Love Is Better Than Ever, 1952
Ivanhoe, 1952
The Girl Who
    Had Everything, 1953
Rhapsody, 1954
Elephant Walk, 1954
Beau Brummell, 1954
The Last Time I Saw Paris, 1954
Giant, 1956
Raintree County, 1957
Cat on a Hot Tin Roof, 1958
Suddenly, Last Summer, 1959

Butterfield 8, 1960
Cleopatra, 1963
The V.I.P.'s, 1963
The Sandpiper, 1965
Who's Afraid
    of Virginia Woolf? 1966
The Taming of the Shrew, 1967
Doctor Faustus, 1967
Reflections in
    a Golden Eye, 1967
The Comedians, 1967
Boom! 1968
Secret Ceremony, 1968
The Only Game in Town, 1970
Zee and Co., 1972
Under Milk Wood, 1972
Hammersmith Is Out, 1972
Night Watch, 1973
Ash Wednesday, 1973
Identikit/
    The Driver's Seat, 1974
The Blue Bird, 1976
A Little Night Music, 1977
The Mirror Crack'd, 1980
Il Giovane Toscanini/
    The Young Toscanini, 1988
The Flintstones, 1994

GENE TIERNEY
The Return
    of Frank James, 1940
Hudson's Bay, 1941
Tobacco Road, 1941
Belle Starr, 1941
Sundown, 1941
The Shanghai Gesture, 1941
Son of Fury, 1942
Rings on Her Fingers, 1942
Thunder Birds, 1942
China Girl, 1942
Heaven Can Wait, 1943
Laura, 1944
A Bell for Adano, 1945
Leave Her to Heaven, 1945
Dragonwyck, 1946
The Razor's Edge, 1946
The Ghost and Mrs. Muir, 1947
The Iron Curtain, 1948
The Wonderful Urge, 1948
Whirlpool, 1949
Night and the City, 1950
Where the Sidewalk Ends, 1950
Close to My Heart, 1951
The Mating Season, 1951
On the Riviera, 1951
The Secret
    of Convict Lake, 1951
Way of a Gaucho, 1952
Plymouth Adventure, 1952
Never Let Me Go, 1952
Personal Affair, 1953
The Egyptian, 1954
Black Widow, 1954
The Left Hand of God, 1955
Advise and Consent, 1962
Toys in the Attic, 1963
The Pleasure Seekers, 1964

LANA TURNER
They Won't Forget, 1937
The Great Garrick, 1937
The Adventures
    of Marco Polo, 1938
Love Finds Andy Hardy, 1938
Rich Man, Poor Girl, 1938
Dramatic School, 1938
Calling Dr. Kildare, 1939
These Glamour Girls, 1939
Dancing Co-ed, 1939
Two Girls on Broadway, 1940
We Who Are Young, 1940
Ziegfeld Girl, 1941
Dr. Jekyll and Mr. Hyde, 1941
Honky Tonk, 1941
Johnny Eager, 1942
Somewhere I'll Find You, 1942
The Youngest Profession, 1943
Slightly Dangerous, 1943
Marriage Is
    a Private Affair, 1944
Keep Your Powder Dry, 1945
Week-End at the Waldorf, 1945
The Postman
    Always Rings Twice, 1946
Green Dolphin Street, 1947
Cass Timberlane, 1947
Homecoming, 1948
The Three Musketeers, 1948
A Life of Her Own, 1950
Mr. Imperium, 1951
The Merry Widow, 1952
The Bad and
    the Beautiful, 1952
Latin Lovers, 1953
The Flame and the Flesh, 1954
Betrayed, 1954
The Prodigal, 1955
The Sea Chase, 1955
The Rains of Ranchipur, 1955
Diane, 1956
Peyton Place, 1957
The Lady Takes a Flyer, 1958
Another Time,
    Another Place, 1958
Imitation of Life, 1959
Portrait in Black, 1960
By Love Possessed, 1961
Bachelor in Paradise, 1961
Who's Got the Action? 1962
Love Has Many Faces, 1965
Madame X, 1966
The Big Cube, 1969
Persecution, 1974
Bittersweet Love, 1976
Witches Brew, 1980
Thwarted, 1991

MAE WEST

Night After Night, 1932
She Done Him Wrong, 1933
I'm No Angel, 1933
Belle of the Nineties, 1934
Goin' to Town, 1935
Klondike Annie, 1936
Go West, Young Man, 1936
Every Day's a Holiday, 1937
My Little Chickadee, 1940
The Heat's On, 1943
Myra Breckinridge, 1970
Sextette, 1978

ESTHER WILLIAMS

Andy Hardy's Double Life, 1942
A Guy Named Joe, 1943
Bathing Beauty, 1944
Thrill of a Romance, 1945
Ziegfeld Follies, 1946
The Hoodlum Saint, 1946
Easy to Wed, 1946
Fiesta, 1947
This Time for Keeps, 1947
On an Island with You, 1948
Take Me Out
  to the Ball Game, 1949
Neptune's Daughter, 1949
Duchess of Idaho, 1950
Pagan Love Song, 1950
Texas Carnival, 1951
Skirts Ahoy! 1952
Million Dollar Mermaid, 1952
Dangerous When Wet, 1953
Easy to Love, 1953
Jupiter's Darling, 1955
The Unguarded Moment, 1956
Raw Wind in Eden, 1958
The Big Show, 1962

NATALIE WOOD

Tomorrow Is Forever, 1946
The Bride Wore Boots, 1946
Miracle on 34th Street, 1947
The Ghost and Mrs. Muir, 1947
Driftwood, 1947
Scudda Hoo! Scudda Hay! 1948
Chicken Every Sunday, 1948
The Green Promise, 1949
Father was a Fullback, 1949
No Sad Songs for Me, 1950
Our Very Own, 1950
The Jackpot, 1950
Never a Dull Moment, 1950
Dear Brat, 1951
The Blue Veil, 1951
The Rose Bowl Story, 1952
Just for You, 1952
The Star, 1952
The Silver Chalice, 1954
One Desire, 1955
Rebel Without a Cause, 1955
The Searchers, 1956
A Cry in the Night, 1956

The Burning Hills, 1956
The Girl He Left Behind, 1956
Bombers B-52, 1957
Marjorie Morningstar, 1958
Kings Go Forth, 1958
Cash McCall, 1959
All the Fine
  Young Cannibals, 1960
Splendor in the Grass, 1961
West Side Story, 1961
Gypsy, 1962
Love with the
  Proper Stranger, 1963
Sex and the Single Girl, 1964
The Great Race, 1965
Inside Daisy Clover, 1965
This Property
  Is Condemned, 1966
Penelope, 1966
Bob & Carol
  & Ted & Alice, 1969
Peeper, 1975
Meteor, 1979
The Last Married
  Couple in America, 1980
Brainstorm, 1983

LORETTA YOUNG

Laugh, Clown, Laugh, 1928
The Magnificent Flirt, 1928
The Head Man, 1928
Scarlet Seas, 1928
The Squall, 1929
The Girl in the Glass Cage, 1929
Fast Life, 1929
The Careless Age, 1929
The Forward Pass, 1929
The Show of Shows, 1929
The Loose Ankles, 1930
The Man from Blankley's, 1930
The Second-
  Story Murder, 1930
Road to Paradise, 1930
Kismet, 1930
The Truth about Youth, 1930
The Devil to Pay, 1930
Beau Ideal, 1931
The Right of Way, 1931
Three Girls Lost, 1931
Too Young to Marry, 1931
Big Business Girl, 1931
I Like Your Nerve, 1931
The Ruling Voice, 1931
Platinum Blonde, 1931
Taxi! 1932
The Hatchet Man, 1932
Play Girl, 1932
Weekend Marriage, 1932
Life Begins, 1932
They Call It Sin, 1932
Employees' Entrance, 1933
Grand Slam, 1933
Zoo in Budapest, 1933
The Life of Jimmy Dolan, 1933
Heroes for Sale, 1933
Midnight Mary, 1933
She Had to Say Yes, 1933

The Devil's in Love, 1933
A Man's Castle, 1933
The House of Rothschild, 1934
Born to Be Bad, 1934
Bulldog Drummond
  Strikes Back, 1934
Caravan, 1934
The White Parade, 1934
Clive of India, 1935
Shanghai, 1935
The Call of the Wild, 1935
The Crusades, 1935
The Unguarded Hour, 1936
Private Number, 1936
Ramona, 1936
Ladies in Love, 1936
Love Is News, 1937
Café Metropole, 1937
Love Under Fire, 1937
Wife, Doctor, and Nurse, 1937
Second Honeymoon, 1937
Four Men and a Prayer, 1938
Three Blind Mice, 1938
Suez, 1938
Kentucky, 1938
Wife, Husband and Friend, 1939
The Story of Alexander
  Graham Bell, 1939
Eternally Yours, 1939
The Doctor Takes a Wife, 1940
He Stayed for Breakfast, 1940
The Lady from Cheyenne, 1941
The Men in Her Life, 1941
Bedtime Story, 1942
A Night to Remember, 1943
China, 1943
Ladies Courageous, 1944
And Now Tomorrow, 1944
Along Came Jones, 1945
The Stranger, 1946
The Perfect Marriage, 1947
The Farmer's Daughter, 1947
The Bishop's Wife, 1947
Rachel and the Stranger, 1948
The Accused, 1949
Mother Is a Freshman, 1949
Come to the Stable, 1949
Key to the City, 1950
Cause for Alarm, 1951
Half Angel, 1951
Paula, 1952
Because of You, 1952
It Happens
  Every Thursday, 1953

ABOUT THE AUTHORS

TEXT
Andrea Sarvady is the author of three other books on popular culture and film, including *The Ultimate Girls' Movie Survival Guide: What to Rent, Who to Watch, How to Deal*.

EDITOR
Frank Miller is a lecturer in theatre at Georgia State University and the author of *Casablanca: As Time Goes By* and *Censored Hollywood: Sex, Sin, & Violence on Screen*.

RESEARCHER
Aubry Anne D'Arminio is a master's student in Film Studies at Emory University. Her work has appeared in the *Journal of Popular Film and Television* and online at the All Movie Guide.

FILM CAPTIONS
Roger Fristoe is retired as the film critic of the *Courier-Journal* in Louisville, Kentucky, and also has written for such publications as the *New York Times* and *Premiere* magazine. He has been a contributing writer for Turner Classic Movies since 1997.

CAROLE LOMBARD IN *TWENTIETH CENTURY*, 1934